FRANZ SCHOBER / TAMIKI KISHIDA / YUKO ARAYAMA (Eds.)

Restructuring the Economy of the 21st Century in Japan and Germany

Schriften zu Regional- und Verkehrsproblemen
in Industrie- und Entwicklungsländern

Herausgegeben von Theodor Dams und Joachim Klaus

Band 65

Restructuring the Economy of the 21st Century in Japan and Germany

Edited by

Franz Schober, Tamiki Kishida
and Yuko Arayama

Duncker & Humblot · Berlin

Die Deutsche Bibliothek – CIP-Einheitsaufnahme

Restructuring the economy of the 21st century in Japan and Germany / ed. by Franz Schober ... – Berlin : Duncker und Humblot, 1999
(Schriften zu Regional- und Verkehrsproblemen in Industrie- und Entwicklungsländern ; Bd. 65)
ISBN 3-428-09935-4

Fotoprint: Werner Hildebrand, Berlin
Printed in Germany

ISSN 0582-0170
ISBN 3-428-09935-4

Gedruckt auf alterungsbeständigem (säurefreiem) Papier
entsprechend ISO 9706 ♾

Dedicated to
Professor Dr. Dr. Kunihiro Jojima

Preface of the Series Editors

This publication presents the revised and updated versions of the papers presented at the 17th Joint Seminar of the Faculties of Economics at the Universities of Nagoya and Freiburg. The seminar marks the twenty-fifth anniversary of the cooperation between both faculties and the twentieth anniverary of conducting joint seminars. The meeting took place in Nagoya/Japan on September 8–10, 1997. It was accompanied by a one-day public session with strong participation and attention from government, industry and the scientific community.

The focus of the papers in this book is relatively broad, compared to most previous seminar topics. It ranges from the state of the general economic system in Japan and Germany to aspects of financial and labor markets to various issues of management and organization. The book reflects some of the most urgent economic problems on the turn of the century. It touches also on some of the recurrent issues treated already in previous seminars, see the appendix in this book.

The Faculty of Economics of the University of Freiburg thanks the Ministry of Science, Research and Arts in Baden-Würtemberg and the corresponding institutions in Japan for their generous financial support. We also thank the Wissenschaftliche Gesellschaft in Freiburg im Breisgau for the grant which made this publication possible. Thanks finally to the scientific, student and secretarial staff from the University of Freiburg who took the burden to proofread the papers and technically shape the publication into its final form.

Freiburg im Breisgau, March 1999

Theodor Dams
Joachim Klaus

Table of Contents

Twenty-Five Years of Cooperation between Nagoya and Freiburg

Theodor Dams[1]

With this 17th Joint Seminar we are celebrating the 25th anniversary of the socio-economic cooperation between the faculties of economics of the universities of Nagoya and Freiburg and 20 years of conducting joint seminars in Japan and Germany. The results of the seminars have been published in 13 seminar proceedings in Germany and 11 in Japan, the former proceedings for many years in German an later in English language, the latter in Japanese language.[2]

Yet the collection of quantitative facts alone cannot sufficiently illustrate the qualitative value of such an intensive cooperation, i. e. the growing mutual scientific confidence among the Japanese and German participants, the creation of an atmosphere of friendship which supports participation from below, the common interest in favour of the academic education of the younger colleagues, and last but not least the common engagement for a higher prestige of our faculties and universities in both countries. And we should not forget the individual benefits for us and our family members by granting a great hospitality that gives more opportunities for arriving at a better understanding of the society in Japan and Germany.

Twenty-five years of cooperation may not be a long span of time within the historical perspective of an university. The Albert-Ludwigs-University has been founded in 1457 and is one of the oldest German academic institutions. The department of economic sciences has been established within the faculty of law in 1896 (from then on as "Rechts- und Staatswissenschaftliche Fakultät"), strongly supported by Max Weber (1864–1920) who had been a faculty member in Freiburg from 1894 to 1897. I mention this because especially Max Weber has contributed to a comparative study of the relationship between religion and economic development, i. e. the rationality in Confucianism and in Protestantism. Colleagues from Freiburg as well as from Meiji University have recently present-

---

[1] This chapter contains an abbreviated version of the key address delivered by the author on September 8, 1997 at the 17th Joint Nagoya/Freiburg Seminar in Nagoya.

[2] See appendix in this book.

ed new interpretations of Max Weber's thinking, and I am sure that this topic will be a field of common interest also in the future.

How can the results of 25 years of cooperation be interpreted and what kind of criteria can be applied in balancing the benefits of our efforts? My subjective view is that we should understand the economic development in Japan and Germany in the context of their respective cultural, social, economic and political environments.

During the last century Japan had, in the western view, considerably diverged from western norms and goals. Today in the context of globalization the Japanese economy has developed one of the highest degrees of competitiveness. This for the western world provocative situation cannot be explained by using traditional Japanese values alone. Therefore, the challenging question is: What are the ethical and cultural forces, values and inner social capabilities of today's Japanese society and how will they support the outstanding efficiency of Japan in the longer run?

As a consequence, Max Weber's concept of rationality in Confucianism and Protestantism has been more and more questioned today, while the ideas of the philosophers of the EDO period before 1867 – especially of Shosan Zuzuki and Baigan Ishida – have been carefully studied in order to explore the impact of their thinking to present problem solving. However, I have the impression, that we still experience a great deficiency in the way we are explaining the present situation by using the results of historical developments and concepts. Yet, there is an increasing awareness for the vertical interdependencies between the different historical periods. In my view, the Nagoya/Freiburg cooperation should take these challenges into account when elaborating the concept of the future program. It should reflect the economic problems in relation to political and social evolution based on historical development.

Let me become more precise by looking upon the present decade and its economic and institutional problems. Both, Japan and Germany, are confronted with the impact of a severe structural adjustment process.

In 1997 the IMF-Journal "Finance and Development" had published an article by Professor Takoshi Ito from Hitotsubashi University entitled "Japan's economy needs structural adjustments". A similar article could easily be published for Germany, too, but with some divergent elements. What are the main conclusions of Ito's article? (a) The economic miracle of Japan seems to "turn pale" (observe the parallel situation in Germany some decades ago). (b) The rapid economic growth in Japan during the 1950–1990 period had been caused – as economist have explained – by specific favourable institutional preconditions such as the life-long employment scheme in enterprises, the banking system and their connection to the enterprises, or the industrial "Keiretsu" on the vertical and horizontal level. All these elements have fostered the economic growth and welfare of the Japanese economy and society. But in the 1990s these elements are no longer the powerful endogenous forces, in contrary, they seem to severely constrain the future development.

The Nagoya/Freiburg cooperation should pick up these challenges of historic development and its economic impact, of turning point analysis and related problems in Japan and Germany, and, by that, hold the doors open for an efficient cooperation also in the future.

After this excursion into a possible future road of the cooperation, let me touch a few facts concerning the past 25 years.

Here, we have to consider that we started the cooperation long time before its official inauguration in form of a written University Contract in 1987. A key event was the grant of an Alexander von Humboldt scholarship to Professor Dr. Dr. Kunihiro Jojima from Nagoya University for the years 1954–57 which he spent at the University of Bonn. Subsequently he had been a Visiting Professor to the Universities of Münster (1962–1963) and Freiburg (1971). Since then, Jojima-sensai has become the essential personality in shaping the cooperation from the Japanese side. He had supported further scholarships to Freiburg, e. g. an Alexander von Humboldt scholarship to Professor Takashi Matsugi and doctoral scholarships to Tetsushi Harada, Naoki Fukuzawa and Kiichiro Yagi who all teach today as professors at Japanese universities. Several further doctoral and other postgraduate exchange programs were initiated comprising some 25 to 30 young scientists equally distributed to both the Japanese and the German side.

Over the two and a half decades our Japanese colleagues have enlarged the cooperation by inviting representatives from neighbour universities, e. g. from Kyoto, Mie, Chubu, Nanzan, Yokkaichi, Nagoya City and Aichi Gakuin University. Japanese scholars sent to Freiburg could add to this list of universities including Keijo, Sophia and Meiji University. This created an efficient network for interdisciplinary research. A good example is the recent book publication by Kiichiro Yagi and Takashi Matsugi entitled "Perspectives and Methods of Social Economics in Germany and Japan". Other examples are the translations of books written by J. Heinz Müller (University of Freiburg) and Tomas Riha (University of Queensland/Australia, Alexander von Humboldt scholar 1985 in Freiburg and frequent visitor to Freiburg also in other years) into Japanese language. These translations were prepared by Kunihiro Jojima, Takashi Matsugi, Tetsushi Harada and others.

Many achievements could be added, also many events and stories which were in some way connected with the Nagoya/Freiburg network, such as the role of the famous philosopher Robert Schinzinger from Freiburg and later academic teacher of the Japanese crown princes, the contributions of Professor Kotaro Araki, the academic teacher of Jojima-sensai, and his wife to the cooperation, the connections between the Arakis and Friedrich August von Hayek, and the "Odyssee" of Joseph Schumpeter's manuscript to his book "Capitalism, Socialism, and Democracy" which crossed our cooperation in a most surprising way and still waits for final evaluation in the library of the Memory Hall of the Mie Province.

Today, the "big family of economists from Nagoya and Freiburg" constitute a self supporting group of scholars who are highly dedicated to their scientific discipline and motivated by the mutual assistance within the cooperation. Since the emeritation of Jojima-sensai from Nagoya University and his acceptance of the presidency of Yokkaichi University, and since my own emeritation several persons have taken over the responsibility of continuing the cooperation, coordinating the joint seminars and editing the proceedings: Professors Masaichi Mizuno, Takashi Matsugi, Tamiki Kishida and Yuko Arayama from Nagoya, Professors Alois Oberhauser and Franz Schober from Freiburg. My sincere thanks to them and my best wishes for another 25 years of successful cooperation.

Envisioning the Japanese Economic System in the 21st Century in Relation to Economies of Network

Masatsugu Tsuji

Introduction

The Japanese economy is facing the longest period of stagnation since the bubble burst in 1990, namely, the poor performance of macroeconomic indicators such as the lowest growth and highest unemployment rates in the post-war period. These problems are due to the current financial crisis; that is, Hokkaido Takushoku Bank, one of ten giant city banks, and Yamaichi Securities, the fourth biggest securities company, went bankrupt one after another in November 1997. The financial crisis is a rather short-term phenomenon. In the long term, the Japanese economy is expected to face more serious problems.

Firstly, economic transformation is taking place as Japan enters the stage of a stable, but low growth economy, with an aging society, and a globalization of the economy. The Japanese economic system is said to have been formed during the era of rapid growth of the 1960s, and its basis lies in the presumption of continuous economic growth. Once the Japanese economy enters a stable growth era as the economy matures, this will result in the collapse of the whole presumption on which the economic system is based. Now it is time to restructure the entire system. Secondly, the basis which was the source of strength of the Japanese economy no longer provides any positive effect. The success of the Japanese economy in the 1970s and 1980s was due to the "Japanese system", which will be discussed later, being based on economies of scale or economies of scope. Since the 1990s, with the development of computer and telecommunications technology, the efficiency of the system has come from "economies of network". From the viewpoint of economies of network, the Japanese system is not structured to exhibit this. For economies of network to be exhibited fully, the system is required to be open, fair, and flexible. That is, people or firms should be able to connect freely, and transmit and receive all kinds of information freely. If not, the system will not be able to exhibit economies of network.

In what follows, we will focus on Japanese economic systems in the areas of employment and production, which are fundamental to Japanese international competitiveness, and discuss their basis of efficiency. Then, in the age of an information society, the source and importance of economies of network will be discussed. Here, we will make a comparison with the U.S. economy, which has an entirely different economic system, and show how the U.S. economy has changed itself to adjust to economies of network. Finally, possible reforms of the Japanese system will be presented in the conclusion.

A. Economies of Network

To begin with, a definition of economies of network in the age of the information society will be provided, and it will be noted as to how it differs from the usual notion of economies of scale and economies of scope, which were dominant prior to the 1990s.[1]

I. Definition

A network is defined by nodes and arcs: in an economy, for instance, the former are economic agents and the latter are channels which interconnect the agents. Firms, consumers, governments, organizations, and groups of nations such as the EU and APEC are examples of nodes, and telecommunications cables, roads, railroads, airlines, and wires for electricity or utility are those of arcs.

The reason why economic agents connect to a network is to receive some service from the network. In telecommunications, by using a telephone we can talk to someone in a distant place. The merit of subscribing to this service is measured in terms of utility. As for a network, in addition to direct utility, agents can receive an extra utility through the network. The more agents participate in the network, the more utility they can perceive. This is the definition of economies of network, or network externality. The latter has the same meaning as the usual external effect in economics, which implies that one's utility is affected by the action of others.[2] In the business world, economies of network are widely recognized, and competition for subscriptions in the broadcasting, newspaper, and telecommunications industries are typical examples.

A network gives rise to negative as well as positive externalities. In case of the usual commodity, one's consumption does not hinder that of others. In some networks, however, congestion might occur. This commonly occurs in a network

---

[1] This chapter is based on Tsuji and Nishiwaki (1996), chapter 2.

[2] This similarity is pointed out by Katz and Shapiro (1985).

with a limited capacity such as telecommunications and public utility. Beyond a certain level of participation rate, negative externality becomes bigger than a positive one. Thus, the utility of the network can be described as shown in figure 1.

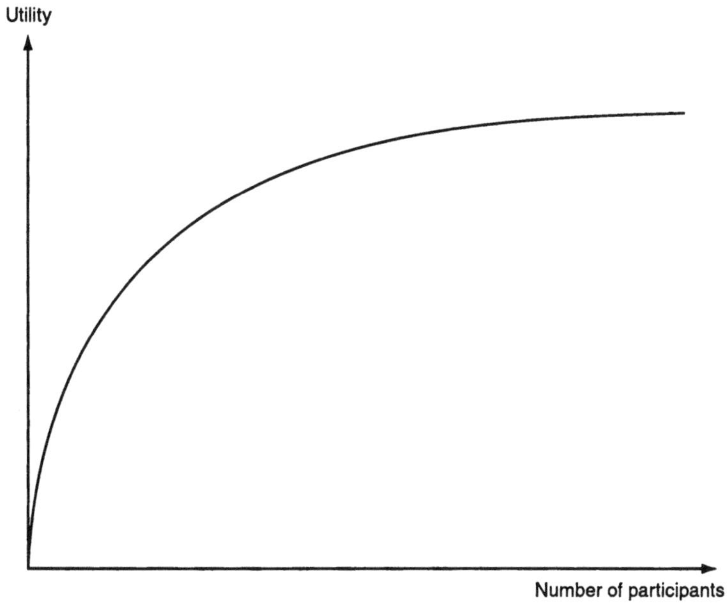

Figure 1: Utility of a Network

II. Contents and Basis of Economies of Network

Economies of network have the following four characteristics: (a) outsourcing of management resources: If agents connect to the network, they can receive all kinds of information via the network, which they themselves do not own. If it is costly for them to obtain those resources by themselves, they can then purchase information from other agents, and thus specialize their own activities. This is a primitive example of efficiency through division of labor; (b) quick response to changes in the environment: Information via the network includes information related to the environment surrounding the agents. They can receive information on ongoing changes in the environment in real time, and thus react to those changes immediately; and (c) economies of speed: Since agents can receive all kinds of information in real time, they can quickly make a decision. Moreover, they can make use of the information to prepare for future or strategic plans according to the information from the market.

The basis of economies of network lies in the development of telecommunications technology. Without this technology, it cannot possibly be realized. Above all, digitalization and multimedia are two key factors; by digitalization, all information can be processed by computer. Contemporary telecommunications technology converges to that of computer. By combining digitalization and optic fibers, a huge volume of information can be transmitted all over the world in seconds. Moreover, multimedia makes it possible to transmit information such as images, letters, and sounds by a single device. Before multimedia, one type of transmitting device could send only one kind of the above data. Thus, with this technological development, agents can receive desired information of the desired amount at the desired time.

III. Economies of Scale and Economies of Scope

In this section, other concepts of efficiency will be examined. Firstly, let us turn to economies of scale, which are related to economies of mass production. That is, when all inputs are increased at the same rate, output is increased even more. In other words, with the increase of production, the average cost is decreased. This can be formalized as follows. Let us define x_q as the total amount of production, and x_i as that of the i-th factory. All factories are assumed to have the same cost function $C = C(x_i)$. The total cost of x_q produced in one factory is thus equal to $C(x_q)$. On the other hand, if it is divided into n factories, the total cost is expressed by $C(x_1) + C(x_2) + ... + C(x_n)$. If the following inequality holds, then there exist economies of scale.

$$C(x_q) < C(x_1) + C(x_2) + ... + C(x_n),$$

where $x_q = x_1 + x_2 + ... + x_n$.

Economies of scale result from the following characteristics: (a) existence of a fixed cost; (b) indivisibility of production plants; and (c) nature of physics. The typical industries of this nature are heavy industries such as steel, chemical, and petroleum. These commonly have production plants of a large scale.

Secondly, another concept is economies of scope. The cost of production of several products at one factory is smaller than if produced separately. This can be expressed in the following way. Let us define $C(x_1, x_2)$ to be the cost of production of commodities 1 and 2 jointly, and $C(x_1, 0)$ and $C(0, x_2)$ the cost of production of the 1st and 2nd commodities separately, which is called stand-alone cost. If the following inequality holds, then there exist economies of scope:

$$C(x_1, x_2) < C(x_1, 0) + C(0, x_2).$$

The characteristics of the cost function are said to be sub-additive. Economies of scope obtain if the cost of joint production is smaller than if produced separately. The source of economies of scope is the existence of a common factor of production. Typical industries which have economies of scope are financial institutions. Banking and securities companies are separate businesses, but they are quite similar in nature. If one branch can handle both businesses of banking and securities together, it would be less costly than doing business separately. Another example is producing different products with common factors of productions. Numerically-controlled (NC) machine tools are of this category, which is a combination of mechanics and electronics. The assembling and processing industry which includes automobiles, household electric appliances, and precision machinery also has this characteristic. Automation of the production process using industrial robots makes the production of different kinds of products on a single assembly line possible.[3]

Similar to the definitions of economies of scale and economies of scope, economies of network might be formulated in the following way. Here, we take an example of the characteristics of outsourcing of management resources. Suppose there are two firms with the following production functions.

$$Y_1 = F_1(x_1)$$

$$Y_2 = F_2(x_2),$$

where Y_i and x_i stand for output and input of the i-th firm, respectively. Since these two firms interconnect with each other, they can make use of the other's outputs as management resources of both firms. When they are able to utilize the outputs of another firm as their inputs, their production function can be formalized as follows,

$$Y_1' = F_1(x_1, Y_2)$$

$$Y_2' = F_2(x_2, Y_1).$$

When economies of network exist, the following inequality holds:

$$Y_1' > Y_1$$

$$Y_2' > Y_2.$$

Each firm can obtain a larger output through the increase of efficiency of production by the outsourcing of management resources.[4]

---

[3] Other examples of economies of scope are electric appliances makers which produce PCs, beer brewers which sell soft drinks, and department stores which offer consumer loans.

[4] The difference between economies of scope and economies of network is that the latter are related to a single firm, while the letter to a larger number of firms.

IV. Industrial Transformation of the Japanese Economy

In any age, economic systems are built for exhibiting the efficiency of the system by adjusting to the economic environment such as production technology and consumers' tastes. In this sense, the process of economic development is the result of seeking the most ideal economic system to exploit efficiency. Modern economies have been shifting industry from agriculture to manufacturing, and from manufacturing to the service sector, and this transformation can be explained as seeking the best economic system that can adjust to the change in the economic environment.

Economic transformation in the post-war Japanese economy is shown in table 1. In the era of rapid growth, the main manufacturing industries were resource-related ones which showed economies of scale. After the oil crises in the late 1970s, the service sector and the assembling and processing industry became dominant, which have the characteristics of economies of scope. Thus, the Japanese economy could successfully transform its industries by making adjustments to them.,

As for economies of network, however, even now no industry has been able to fully adapt itself to it. It is for this reason that the performance of the current Japanese economy is so poor, as previously mentioned. In the following sections, we will analyze why this is so.

B. Japanese System I – Employment System

The Japanese system consists of several subsystems, as shown in figure 2: (a) the employment system, which relates to households and firms; (b) industrial groups which connect firms with other firms; (c) the relation between firms and the government sector; and (d) the political relationship of the government sector with the households who are the voters.

I. Characteristics of the Japanese Employment System

The most important economic system in an economy is the employment system, since it is the basis of not only economic but also social life. The differences

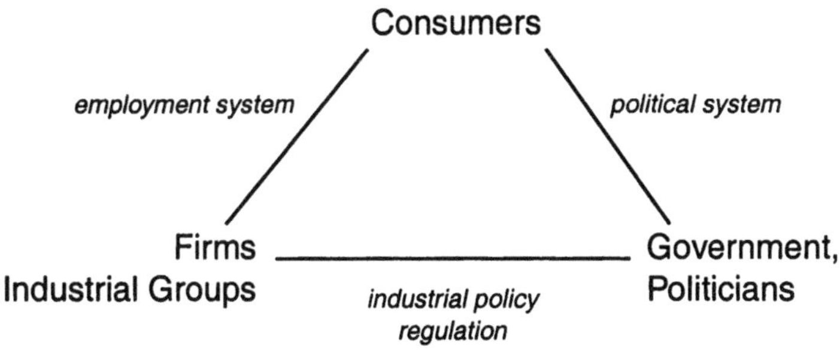

Figure 2: The Japanese System

Table 1

Transformation of the Japanese Economy

Period	Rapid Growth	Oil Crises	Bubble	Post-Bubble
Macroeconomy				
Growth rates	9.0%	3.9%	4.7%	0.9%
Factors of growth	domestic demand	foreign and government	domestic demand	foreign and government
Demand	not sufficient	variety of taste	high grade	low
Consumer attitude	disposable	Oshin syndrome	ecology	thrift
Constraints	trade balance	natural resources	strong yen	economic system
Industries				
Economies	economies of scale	economies of scope	economies of scope	econonomies of network
Innovation	process innv.	process innv.	product innv.	product innv.
Production	mass production	mass variety and small amount	variable variety and amount	variable variety and amount
Pattern of industry	natural resources	processing and assembling	processing and assembling service	telecom. and information
Leading industry	steel and chemical	auto and elec. appl.	auto and finance	multimedia
Method of prod.	automation	FMS	CIS	CALS
Industrial policy	heavy industry	conservation energy	mega-technology	venture business

of the employment systems of Japan and the Western economies is given in table 2.[5]

Table 2
Comparison of Two Employment Systems

Japanese Economy	Western Economies
Lifetime employment	Lay-off
Seniority	Ability
Bonus system	Only for executives
Retirement payment	None
Company union system	Union system

The seniority system implies that wage levels and promotions are based on the years contributed to the specific firm where they have been employed. Changing jobs results in losing seniority and the wage level will be lower. Lifetime employment and seniority systems are meaningful when both are in effect.

II. Economic Foundations of the Japanese Employment System

The economic explanation of the Japanese employment system is characterized by a long-term implicit contract relationship rather than the market mechanism of the Western economies. Without signing a formal contract, the workers and firm implicitly agree that labor will be supplied and the firm can hire them until retirement. Promotions and wage levels are determined inside the firm, and it is very rare for the firm to recruit middle management, for instance, from the market when a vacancy occurs. Thus, human resources are allocated inside the firms, and firms serve as a resource allocation mechanism, which is referred to as the internal labor market. A long-term implicit contract relationship is a system which does not use the market mechanism. On the other hand, in a Western firm, as in the above example, the vacancy of a particular position is usually filled by hiring an outside person, instead of promoting a person in the firm. The allocation of human resources is based on the market in a competitive way.

Both economies thus have polar systems and show marked contrast. Which is more efficient? We can compare them from the viewpoint of the cost of transactions and information in the market. In order for firms to carry out smooth transactions, they have to bear costs, among them, the cost of information. In the case

---

[5] For a concise exposition of the Japanese employment system, see Ito (1992), chapter 8.

of hiring a worker, it would be too late for the firm to realize that the new worker is not very capable, after he is hired. The firm thus spends time and energy in examining the workers prior to hiring them. On the other hand, when the firm promotes particular workers who have already been working at the firm, it is already well-informed about their background. This merit of the Japanese employment system thus saves the cost of transactions and information.[6]

In addition, since workers remain in one company over a long period of time, it is worthwhile to invest in human resources, which becomes the basis of the promotion of productivity. It is rather risky for a Western firm to invest in that way, since workers with higher productivity can easily leave the firm for higher wages. The firm invests in increasing a specific ability which can only be applied in the firm.

The most important mechanisms for maintaining the morale of the workers in the system are incentives and monitoring. In a Japanese firm, the bonus system provides an incentive for workers to contribute to the profit of the firm. The higher the profit of the firm, the larger the bonus workers receive. The bonus thus depends on the amount of profit. Transactions in the market have to be monitored all the time.[7] In a market economy, if there is no concrete monitoring system, morale hazards and adverse selection always occur due to the asymmetry of information. In order to prevent these phenomena, the firm has to spend lots of resources. A long-term relationship between the firm and its workers can save all of these costs.

C. Japanese System II – Industrial Group

Firms do not exist by themselves, but are interconnected with one another and form groups. Japanese firms form groups in a unique way, and it is these industrial groups that make Japanese management more competitive than that of other economies. There are two kinds of industrial groups, and in what follows, their definitions and economic functions will be presented.

---

[6] For a more detailed discussion, refer to papers in Aoki (1988), and Aoki and Dore (1994).

[7] For an extensive analysis of the bonus system from various aspects, see Freeman and Weizman (1987). The relation between the bonus and the Japanese savings rate has been analyzed by Ishikawa and Ueda (1984), for instance.

I. Horizontal Group: *Zaibatsu* Group

The first category is the horizontal group. There are six major industrial groups in this category, namely, Sumitomo, Sanwa, Mitsui, Mitsubishi, Fuji, and Ikkan. The historical background of these groups can be traced back to Zaibatsu before the Second World War. By the democratization of the economy under the allied forces, the holding companies of Zaibatsu were abolished. Soon after the end of the occupation, however, Zaibatsu groups reorganized again. Banks became the center of those groups instead of the holding companies, and each group was named after these banks. This system is referred to as the "main bank system", and those banks are called the "main banks".[8]

Horizontal implies that firms of all kinds of industries are members of the group, and this is quite in contrast to the vertical group which will be discussed later. They make close connections with each other by having interlocking directors and mutual shareholding. The reason for the formation of horizontal groups is not to make a larger profit through the exclusion of outsiders. Rather, it can be summarized as follows: (a) long-term contract relationship: As mentioned in the previous section, this was aimed at saving the cost of transactions and information. CEOs of major firms in these groups meet regularly, and they exchange information and discuss new joint projects, etc.; (b) risk-sharing: By combining with firms of different industries they can diversify the risk of management.[9] Risk also includes being taken over by others; and (c) growth-sharing: One can never be certain as to which industry will become a major one in the future. Since the group has firms in all industries, they can shift funds and human resources to a budding industry from the smokestack sector, and the group as a whole can adjust to new environments and enjoy continuous growth.[10] .

II. Vertical Group: Hierarchical Production Structure

Another category is referred to as the vertical group, and firms in this group are interconnected according to the distribution flow of materials, parts, and final

---

[8] The main bank is defined as the bank which has provided the largest share in loans. The relation between firms and the main bank are also that of a long-term implicit contract. The economic foundations of the main bank system are as follows: (a) saving the cost of transactions and information; (b) risk sharing; and (c) delegated monitoring. (c) asserts that the main bank representatively monitors firms for other banks. For further discussion, see Aoki and Patrick (1994).

[9] As for the risk-sharing hypothesis among firms in horizontal industrial groups, refer to Nakatani (1982).

[10] An example of growth-sharing in the Japanese automobile industry is discussed later in section C.III.

products. Typical examples are found in the assembling and processing industry. The characteristics of this industry is that their products consist of a tremendous amount of parts. The efficiency of production depends heavily on how these parts suppliers are organized. The solution of Japanese firms is the hierarchical production system. Parts suppliers are called subcontractors or "Keiretsu". The structure of Toyota, for example, is shown in figure 3.[11]

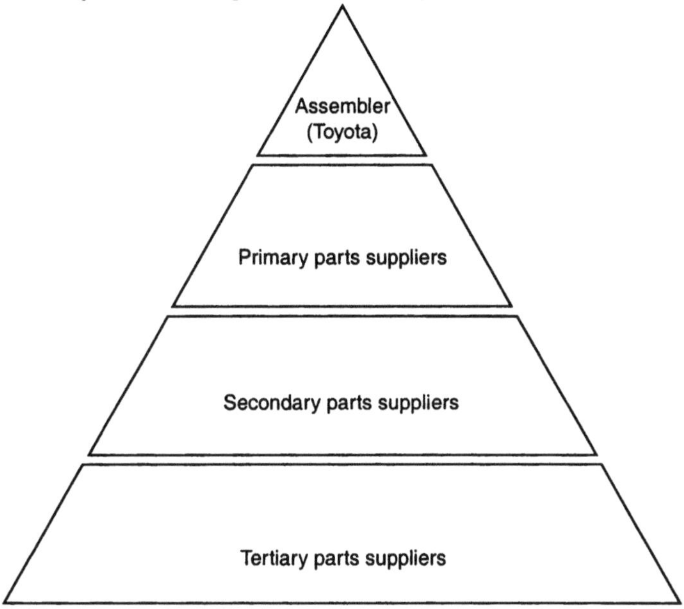

Figure 3: Hierarchical Production System

According to this figure, related firms of Toyota can be classified as follows:

(1) primary parts manufacturers

The firms in this category supply parts directly to Toyota. They supply complete parts such as air conditioners, clutches, brakes, and shock absorbers. These firms are quite big, and some are independent from Toyota. Toyota owns part of their stocks and sends directors. Toyota currently has 168 primary parts suppliers.

(2) secondary parts suppliers

Manufacturers of this type supply secondary parts such as clutches, cylinders, break linings, and thermostats to Toyota. The size of these firms is generally me-

[11] The reality is much more complicated. More detailed classification of parts suppliers and their relation with Toyota is presented in Tsuji (1991).

dium to small. Secondary parts suppliers have a strong tie with primary parts suppliers. There are 5,437 parts suppliers in this category.

(3) tertiary parts suppliers

Firms in this category are of a small size, and depend on family labor. As subcontractors of secondary parts suppliers, their main business is of a processing nature such as casting and forging. These are labor intensive and their productivity is low. The number in this category is the largest and totals more than 40,000.

Thus, Toyota has nearly 36,000 parts suppliers omitting double accounts. Toyota, however, purchases parts directly from less than 200 firms. Next, let us compare Toyota with GM, whose production structure is shown in figure 4. The production structure of GM is non-hierarchical, and it has only 12,000 parts suppliers. This implies that the ratio of domestic production is much higher than that of Toyota. A comparison of the two systems is summarized in table 3.

Table 3

Comparison of Toyota's and GM's Systems

Toyota	GM
Low domestic production: 20%–25%	High: 40%–50%
200 trade partners	Much larger number
Toyota dominates parts suppliers	Equal partners
Long-term commitment on quality and price	Market-based relationship
Parts suppliers' investment in specific equipment	General equipment

How does Toyota organize its huge hierarchical structure? It can be summarized as follows: (a) "Kanban Method" or just-in-time system, which implies the synchronization of production. This is a system of delivering the right parts to the right places at the right time. This enables saving the cost of inventories. Because of this, most factories of its parts suppliers are located close by to Toyota production factories; and (b) joint activity such as R&D, quality control (QC), and total quality control (TQC). The latter two are famous as "Kaizen". Primary parts suppliers include eleven firms called the "Toyota Group" whose businesses are related to the automobile industry. Their relationship with Toyota is so close that they engage in joint activities such as R&D, and improving the quality of parts through QC and TQC. These are the basis for the high quality of Toyota products. Toyota also has cooperative organizations of parts suppliers such as "*Kyohokai*" and "*Kyoeikai*". Their ties with Toyota are also strong.

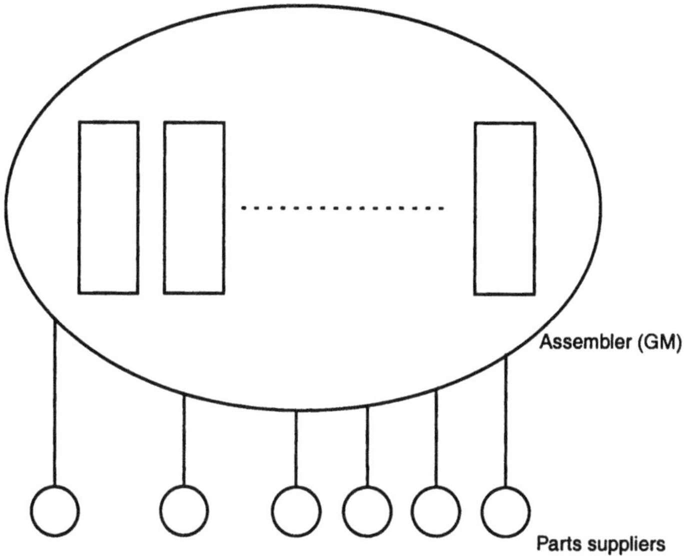

Figure 4: Non-Hierarchical Production System

III. Economic Basis of the Hierarchical Production System

The relationship of parts suppliers with Toyota can be explained by the long-term implicit contract. Once Toyota opens trade with a certain parts supplier, it implies that Toyota will make purchases from that parts supplier over a long period. Again, this long-term relationship can save the costs of transaction and information. Parts suppliers can invest in specific equipment for the production of Toyota parts only. In addition to this, the efficiency of the hierarchical production structure can be explained by the "principal-agent model". Toyota is the principal and the parts suppliers are agents. It is not necessarily efficient for Toyota to produce all kinds of parts by itself. It is more efficient to hire certain firms as agents and to make a contract with them for production, since those firms have more information on manufacturing-related parts than the principal has. Subcontracting is commonly adopted in industries such as construction, since subcontracting improves the efficiency of a large organization.[12]

The Toyota production system is a multi-layered principal-agent relationship. In the Toyota system, Toyota is the single and ultimate principal in the whole sys-

---

[12] For more detailed discussions on the economic explanation of the hierarchical production structure, see Asanuma (1992) and Tsuji (1991).

tem, but the primary parts suppliers are the principal and the secondary parts suppliers are agents at the second stage; secondary parts suppliers are the principal and tertiary parts suppliers are agents at the third stage. According to Coase (1937) and Williamson (1989), the optimal length of the stages in this context is determined by either the transaction costs or the information structure of the system to prevent opportunism and bounded rationality. Toyota can determine the optimal length of layers.

In order for a hierarchical production system using a principal and agent relationship to function effectively, the following two factors are required: (a) monitoring, and (b) an incentive scheme. As for the former, Toyota can easily check the quality of the parts, and continuously supervise these parts suppliers. Since all parts are manufactured by its subcontractors, the quality of its parts determines the quality of Toyota automobiles. As for the latter, the incentive for nearly 36,000 subcontractors to support the hierarchical production system is "growth-sharing", that is, when Toyota grows, the parts suppliers also grow.[13] As a matter of fact, parts suppliers grow in step with Toyota, and most Toyota Group firms are now world-scale enterprises. An interesting relationship can be found in the negotiation of pricing of parts between Toyota and its parts suppliers. Toyota is said to be very strict in the pricing of parts. Prices are basically based on the calculation of costs, but the profit margin of parts suppliers is not subject to price negotiation, but rather based on some historical value, since a severe price-cut would spoil the incentive to work with Toyota.

D. Economies of Network and the Japanese System

In this section, we attempt to analyze the Japanese system in the context of information and network. We also show that the system which fully exhibits economies of scale and economies of scope might not be the best system for economies of network. In contrast to Japanese firms, firms in the U.S. have been utilizing EDI (electric data interchange) and Intranet, and seem to take advantage of the information society. The current economic boom in the U.S. has been inspired by these innovations. We analyze why this is not the case for Japanese firms.

[13] The growth of the firms in the Toyota Group in terms of the amount of capital and the number of employees is analyzed also by Tsuji (1991).

I. Traditional Information Interchange inside Japanese Firms

The essence of economies of network has been summarized as follows: (a) outsourcing of management resources; (b) adjustability to change in the economic environment; and (c) economies of speed. The transmission mechanism of information inside Japanese firms is basically based on paper through hierarchy, and importance is placed on face-to-face communication. In this transmission process, an important aspect should be noted which is particular only to Japanese firms; namely, "groupism" or "*Nemawashi* (rooting)". This is related to the harmonious relationship between labor and management. Through this system of sharing information in the firms, labor can feel that they are participating in the decision making, and have the incentive to contribute to the firms. Japanese workers belong to a particular section of management, and they work jointly as a team. All this results in the "groupism" of Japanese firms. This would not be possible without the lifetime employment and seniority systems.

It should be noted, however, that there is a risk of sectionalism and bureaucracy in management. Information might be kept only in a certain section and not revealed or transmitted to other sections. Information is thus made use of only for the members of a group. In this context, the Japanese system is a closed network. As mentioned in previous sections, the Japanese system does not use the market mechanism, and it tends to be less transparent in terms of information. Asymmetric information between insiders and outsiders is much wider than in economies with the market mechanism. Lack of corporate governance widely reported these days in the context of the corruption of Japanese firms is due to this asymmetric information. Non-performing loans of banks are typical. When tax money was introduced as a way to cover such loans, the authorities and banks promised to reveal information on them. No concrete information has yet been revealed.

II. LAN in Japanese Firms

Information innovation has been gradually penetrating Japanese firms. In some industries such as the distribution sector, for instance, POS is widely utilized to save the costs of inventories by acquiring sales information in real time. Moreover, LAN (Local Area Network) has been put into practice in various industries. In Kao's system, for instance, all operations related to production in the Kyushu branch factory can be controlled by the headquarters located far away. Multinational companies such as Toyota, Sony, and Honda have already established a global network of information all over the world. These are, however, rare examples of utilizing the network.

Though Intranet and LAN are gaining in popularity, it is not at the same level as in the U.S, where firms use e-mail or voice mail extensively as a means of sharing information between all positions in the firm in the following way: (a) exchange of ordinary business information among workers; (b) sending reports or proposals to upper management; (c) transmission of PC data; and (d) exchange of information related to clients and customers. One can directly access other worker's computers to check their schedule, etc.[14] These innovations in the 1990s not only speed up decision making, but also reduce manpower and labor costs.

The success of U.S. firms in the 1990s lies in their management system. In contrast to Japanese firms, the U.S. system is rather top-down in decision making. In such cases, all business decision making is efficiently transmitted by the above-mentioned information system to all sections. Moreover, there is no need for middle management, since all workers are directly interconnected to top management. Thus, the organizations tend to be flat in structure. There are no obstacles arising from making organizations flat, since they have a more flexible system. Because of the flat structure, savings can be made in the cost and time of transmitting information and decision making.

Japanese firms now own the same ratio of PCs including word processors per worker as in the U.S. The problem here is that they are not interconnected with each other, and exist separately. Moreover, the decision making method through e-mail, for instance, does not necessarily fit the traditional business culture of Japanese firms, such as the bottom-up decision making process or the harmonious relationship between labor and management. The latter can function effectively with face-to-face communication. Business organization must be changed in order for economies of network to be fully exhibited.

III. Transformation of the U.S. Economy and Economies of Network

Currently, the U.S. economy is enjoying an economic boom which began in 1991. The U.S. economy is said to have entered a new stage of development, that is, entered a "New Economy". The assertion of a New Economy and the recovery of the U.S. in the 1990s have resulted in information innovation to exploit economies of network. In what follows, two cases have been selected to examine the

---

[14] These are examples of Hewlett-Packard Japan. Through interviews with officers in charge of its information system, it seems that HP Japan utilizes e-mail most extensively among Japanese firms.

above-mentioned phenomena, namely, concurrent engineering in the automobile industry and venture business.

(1) Concurrent engineering. During the 1980s, the Japanese automobile industry showed its supremacy over the U.S. All technological innovations introduced in the U.S. automobile industry in the fifteen years since the late 1970s are said to have come from Japan, namely, just-in-time production and QC (Kaizen). In 1993, however, Chrysler announced the "Neon" to the market, which shocked the Japanese automobile industry since it had a 2,000cc engine but was priced at only ¥1,000,000. The price of a Japanese automobile with the same engine size was more than twice this amount. The secret to this low price was concurrent engineering, that is, sharing information among different sections of the firm such as production, R&D, and design. In the development of the Neon, Chrysler could cut the R&D period and costs dramatically: thirty-one months and $1 billion.[15] The average period for Japanese assemblers is forty-two months, and that for the U.S. sixty-two months. GM Saturn needed seven years and $3.5 billion, and the Ford Escort required four years and $2 billion for R&D.

Concurrent engineering is the method of developing a new automobile in such a way that different sections engaged in R&D are interconnected with each other through a network of computers, and each can monitor or trace the current stages of development of the others. The usual method of development is linear, that is, passing the results of R&D in each section to the other, one by one.[16] If one section finds mistakes or something to improve, it is returned to the previous section. Concurrent engineering, on the other hand, is multidimensional, and all sections can be engaged in the development simultaneously via computer displays.

Another factor leading to the recovery of the U.S. automobile industry is obtaining parts from all over the world, namely, Taiwan, Korea, and Hong Kong. Since they do not have fixed subcontractors like Japanese assemblers, they can choose parts suppliers of better quality and cheaper prices from the market. They can freely extend the network of parts suppliers. The same strategy is also employed by U.S. PC makers, which can sell PCs at far cheaper prices than Japanese makers. In sum, the U.S. industry takes advantage of not hiring fixed subcontractors, or *Keiretsu.*

(2) Venture business. Another factor of economic growth in the U.S. is the venture business, which is defined as a small business oriented exclusively to high-technology or R&D activities. It is also a young business, not an established large corporation. A tremendous amount of venture businesses can be found in

---

[15] Neon is not yet sold in Japan. It is said that its quality is not of a level satisfactory to the Japanese consumers, since they are more interested in quality than price.

[16] R&D teams of Toyota and its group companies meet regularly on a face-to-face basis when they develop new automobiles. The long-term relationship makes this possible.

industries related to computers, computer software, bio-technology, telecommunications, and new materials. In these industries, the deregulation of business activities during the Reagan administration in the early 1980s is one factor for promoting venture businesses. In addition to this, there are other factors which can be summarized as follows: (a) labor market: There must be a large number of entrepreneurs to start a new business. Since a venture business is related to technology, entrepreneurs starting it up are likely to be engineering specialists, and they need persons to take care of management. The highly flexible labor market can supply those specialists; (b) transfer of new technology: Venture businesses require new technology, which is partly supplied by universities. Universities have technology transfer centers which supply new technology to be commercialized. An example of this can be found in the relationship between Stanford University and Silicon Valley, or MIT and Route 128.[17] Universities are the core of research parks, and play a coordinating role by interconnecting the new technology of university laboratories and entrepreneurs; and (c) funds: The U.S. financial market has already been deregulated and there are many different distribution channels of funds for venture businesses. Those are angles, venture capitals, NASDAQ, and public funds. Thus, in the U.S., there is an abundance of funds for investing in venture businesses which seek high returns by taking risks.

E. Concluding Remarks: The Japanese System in the 21st Century

Thus far, we have analyzed the economic basis of the Japanese system, and how it plays a role in economic development. In addition, the Japanese system does not suit the current economic transformation of a stable, aging, and globalizing economy. The efficiency of an economy in the age of the information society can be found in economies of network. Here, we will discuss possible reforms for shifting the Japanese economy towards becoming one which can exhibit economies of network.

---

[17] The Ministry of Education deregulated the activities of universities. Some private universities started the scheme to commercialize their technology in the same way as in the U.S. National universities have been establishing joint research centers to accept researchers and research funds from the private sector. It will take more time for these institutions to be in full operation.

I. Transformation of the Japanese Economy and the Japanese System

The economic transformation of the Japanese economy is summarized by a low growth rate, aging, and globalization. The Japanese system is not constructed to cope with these factors. On the contrary, these factors will destroy the basis of the Japanese system.

As for the employment system, the lifetime employment and seniority systems are based on the continuous growth of the economy, that is, growth implying the larger size of firms, and more positions guaranteed to workers. Under the seniority system, wages increase as workers become older. The Japanese employment system makes this possible since the younger generation which receives relatively low wages subsidizes the older generation who have relatively high wages; that is, it is an intergenerational subsidy system. However, the aging economy implies that those who comprise the younger generation are shrinking in number. Thus, firms have to bear more costs, and this has become a burden. Due to this, more firms have shifted from a seniority system to one in which wages are based on working ability. In addition, senior workers are either forced to leave the firms for affiliated ones, or are simply fired.[18]

Globalization is another challenge to the Japanese system. Japanese firms have been shifting their activities overseas by means of direct investment. This is not simply because they aim to exploit lower wages and weaker exchange rates, but because they have to take this strategy in order to survive in an intensive, mega-competitive environment. They have to take into account where to build a factory, where to sell a product, where to engage in R&D activity, etc. Globalization makes it necessary for Japanese labor to compete with the low-waged labor of LDCs. This will have a serious effect on the Japanese employment system.

Japanese automobile assemblers have been increasing overseas production. In the host countries, they are levied on local content, that is, some portion of the parts have to be purchased from local firms. In this aspect, it has become harder to maintain *Keiretsu* in Japan. The hollowing of the economy is now a reality.

II. Possible Reform of the Japanese System

As shown in the previous section, the U.S. economy recovered from nearly twenty years of stagnation since the oil crises of the mid–1970s by information innovation and the venture business. A key factor is that the system was changed

[18] The effect of an aging economy is analyzed, for instance, by Hurd and Yashiro (1997).

in such a way as to exhibit economies of network. We have also shown that the Japanese economy cannot rely on these strategies, since the conditions under which they work have not yet been established. As for the information-sharing system in firms, the traditional scheme is still firmly rooted. As for venture businesses, the Japanese system is too conservative for ambitious entrepreneurs to emerge from the Japanese employment system. Students still want to find a job in traditional larger firms. Banks do not wish to invest in risky venture businesses, and they ask for real estate as collateral. The idea or the know-how of venture businesses are not appreciated as collateral. The local as well as central governments provide public funds to venture businesses, but the procedure for applications is too bureaucratic, and the funds are not in great demand by venture businesses.[19]

Under these circumstances, what reforms are possible? As shown in section D.III., economies of network can only be fully exhibited in a flexible and diversified economy, since networks interconnect economic agents in many different ways. One essential reform is deregulation. Free and competitive activities by the private sector are the only source of affluent and diversified networks. The government cannot create such flexibility. In the underlying context of the information society, deregulation is urgent in the telecommunications industry and the labor market. The number of people connected to the Internet is growing rapidly, but the ratio per population is the lowest among developed economies. This is due to the high charges for telecommunications services. The speed of Intranet usage in management also depends upon ISDN charges. Deregulation in the labor market makes it more flexible and leads to higher labor mobility.[20]

The reform of the educational system is also important. In the age of the information society, creativity is most valuable. In an economy with economies of scale or economies of scope, the supremacy of physical commodity determines competitiveness. The Japanese educational system has so far succeeded in reaching the highest level, but it is standardized. Everyone thinks in the same way, and there is no room for individuality. This educational system is suited to economies of scale, since it can produce masses of uniform laborers with a certain level of education. The importance of technology has shifted from process innovation to product innovation, and creativity is essential for the latter.

---

[19] Typical examples of successful venture businesses are Sony and Honda. Most new or venture businesses emerge from industrial groups, as analyzed in section C. They take the form of affiliated companies, and usually funds and manpower are supplied by their parent companies. Thus, venture business as in the U.S. is very rare in Japan.

[20] The Ministry of Posts and Telecommunications now plans to implement a new scheme of price regulation, that is the price-cap regulation. The U.S. and the U.K. adopted it more than ten years ago.

The socioeconomic system is the last to be changed, since it is based on the old structure. The strongest obstacle to an information society is our way of thinking, that is, inertia and holding on to the old system. We tend to like to stick with tradition, since it is rather comfortable doing so. Friction is to be encountered when mastering or confronting a new system. This is the true reason why Japanese firms are reluctant to make use of e-mail or Intranet. It is necessary not only for organizations but for ourselves as well to undergo change in order to capture economies of network.

Acknowledgment

The author expresses his deep gratitude for the comments and suggestions received from the participants of the 17th Joint Nagoya-Freiburg Seminar.

References

Aoki, M. (1988): Information, Incentives, and Bargaining in the Japanese Economy, Cambridge University Press.

Aoki, M., and H. *Patrick* (eds.) (1994): The Japanese Main Bank System: Its Relevance for Developing and Transforming Economies, Oxford University Press.

Aoki, M., and R. *Dore* (eds.) (1994): The Japanese Firm: The Sources of Competitive Strength, Oxford University Press.

Asanuma, B. (1992): Risk Absorption in Japanese Subcontracting: A Microeconometric Study of the Automobile Industry, Journal of the Japanese and International Economy, Vol. 6, No. 1, pp. 1–29.

Coase, R. H. (1937): The Nature of the Firm, Economica, 4, pp. 386–405.

Freeman, R. B., and M. L. *Weizman* (1987): Bonus and Employment in Japan, Journal of the Japanese and International Economies, Vol. 1, pp. 168–94.

Hurd, M., and N. *Yashiro* (eds.) (1997): The Economic Effects of Aging in the United States and Japan, NBER.

Ishikawa, T., and K. *Ueda* (1984): The Bonus Payment System and Japanese Personal Savings, in Economic Analysis of the Japanese Firm, ed. by M. Aoki, North Holland.

Ito, T. (1992): The Japanese Economy, MIT Press.

Katz, M. L., and C. *Shapiro* (1985): Network Externality, Competition, and Compatibility, American Economic Review, Vol. 75.

Nakatani, I. (1982): Risk-Sharing and the Role of Business Groups in Japan, Osaka Economic Papers, Vol. 32, No. 2–3, pp. 219–45.

Tsuji, M. (1991): Structural Shift in the Japanese Economy and Regional Adjustment: Tokai Region and Automobile Industry, Proceedings of the First Pacific Rim Conference on the Resource Management, National Chiao Tung University, Taiwan.

Tsuji, M., and T. *Nishiwaki* (1996): Nettowa-ku Nirai (Future of Network), Nihonhyoron-sha (in Japanese).

Williamson, O. E. (1989): Transaction Cost Economics, in R. Schmalensee and R. Willig (eds.), Handbook of Industrial Organization, Vol. 1, North Holland.

Nominal Wage Setting and Employment at the Aggregate and Sectoral Level

Jürgen Jerger

A. Introduction

For more than two decades, the fight against unemployment is one of the top priorities on the agenda of economic policy. Nevertheless, unemployment figures continue to rise to ever new record levels from one business cycle to the next. This is not only true for Germany and most other European economies, but also – albeit at a substantially lower level – for Japan.

Modern explanations of this development focus on the interpretation of the labour market as a mechanism to balance the distributional aspirations of different interest groups (Landmann 1989, Layard et al. 1991, Lindbeck 1993, Franz 1996). Since distributional aspirations are *real* magnitudes, these models are cast in terms of real wages and hence the role of nominal wage setting is not made explicit. Nominal wage setting, however, is the operational level at which firms and workers (or their respective unions) determine the labour market outcome to a large extent.

This paper analyses the effects of nominal wage setting at both the sectoral and aggregate level. After a short review of the relevant literature (section B), a simple model is presented that brings together the traditional classical and Keynesian explanations of the labour market (section C). In this setting, it is possible to assess the relative merits of Keynesian (nominal) demand policy and (nominal) wage policy. In section D, the model is confronted with both aggregate and sectoral data of the German economy. From a practical point of view, the sectoral results are especially relevant with regard to the present discussion about the structure of wage bargains in Germany. Section E offers some conclusions.

B. Nominal Wages and Employment

The political discussion of wage setting centers around two issues, which both remain highly relevant in the face of persistent high unemployment. First, there is an argument about the "purchasing power" vs. "cost" aspects of wages, that questions the very sign of the correlation between wages and employment. Second, there is a large literature which tries to give a "scientific" benchmark for the determination of "appropriate" nominal wages. Since the results of this paper pertain to both aspects, I will briefly review these two strands of discussion.

I. Purchasing Power vs. Cost Aspect of Wages

The so-called "purchasing power argument" describes a *positive* correlation between wages and employment, since – as the argument goes – higher wages lead to higher demand on the goods markets and hence to more employment. In the face of sluggish and/or incomplete adjustment of prices to nominal wage claims, an increase of the latter could simultaneously boost real wages and employment. The cost aspect of wages leads to exactly the opposite conclusion, since higher real wages depress labour demand according to standard neoclassical theory. Despite the obvious policy relevance, the purchasing power aspect is widely ignored in the political and scientific discussions. The German Council of Economic Advisors may serve as a typical example (SVR 1977, Tz. 291 ff.). Some twenty years ago, it was simply stated that the purchasing power argument is wrong (SVR 1977, Tz. 292), without even an attempt to give (or at least to cite) a rigorous analysis. Since then, the statement was repeated sometimes (the last time in SVR 1995, Tz. 266), but never given a deeper analytical treatment.[1]

This remarkable absence of theoretical and empirical work is also reflected in the academic literature. The paper by Rohwedder/Herberg (1984) is an important exception, although their model is mainly descriptive and not based on some kind of optimizing behaviour of economic agents. Hence, despite the discussion of a host of possibilities – reaction of monetary policy, price adjustment etc. –, the sign of the wage-employment correlation remains unclear: "Not surprisingly, our main conclusion is that neither the PPA [Purchasing Power Argument, J. J.] nor

---

[1] The famous OECD Jobs Study treats this issue in a very similar way. The employment-wage nexus according to the purchasing power argument is stated in the subjunctive, the dominance of the cost aspect is simply stated: "The positive labour demand effects of wage cuts *may* be moderated by the lower purchasing power of the employees in the short run." (OECD 1994, p. 2, italics added). After this remark, the purchasing power aspect is totally ignored.

the PCA [Production Cost Argument, J. J.] is generally valid." (Rohwedder/Herberg 1984, p. 587).

The state of empirical knowledge mirrors the theoretical confusion or neglect of the issue. Schuster/Weiß (1991) attempt to tackle the question via the joint estimation of employment and (consumption goods) demand equations for German data. Employment is treated as a function of both the wage cost and goods demand, the latter is a function of labour income, i.e. the product of wages and employment. However, there is neither an endogenous price adjustment nor a (demand) policy reaction function and hence the results are quite difficult to interpret. In fact, for Schuster/Weiß (1991) it was difficult to find any clear-cut result, since they could not identify a large impact of nominal wages on employment. Like in the paper of Rohwedder/Herberg (1984), the problems stem from the lack of a coherent theoretical framework. This poor "state of the art" explains pretty well, why the "purchasing power vs. cost aspect discussion" of wages is used and abused by different interest groups for their own concerns, leaving the economics profession in the uncomfortable – although familiar – position of an undecided referee.[2] The perception of the "two-handed" economist on this question is quite common, although the main advisory institutions reject the implications of the purchasing power idea. It is one result of this paper that nominal wage restraint will boost employment also if and – as it will turn out somewhat paradoxically – *especially* if the purchasing power aspect of wages is taken into account.

II. Nominal Wage Setting Rules

A second strand of the policy discussion is concerned with a variety of "scientific" rules which are designed to find an "appropriate" nominal wage (increase) in the wage bargains. Since its very first report (SVR 1965, Tz. 248), the German Council of Economic Advisors repeatedly advocated the concept of "cost neutral wage policy". This concept requires nominal wages to be set such that unit labour

[2] Even a very superficial scan of (political) statements reveals the importance of the purchasing power aspect of wages in everyday thinking. In an advertisement published in "The Economist" (July, 26th 1997, p. 54), the Commerzbank tried to answer the headline question: "Has wage restraint *aggravated* Germany's employment crisis?" (italics added). In a recent expert hearing (April, 27th 1997) of the Deutsche Bundestag, union representatives explicitly denied that high wages are at the root of the employment problem and a recognized economist even said that higher wages will lead to positive employment perspectives. Similarly, Oskar Lafontaine, the chairman of the German Social Democratic Party, in a recent letter to party members disagrees with the call of the government for low wages by invoking the reasoning of the purchasing power argument.

cost are constant in nominal terms. Hence, the nominal wage increases have to be in line with productivity growth[3] adjusted for variations in the cost of other factors of production. In this way, the wage policy avoids the danger of a cost push inflation.[4] Similar reflections lead to the recommendation of the European Commission (Europäische Kommission 1996, p. 62) that an appropriate *real* wage target can be found by the rule of thumb "productivity growth less 1 percent", where the "less 1 percent"-part is intended to contribute to the fight against unemployment.

There are, however, at least two problems with this kind of policy guideline: First, it requires an estimate of employment neutral productivity growth in order to avoid rising real wages in perfect harmony with productivity figures but at decreasing employment. Even if wage increases are employment neutral in this sense, this may be too aggressive in the face of an expanding labour force. The increasing labour force of the 1980s in Germany, for example, due to the baby boom some twenty years before and higher participation rates among women, only partly translated into higher employment. Second, the exclusive focus on the rate of technical progress neglects the possible influences of other factors such as rising capital cost and the related decrease of the optimal capital-labour ratio.[5]

Both problems can lead to serious problems at a practical level. The problem to estimate the appropriate rate of technical progress may be best illustrated by pointing to the ongoing discussion about the causes of the productivity slowdown since the mid–1970s.[6] Another striking example for the associated problems is the overestimation of future productivity growth after the German reunification and the resulting timetable for the equalization of wages in both parts of Germa-

---

[3] Productivity growth refers to increases of (marginal) labour productivity *at a given level of employment*. To speak in familiar theoretical terms, it is the shift of and not the movement along a given labour demand schedule that gives room for employment neutral wage increases. This shift is the result of either capital formation or technical progress.

[4] More recently, the German Council of Economic Advisors disavows such strict rules: "There is no general formula for an economically optimal wage setting, but one can give a guideline." (SVR 1995, Tz. 370, translation by the author)

[5] The effects of rising capital cost and labour force are analyzed in Jerger (1993) and Landmann/Jerger (1993) with German data.

[6] A recent attempt to deal with this question with a series of country studies is the volume edited by Crafts/Toniolo (1996); see also Crafts (1996). The upshot of this work is the idea that the high growth rates after World war II until the oil shock of the 70s can be understood in terms of Solovian catch up, whereas the lower growth rates thereafter mark an episode of "steady state" growth. The main challenge to this analysis is the notion that there was no such thing like a slowdown in productivity growth, but an increasing problem of price index mismeasurement (Boskin/Jorgenson 1997).

ny. This (partial) equalization led both to huge transfers to East Germany and a massive decline of employment.[7]

Even within the economics profession, the issues are not always clear. A recent publication of the ifo-Institute (Köddermann 1996), for example, compares international data on unit labour cost and concludes that the high level of German wages is more or less fully justified by corresponding productivity differentials. It is clear that this is the case *at the actual level of employment*. This, however, is not very soothing in the face of two-digit numbers of the unemployment rate. Similarly, one can find the opinion that a weakening capital formation is *good* news for an increasing labour force (e. g. Kromphardt 1995, p. 23–24).

These statements more than justify to think again about the preconditions for growing employment. In the rest of the paper, we will ask whether and to which extent unemployment can be reduced by nominal wage restraint and whether one can formulate a rule that helps to translate nominal wage variations into changes of employment.

C. Sectoral and Aggregate Effects of Nominal Wage Variations

I. Some Preliminary Remarks

In this section, I intend to develop a model that captures the consequences of nominal wage variations for the key macroeconomic variables, namely output, employment and the price level.

Besides nominal wages, the second major exogenous variable in the model is aggregate *nominal* demand, which is assumed to be (partly) controlled by fiscal and monetary authorities. Although the model is well suited for an analysis of the interdependence between (union) wage setting and aggregate demand management, I do not pursue this in any detail.

The survey of the preceding section showed that – at least at the political level – the argument between cost and purchasing power aspect is still going on. Since the positive employment effects of nominal wage restraint will be one of the central results, the possibility of demand effects of wages has to be modeled explicitly. This is done by specifying real aggregate demand as a function of real labour income (i. e. the product of real wages and employment). It can be shown that this explicit modeling of the purchasing power aspect of wages does not weaken the

[7] The authoritative analysis of Sinn/Sinn (1993) pointed very clearly – and in time – to the potential problems of this "high wage/high tech strategy".

negative employment effect of nominal wage increases. Quite to the contrary – and somewhat paradoxically –, the employment effects of nominal wage variations are reinforced by the demand effect of labour income.

Even without any formal analysis, it is quite obvious that the effects of nominal wage variations depend on whether we are looking at the sectoral or aggregate level. In order to explore these differences in more detail, the starting point of the following model is the sectoral level from which an aggregate solution will be derived in a second step.

The main innovation of the model in this paper relative to the existing literature is the explicit treatment of the demand effects of labour income. Apart from this point, at the sectoral level the model proceeds along the lines of the by now familiar monopolistic competition framework. The aggregate model that can be derived from this, has the structure of a standard aggregate supply/aggregate demand (AS/AD) model. Solow (1986) and Manning (1990, who, however, is interested in the effects of a technology with increasing returns) are the references that come closest to the spirit of the following model.

One further result of the analysis will be a "rule" for nominal wage setting, that has been suggested in the German literature before (Koll 1988, Lehment 1991, 1993). However, these papers failed to derive the wage rule from a formal model of the labour demand decision with or without demand effects of labour income. The rule states that a nominal wage increase leaves employment unaffected if the growth rate of nominal wages equals the growth rate of nominal demand. Accordingly, "wage restraint" is defined by a positive differential between the growth rates of nominal demand and nominal wages. Vice versa, employment will fall, if nominal wages grow faster than nominal demand.

The following section C.II develops the model at the sectoral level, before I go on to the aggregate level in C.III. Section C.IV presents and discusses the main results of the analysis.

II. The Sectoral Level

Consider an economy consisting of S sectors $i = 1, \ldots, S$, each of which produces a single, differentiated good according to

$$Y_i = N_i^{\alpha} A_i^{1-\alpha} e^{u_i} \qquad \forall i \tag{1}$$

N_i denotes the amount of sectoral employment, u_i a sector-specific productivity shock with zero mean and finite variance: $u_i \sim (0, \sigma_{u_i}^2)$, respectively. A_i is a catchall for other factors of production (capital stock, technology), which are treated as exogenous. In order to purge the aggregate results from an effect of the number of sectors, it is assumed that the production function exhibits constant returns with respect to N_i and A_i. The specific form of the Cobb-Douglas function enables the computation of a closed-form solution.

Aggregate real demand is specified as follows:

$$Y^d \equiv D = \frac{M}{P} \cdot \left(\frac{WN}{P}\right)^{\beta} \qquad 0 \le \beta < 1 \tag{2}$$

M, W and P denote an index for aggregate nominal demand management (i. e. some joint measure of fiscal and monetary policy), the aggregate nominal wage and the aggregate price level, respectively. This specification can be considered as a generalization of a demand function which can be derived from the equation of exchange.[8] For $\beta > 0$, real demand is a positive function of real labour income in the economy.[9] Although (2) is essentially ad hoc, i. e. without explicit microfoundations, it should capture the notion of the purchasing power aspect of wages quite adequately. At the same time, the comparison of the results with and without this role of labour income is very easy.

In order to derive the sectoral demand functions, a further assumption about the utility function of the representative consumer is necessary. I assume that the sectoral outputs are perceived as imperfect substitutes with an identical and constant elasticity of substitution $\sigma > 1$ between all pairs of goods. This assumption constitutes the well-known love-of-variety approach. The utility function conforming to this description is given by:

$$U = \left(\sum_{i=1}^{S} Y_i^{\frac{\sigma-1}{\sigma}}\right)^{\frac{\sigma}{\sigma-1}}$$

Furthermore, we assume that the number S of differentiated goods is large enough to preclude strategic interdependencies between the different sectors, and hence the S sectors are monopolistic competitors. The demand function for a single sector can be derived from these assumptions as (Dixit/Stiglitz 1977, Blanchard/Fischer 1989, ch. 8.1):

$$Y_i^d \equiv D_i = \frac{1}{S}\left(\frac{P_i}{P}\right)^{-\sigma} D \tag{3}$$

where the price index P can be computed from the dual cost minimization problem:

[8] The equation of exchange results from (2) for $\beta = 0$, if M is interpreted as nominal money stock and the velocity of money is normalized to unity.

[9] The elasticity of real demand with respect to (M/P) is normalized to unity for convenience only. Nothing of substance would change with a more general specification.

$$P = \left(\frac{1}{S}\sum_{i=1}^{S} P_i^{1-\sigma}\right)^{\frac{1}{1-\sigma}}$$

In this setup, the price elasticity of demand is equal to the elasticity of substitution between the different varieties.

Inserting (3) into (1) yields an equation which gives sectoral employment as a function of aggregate demand and the relative price of variety *i*:

$$N_i = \left[\left(\frac{D}{S}\right)\left(\frac{P_i}{P}\right)^{-\sigma} A_i^{\alpha-1} e^{-u_i}\right]^{\frac{1}{\alpha}}$$

In each sector, the firm chooses P_i such that profits are maximized. Hence the following problem has to be solved:

$$\text{(4)} \qquad \max_{P_i} \Pi_i = \frac{Y_i P_i}{P} - \frac{W_i N_i}{P} = \left(\frac{D}{S}\right)\left(\frac{P_i}{P}\right)^{1-\sigma} - \frac{W_i}{P}\left[\left(\frac{D}{S}\right)\left(\frac{P_i}{P}\right)^{-\sigma} A_i^{\alpha-1} e^{-u_i}\right]^{\frac{1}{\alpha}},$$

where Π_i represents real profits (where the aggregate price level is used to deflate nominal profits).

Since the number of sectors S is assumed to be large enough to rule out strategic interactions, the decision about P_i does not take into account the feedback to the aggregate price level. The same holds true for W and N and hence for aggregate demand D. Under these assumptions, the solution to (4) is given by

$$\text{(5)} \qquad (p_i - p) = \frac{1}{\Delta_1}[-\alpha\mu + (1-\alpha)(d-s) + \alpha(w_i - p) - (1-\alpha)a_i - u_i],$$

where $\Delta_1 \equiv \sigma(1-\alpha) + \alpha > 1$ and $\mu \equiv \log\left(\frac{(\sigma-1)\alpha}{\sigma}\right)$. Lower case letters denote logs of the corresponding level variables introduced in upper case letters above.

Together with the production function (1) and the sectoral demand function (4), eq. (5) allows to compute the reduced form solution for the endogenous variables Y_i, N_i and P_i. In log-linear form, we obtain

$$\text{(6)} \qquad \begin{bmatrix} y_i \\ n_i \\ p_i \end{bmatrix} = \frac{1}{\Delta_1} n \begin{bmatrix} \alpha & -\alpha & \alpha\beta & -\alpha\sigma & \alpha\beta & \alpha(\sigma-\beta-1) & \sigma & \sigma(1-\alpha) & \alpha\sigma \\ 1 & -1 & \beta & -\sigma & \beta & \sigma-\beta-1 & \sigma-1 & (\sigma-1)(1-\alpha) & \sigma \\ 1-\alpha & -(1-\alpha) & \beta(1-\alpha) & \alpha & \beta(1-\alpha) & (1-\alpha)(\sigma-\beta-1) & -1 & -(1-\alpha) & -\alpha \end{bmatrix} \cdot x_i$$

where $x_i = \begin{bmatrix} m & s & w & w_i & n & p & u_i & a_i & \mu \end{bmatrix}'$.

In this system, aggregate employment and the aggregate price level are still exogenous, since they are given for every single sector. The aggregate model has to endogenize these variables, of course. However, the following observations can already be made at this stage:

A (non-coordinated) nominal wage increase at the sectoral level leads to an equiproportionate change of the relevant real wage $(w_i - p)$, since – by assumption – the aggregate variables are unaffected by sectoral changes. The higher real wage cost are partly translated into higher prices for the sectoral output, which in turn depresses demand and hence employment in this sector. Thus, the labour income is influenced by two counteracting forces. Under the assumptions of this model, the negative effect on employment more than eliminates the positive effect of higher nominal wages and hence the sectoral labour income declines:

$$\left.\frac{\partial(w_i + n_i - p)}{\partial w_i}\right|_{dw=0} = \left.\frac{\partial(w_i + n_i)}{\partial w_i}\right|_{dw=0} = -\frac{\alpha(\sigma-1)}{\Delta_1} < 0$$

Positive sectoral productivity shocks lead to a lower relative output price and hence boost demand. Since the elasticity of output with respect to the shock is larger than unity, the higher productivity also boosts employment.

One might argue from (6) that the purchasing power from wages paid outside the sector *i* could boost employment in *i*. This observation is misleading, however, since it does not take into account the feedback of aggregate nominal wages on aggregate prices and employment. To explore these effects, we now have to turn to the aggregate model.

III. The Aggregate Level

The aggregation of the sectoral models is achieved most easily by using some simple symmetry assumptions. Eq. (7) contains the aggregation rules:

$$(7) \qquad \begin{bmatrix} y \\ n \\ a \\ w \\ p \\ u \end{bmatrix} = \begin{bmatrix} s + y_i \\ s + n_i \\ s + a_i \\ w_i \\ p_i \\ u_i \end{bmatrix}$$

u now denotes an aggregate productivity shock and *a* is (the log of) an index of the aggregate capital stock and technology.

The aggregation rules stated in (7), the production function (1), the first order condition (5) and the aggregate demand function (2) yield a solution for aggregate output, employment and the price level:

$$(8)\qquad \begin{bmatrix} y \\ n \\ p \end{bmatrix} = \frac{1}{\Delta_2}\begin{bmatrix} \alpha & -\alpha & 1-\alpha & 1 & \alpha(1+\beta) \\ 1 & -1 & \beta(1-\alpha) & \beta & 1+\beta \\ 1-\alpha & \alpha(1-\beta) & -(1-\alpha)(1-\beta) & \beta-1 & \beta-\alpha \end{bmatrix} \begin{bmatrix} m \\ w \\ a \\ u \\ \mu \end{bmatrix}$$

where $0 < \Delta_2 \equiv 1 - \alpha\beta < 1$.

Eq. (6) and (8) describe all effects on both the sectoral and aggregate level. The most important results are discussed in the following section.[10]

IV. Results

The main result of the model is the positive employment effect of nominal wage restraint at both the sectoral and aggregate level which holds true despite the demand effect of labour income.

In section C.II we pointed to the – intuitively plausible – possible positive employment effects at the sectoral level in response to a nominal wage increase in the rest of the economy. From (6), however, we compute

$$\left.\frac{\partial n_i}{\partial w}\right|_{dw_i=0} = \frac{\beta}{\Delta_1} + \frac{\partial n_i}{\partial p}\frac{\partial p}{\partial w} + \frac{\partial n_i}{\partial n}\frac{\partial n}{\partial w} = \frac{\alpha^2[\sigma(1-\beta)-1]}{\Delta_1\Delta_2},$$

where eq. (8) was used to compute the effects of w on n and p.

This equation reveals the following paradox: If the purchasing power aspect of wages is neglected (i. e. $\beta = 0$) employment in the sector i rises in response to wage increases in the rest of the economy. The intuition for this result is straightforward: The higher wage demands in the rest of the economy are partly shifted to higher prices. Hence, the relative price in sector i falls, thereby generating additional demand and employment. For a sufficiently high value of β, to be precise: for $\beta > \frac{\sigma-1}{\sigma}$, the sign of this reaction is actually reversed. In other words: Precisely in the case when real goods demand depends on labour income, even the somewhat artificial experiment of an isolated nominal wage increase in the rest of the economy leads to a *decrease* of employment in sector i. We will come back to the explanation of this paradox later.

---

[10] A more detailed discussion of the effects at the aggregate level can be found in Jerger (1996).

A more realistic scenario is the increase of nominal wages in the whole economy, i. e. including the sector under consideration ($dw=dw_i$). In this case, (6) and (8) yield

$$\left.\frac{\partial n_i}{\partial w}\right|_{dw = dw_i} = \frac{\partial n}{\partial w} = -\frac{1}{\Delta_2}.$$

The sign of this reaction is unaffected by the inclusion of labour income in the aggregate demand function. The size of the effect is larger, however, the bigger this impact is:

$$\frac{\partial((\partial n)/(\partial w))}{\partial \beta} = \frac{-\alpha}{\Delta_2^2} < 0 .$$

These results imply that the nominal wage setting can indeed help to fight the unemployment problem by wage restraint.[11] At the aggregate level, the effects of the wage policy are the exact mirror-image of aggregate demand management. Therefore, the success of nominal wage restraint crucially depends on the behaviour of nominal demand management and vice versa. Expansionary demand policies can be completely frustrated by an equiproportionate nominal wage increase, leaving all real variables unchanged with a price increase as the only consequence. By the same token, nominal wage restraint does not yield the positive employment effects if it is accompanied by a restrictive macroeconomic policy stance.[12]

From these reflections, it is straightforward to derive a measure for the employment effects of nominal wage setting: Given the other variables, a nominal wage increase will boost employment to the extent that it falls short of the growth rate of nominal demand. For $\beta = 0$, this can be directly observed from the employment equation of (8). The same holds true for arbitrary values of β, however. From (2) and (8), one can compute

(9)

$$n = \underbrace{y+p}_{\text{nominal demand}} - \underbrace{w}_{\text{nominal wage}} + \mu$$

[11] This clarification does not, of course, solve the problem of why the wage setters are not willing to accept lower wages. This question is the hallmark of a good deal of modern labour market theory, e. g. in Lindbeck/Snower (1989), Solow (1990) and Saint-Paul (1995).

[12] It is easily checked that the model exhibits the property of the classical dichotomy, i. e. the real variables are homogenous of degree 0 in the nominal exogenous variables (*W* and *M*).

At the sectoral level the basic message is pretty much the same, although some qualifications are in place. Inserting (2) and (3) into the employment equation of (6) yields

$$(10) \quad n_i = \frac{1}{\Delta_1}[(y_i + p_i - w_i) - (\sigma - 1)(w_i - p_i) + (\sigma - 1)(1 - \alpha)a_i + (\sigma - 1)u_i + \sigma\mu]$$

The first term at the RHS of (10) corresponds to the message of eq. (9), i. e. employment is determined by the ratio of nominal demand and nominal wages in the respective sector. Depending on the elasticity of substitution between the different varieties associated with the sectors, there is an additional effect of the sectoral real wage (measured in sectoral prices) and the sectoral productivity shock and technology variables. Note that in eq. (10), there is no need to distinguish between $\beta = 0$ and $\beta > 0$, since the sectoral demand equation is directly substituted.

These results can be formulated as a very simple (although not trivial) rule which allows to infer the employment consequences of a given stance of nominal wage policy. Of course, this rule can not avoid the general problem that nominal wages are set *ex ante* and hence the bargaining parties have to rely on forecasts of nominal demand. For most industries, however, such forecasts exist since the firms need this information for production planning and marketing decisions anyway. Hence, the requirement of demand forecasts should not prove to be a major obstacle in implementing this rule. We already commented on the difference of this rule and the familiar "productivity rise + compensation for inflation" rule in section 2 above.

The next question is how technological progress and capital formation (the parameter a of our model) affect employment. At the aggregate level, we obtain:

$$\frac{\partial y}{\partial a} = \frac{1-\alpha}{\Delta_2}; \qquad \frac{\partial n}{\partial a} = \frac{\beta(1-\alpha)}{\Delta_2}; \qquad \frac{\partial p}{\partial a} = -\frac{(1-\alpha)(1-\beta)}{\Delta_2}$$

For $\beta = 0$ ($\Rightarrow \Delta_2 = 1$) real output is proportional to a, leaving employment unaffected. Given m, the higher real demand is made possible by a declining price level. If labour income directly affects demand ($\beta > 0$), employment is *positively* related to a. This result is another paradox in view of the policy debate, since proponents of the purchasing power aspect of wages are very likely to promote the view that technical progress and capital formation lead to *lower* employment. The model shows, however, that employment will *rise* if and only if the purchasing power aspect is properly taken into account. The only way to justify the opposite result is to postulate saturation, i. e. an exogenously limited real demand. This saturation scenario, however, is not perceived to be an accurate description of the real world – at least beyond the time horizon of a business cycle.

Before we turn to the empirical part of the paper, we have to solve the paradox that the purchasing power aspect does indeed *strengthen* the positive employment effects of nominal wage restraint instead of reversing or at least weakening it. The reason for this is the fact that the real wage sum (and hence demand) is negatively affected by the nominal wage increase, although only a part of it is shifted to higher prices. Since this means higher real wages, employment is a negative function of nominal wages. Under the assumption of a Cobb-Douglas technology, the employment effect more than offsets the positive real wage effect and hence the wage sum decreases:

$$\frac{\partial(w+n-p)}{\partial w} = -\frac{\alpha}{\Delta_2} < 0 \ .$$

This result leaves open the question, why unions may find it attractive to rise nominal wages. The answer to this question is, that the nominal wage increases translate into higher real wages and hence the (yet) employed will benefit. Although this result verges on the trivial at least at the sectoral level[13], it contradicts the widespread perception that unions can not do very much about *real* wages since they are unable to set prices. Even at the aggregate level, higher nominal wages are not fully offset by higher prices:

$$\frac{\partial(w-p)}{\partial w} = \frac{1-\alpha}{\Delta_2} > 0 \ .$$

Hence, the employed are able to benefit at the expense of the unemployed. This reasoning is at the centre of all bargaining models that distinguish between insiders and outsiders. In this model, I showed that the purchasing power aspect is not an excuse for the insiders to insist on high nominal wages in the face of a dismal employment record.

D. An Empirical Analysis of Sectoral Data for Germany

The model of the previous section yielded a clear-cut and testable result – namely that employment is a function of the ratio of nominal demand and nominal wages. Now we will confront this hypothesis with a fairly large sample from the sectoral database of the Statistisches Bundesamt. This database gives a breakdown of figures on value added, wages and employment for 58 sectors plus a number of sub-aggregates of sectors. All data refer to West Germany (i. e. East Germany is excluded also for the post-1990 period). For most of the sectors, annual data are available from 1960 up to 1995. In addition, I use the quarterly data

---

[13] If the sectoral real wage is measured in terms of the aggregate price level, the latter being unaffected by the action of a single sector, it is straightforward that $\partial(w_i - p)/\partial w_i = 1$.

from 1968:1 to 1997:1 that exist for a small number of sectoral sub-aggregates.[14] Table 1 specifies the sectors.

Table 1

Sectoral Breakdown of the German Economy

No.	Sector
q)1	Agriculture, forestry and fishing
2	Agriculture and livestock production
3	Gardening, animal raising, forestry and fishing
q)4	Production industries
5	Electricity, gas, steam and water supply, mining
6	Electricity, gas, steam and water supply
7	Electricity, steam and hot water supply
8	Gas supply
9	Water supply
10	Mining
11	Coal Mining
12	Other mining
13	Manufacturing
14	Chemical Industries
15	Mineral oil refining
16	Manufacture of plastic products
17	Manufacture of rubber products
18	Quarrying, extraction and working up of stones and earths
19	Manufacture of ceramic goods
20	Maunfacture and processing of glass
21	Iron and steel industry
22	Non-ferrous metal industry
23	Foundries
24	Drawing plants, cold rolling mills
25	Manufacture of structural metal products, rolling stock
26	Mechanical engineering
27	Manufacture of office machinery and data processing equipment
28	Manufacture of road vehicles
29	Shipbuilding
30	Manufacture of aircraft and spacecraft
31	Electrical engineering
32	Manufacture of precision and optical instruments, etc.
33	Manufacture of tools, finished metal goods
34	Manufacture of toys, games, jewellery, etc.
35	Wood-working
36	Manufacture of wood products
37	Manufacture of pulp, paper and board
38	Processing of paper and board
39	Printing and duplicating
40	Manufacture of leather and leather goods
41	Textile industry

[14] All data can be taken from Statistisches Bundesamt (jährlich). It is also possible – and much more convenient –, however, to extract the data directly from the database of the Statistisches Bundesamt via the WorldWideWeb. For all the results on quarterly data reported below I used seasonally adjusted series. The adjustment was done with the EZ X-11 software.

Table 1 (contd.)

Sectoral Breakdown of the German Economy

42	Clothing industry
43	Food industries
44	Beverage industries
45	Tobacco industry
46	Construction
47	Construction (excl. installation, etc.)
48	Installation and building completion work
◊ 49	Wholesale and retail trade, transport and communication
50	Wholesale and retail trade
51	Wholesale trade and commission trade
52	Retail trade
53	Transport and communication
54	Railroad transport
55	Water transport
56	Communication (Deutsche Bundespost)
57	Other transport
◊ 58	Service enterprises
59	Financial and insurance institutions
60	Credit institutions
61	Insurance enterprises
62	Housing (incl. owner-occupied dwellings) †
63	Other service enterprises
64	Hotels and resturants, homes and hostels
65	Education, science, culture services, publishing
66	Medical care and health services, veterinary services
67	Other service enterprises, N.E.C.
68	All enterprises
◊ 69	General government, households
70	General government
71	Central and local goverment
72	Social security funds
73	Households and private non-profit institutions
74	Households
75	Private non-profit institutions
◊ 76	Total of sectors

Notes: ◊ Quarterly data available
† To this sector, the Statistisches Bundesamt imputes value added, but no employment (and hence no labour income). Hence no further results for this sector are reported.

Figure 1 gives a broad picture of the sectoral composition of employment in 1995 and an idea of the breakdown for which data are available.[15] It is interesting to note in passing that for the manufacturing sector, no less than 32 subsectors are covered, whereas only 7 are availabe for the services sector. This clearly reflects a lag of the identification of statistical entities behind reality, although in 1995 there are still almost twice as many workers in manufacturing than in services.

---

[15] The numbers are percentage shares and add to 100% along a horizontal branch. Where appropriate, the second number indicates how many subsectors are aggregated in the respective sub-aggregate.

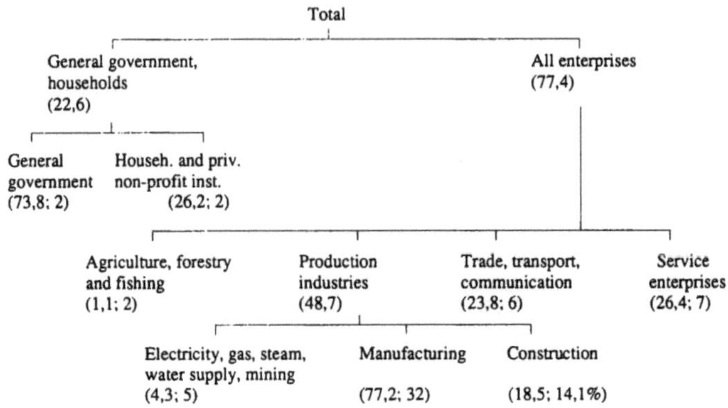

Figure 1: Shares of Employment in 1995 for the Main Sectoral Aggregates

The change of the composition of employment across the different sectors can be seen in figure 2, where the most important aggregates of subsectors are shown. It is clear that employment shifted away from the agricultural sector and the production industries to the service sector and also to the public sector.

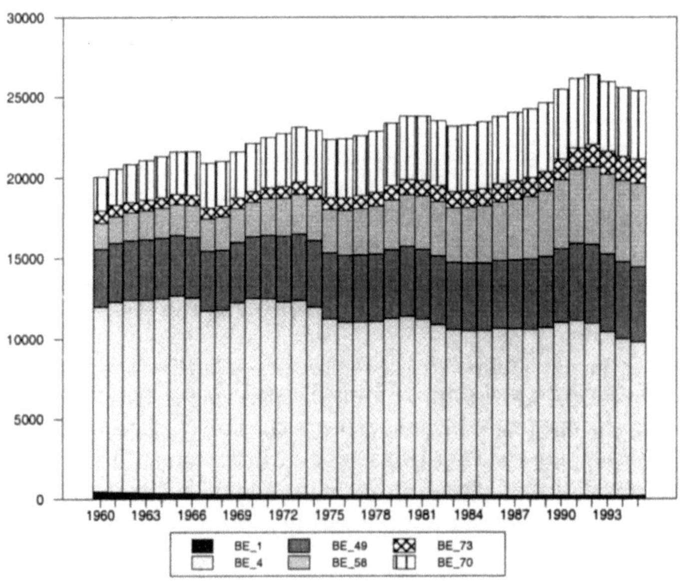

Figure 2: Sectoral Employment, 1960–1995

Figure 3 displays the relative wages across different sectors from 1960 to 1995. Despite the wide-spread belief that wage structures in Germany are rigid, quite substantial shifts of sectoral relative wages took place.[16]

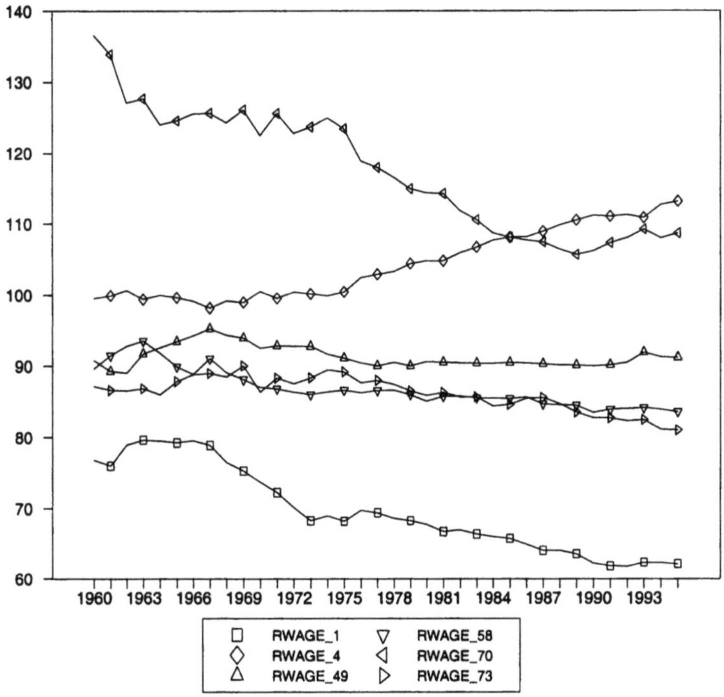

Figure 3: Sectoral Relative Wages, 1960–1995

After this brief description of the data, I will use the employment equations (9) and (10), respectively, for the empirical analysis. Due to data limitations, no allowance is made for sector-specific differences of the technology variable.[17]

Data for sectoral gross value added in current prices are directly available, whereas wages have to be calculated as the ratio of compensation of employees

---

[16] The data do not, however, permit to trace back relative wages and their changes to different skill levels across industries and over time.

[17] The omission of this variable would be correct at the aggregate level if $\beta = 0$.

and the number of employees. The compensation figures include all contributions to the social security system (also the employers' share) as well as wage taxes. We do not distinguish between wage cost (the "producer wage") and (net) take home pay (the "consumer wage") and hence do not take into account the rising wedge between these two magnitudes. This distinction can and should be made explicit in future research. For the present analytical purpose, however, it is only relevant insofar as the government and consumers exhibit different spending habits. In this case, the demand effects of (wage) tax payments to the government and wages paid to the private sector would make a difference. A further conceptual drawback of the data stems from the fact that a reduction of work-time does not show up as a wage increase since for the nominator of the ratio described above, only the annual (or quarterly) wage sum is available.

The first step in an econometric analysis of time series is to look at the univariate properties of the data. In particular, it is important to know, whether the data are stationary or contain a unit root. Since the seminal work of Fuller (1976), a host of unit root tests was developed that allow for different deterministic components, different degrees of autocorrelation etc.. For this paper, I adopted a sequential testing strategy – suggested e. g. by Perron (1988) and Enders (1995) – by first specifying the univariate model with a constant and a trend as deterministic components and then "testing down" whether or not the specification is appropriate.[18] The results for (the logs) of sectoral employment n_i and sectoral wage restraint $(y_i + p_i - w_i)$ are contained in the right-hand part of table 2. From the 75 sectors (and sub-aggregates) for which annual data are available, exactly 25 display stationarity of both variables, non-stationarity of both variables and mixed conclusions, respectively, for (n_i) and $(y_i + p_i - w_i)$. Taken literally, this result is discouraging, since the last category – which accounts for one third of all cases – does not make any *economic* sense. The poor performance of unit-root-tests with regard to the power to distinguish between the null of non-stationarity and near-unit-root series or trend-stationary series is well-known, however (e. g. Campbell/Perron 1991), and hence, I proceed with the analysis – albeit with caution. This caution is reflected in reporting both traditional t-tests for the siginifcance of coefficients (which are appropriate if both series are stationary) and co-integration tests (which are appropriate if both series are non-stationary).

Another econometric problem with the data at hand is the very likely comtemporaneous correlation between the left-hand and right-hand variable. After all, one should expect that employment and real output (which is part of the wage restraint variable) are positively correlated. This problem is tackled by employing

[18] The calculations were done using a RATS-procedure, which can be obtained from the author upon request.

an instrumental variable approach, where for each regression, the right-hand side is instrumented by the lagged dependent variable and a constant term. By construction, the lagged dependent variable is uncorrelated with the disturbance term if the latter is assumed not to be autocorrelated.

The third column of table 1 reports the coefficient of an IV-regression of n_i on $(y_i + p_i - w_i)$ and a constant term. Virtually all of the coefficients are highly significant and in the expected range between zero and unity. Depending on the univariate time series properties, the $\bar{R}^2$ measure is usually quite high and the standard error of estimation (SEE) in an acceptable range.[19]

Nevertheless, in some cases the time series properties described above pose some major problems. The regression with annual data for sector No. 49 (Wholesale and retail trade, transport and communication), for example, yields a negative coefficient, which is – as the breakdown makes clear – due to wholesale trade (No. 50) and retail trade (No. 51). This can be explained by the fact that value added in trade is not very good described by a production function like eq. (2) on which all of the subsenquent analysis is build. For quarterly data, however, the coefficient of the respective regression is significant and in the expected range.

Two other problems have to be made explicit:

First, in some of the sectors, output and input can not be measured independently, i. e. output is more or less measured by inputs. This is partly the case in the government sector,[20] and fully in the household sector (No. 74, see remark in table 2). Admittedly, this "biases" the results for those sectors towards the hypothesis put forward in this paper.

Second, some sectors are not best characterized by a market model with profit maximizing firms, but are highly regulated. This helps, for example to explain the negative results for sectors No. 3, 6 and 9. In these sectors, prices are regulated, and hence "output in current prices" does not necessarily depend on factors stressed in the framework of the above model.

A somewhat less formal approach to the data is to use double-scaled diagrams for n_i and $(y_i + p_i - w_i)$. This is done in figure 4 for the main sectoral subaggregates for quarterly data from 1968–1997.

---

[19] Since the data are in logs, the SEE can be interpreted as relative error with respect to the level of the LHS variable. The regression for the total of sectors (No. 76) using quarterly data implies, for instance, that employment is explainded by the regression with a standard error of 2.9%.

[20] The productivity measure of national accounting for an economist at a state university – for example – is *not* the number of articles in refereed journals, but simply her or his wage.

Table 2

Empirical Results

IV-Regression and Cointegration test							Unit root test	
S	No.	Coeff.	t-Stat.	$\bar{R}^2$	SEE	DF-CI	log (employment)	log (wage restraint)
Annual Data (mostly 1960-1995)								
1	35	0.546	12.592	0.825	0.083	-1.811	$\hat{\tau}_{\mu}$ = -6.137 S	$\hat{\tau}_{\tau}$ = -3.495 S
2	17	0.635	4.618	0.538	0.058	-1.932	$\hat{\tau}$ = -2.554 S	NS
3	17	-0.065	-0.646	-0.039	0.024	-1.545	NS	NS
4	37	0.449	14.255	0.856	0.027	-2.481	$\hat{\tau}_{\tau}$ = 4.014 S	$\hat{\tau}$ = -3.005 S
5	37	0.815	23.866	0.944	0.032	-3.118	$\hat{\tau}$ = -2.926 S	$\hat{\tau}$ = -3.431 S
6	36	-0.785	-2.098	0.030	0.100	-1.563	$\hat{\tau}_{\mu}$ = -5.329 S	NS
7	26	0.229	1.201	-0.048	0.045	-1.591	NS	NS
8	26	0.571	12.272	0.881	0.074	-3.169	$\hat{\tau}_{\tau}$ = -4.299 S	NS
9	26	-0.176	-0.424	-0.219	0.079	-3.461	NS	$\hat{\tau}_{\mu}$ = -3.388 S
10	36	0.682	37.050	0.976	0.051	-2.880	$\hat{\tau}$ = -3.761 S	$\hat{\tau}$ = -2.063 S
11	36	0.631	32.001	0.969	0.058	-2.720	$\hat{\tau}$ = -3.878 S	$\hat{\tau}$ = -4.476 S
12	36	0.863	10.862	0.769	0.184	-2.006	NS	$\hat{\tau}$ = -2.079 S
13	37	0.394	11.709	0.800	0.030	-2.270	NS	$\hat{\tau}$ = -2.730 S
14	36	-0.044	-0.710	-0.014	0.043	-2.602	$\hat{\tau}_{\mu}$ = -2.697 S	$\hat{\tau}_{\tau}$ = -3.749 S
15	36	1.252	4.411	0.206	0.184	-1.018	NS	NS
16	36	1.497	17.725	0.905	0.096	-2.060	NS	NS
17	36	0.473	7.153	0.620	0.056	-1.889	NS	NS
18	36	0.696	24.149	0.946	0.045	-1.523	NS	$\hat{\tau}$ = -2.386 S
19	36	0.711	46.138	0.985	0.022	-3.130	$\hat{\tau}_{\tau}$ = -4.107 S	$\hat{\tau}$ = -3.232 S
20	36	0.708	17.932	0.907	0.040	-2.531	NS	NS
21	36	0.799	23.952	0.946	0.079	-3.168	NS	$\hat{\tau}_{\tau}$ = -3.982 S
22	36	0.709	9.537	0.745	0.068	-3.315	$\hat{\tau}_{\tau}$ = -2.681 S	NS
23	36	0.729	29.628	0.966	0.039	-1.669	$\hat{\tau}_{\tau}$ = -4.784 S	$\hat{\tau}_{\tau}$ = -3.602 S
24	36	0.251	6.260	0.561	0.034	-3.100	NS	NS
25	36	0.533	6.939	0.649	0.055	-3.079	NS	NS
26	36	0.211	2.543	0.127	0.043	-2.456	$\hat{\tau}_{\mu}$ = -3.117 S	NS
27	36	0.704	4.590	0.313	0.139	-2.334	$\hat{\tau}_{\mu}$ = -2.836 S	NS
28	36	2.374	5.674	0.286	0.134	-1.965	$\hat{\tau}_{\mu}$ = -2.857 S	$\hat{\tau}_{\mu}$ = -2.869 S
29	36	0.898	20.351	0.927	0.090	-3.236	$\hat{\tau}$ = -4.206 S	$\hat{\tau}$ = -2.143 S

Table 2 (contd.)

Empirical Results

30	36	1.237	8.104	0.622	0.186	-2.571	$\hat{\tau}_\tau$ = -6.709	S		NS
31	36	0.842	4.122	0.201	0.056	-2.366		NS		NS
32	36	1.431	3.252	0.009	0.094	-0.810		NS		NS
33	36	0.534	14.406	0.869	0.032	-2.041		NS		NS
34	36	1.018	14.587	0.864	0.071	-2.312	$\hat{\tau}$ = -2.500	S	$\hat{\tau}_\tau$ = -2.612	S
35	36	0.777	28.999	0.962	0.045	-3.303	$\hat{\tau}$ = -3.848	S	$\hat{\tau}$ = -2.601	S
36	36	0.475	5.830	0.540	0.045	-2.465	$\hat{\tau}_\tau$ = -3.894	S		NS
37	36	0.737	12.973	0.826	0.077	-2.300		NS		NS
38	36	0.410	9.805	0.737	0.054	-2.220		NS		NS
39	36	0.582	6.785	0.558	0.044	-1.735		NS		NS
40	36	0.940	52.947	0.988	0.056	-2.175	$\hat{\tau}$ = -2.689	S	$\hat{\tau}$ = -6.211	S
41	36	0.787	40.317	0.980	0.059	-1.404	$\hat{\tau}$ = -2.492	S	$\hat{\tau}$ = -5.715	S
42	36	0.853	38.976	0.979	0.054	-1.220	$\hat{\tau}$ = -2.390	S	$\hat{\tau}_\tau$ = -3.532	S
43	36	0.603	7.177	0.535	0.046	-3.573		NS		NS
44	26	0.671	21.587	0.953	0.039	-1.299	$\hat{\tau}_\tau$ = -3.609	S	$\hat{\tau}$ = -4.522	S
45	36	1.033	36.643	0.976	0.072	-2.799	$\hat{\tau}_\mu$ = -7.165	S	$\hat{\tau}$ = -4.469	S
46	37	0.623	13.372	0.836	0.040	-2.531	$\hat{\tau}_\tau$ = -3.613	S		NS
47	36	0.721	24.565	0.948	0.043	-2.309	$\hat{\tau}_\tau$ = -3.489	S	$\hat{\tau}_\tau$ = -3.205	S
48	36	0.882	4.831	0.428	0.092	-2.465	$\hat{\tau}_\tau$ = -3.297	S		NS
49	37	-0.357	-2.203	0.033	0.082	-0.261	$\hat{\tau}_\tau$ = -4.607	S		NS
50	37	-0.505	-4.837	0.364	0.083	-0.543	$\hat{\tau}_\tau$ = -3.549	S		NS
51	26	0.435	3.282	0.317	0.048	-1.292	$\hat{\tau}$ = -2.643	S		NS
52	26	0.163	0.408	-0.034	0.092	-1.638	$\hat{\tau}_\tau$ = -3.281	S		NS
53	37	0.380	5.560	0.537	0.033	-2.112	$\hat{\tau}_\tau$ = -5.217	S	$\hat{\tau}_\tau$ = -2.321	S
54	36	0.535	15.298	0.877	0.087	-1.180	$\hat{\tau}$ = -2.526	S	$\hat{\tau}$ = -6.293	S
55	26	1.104	12.644	0.871	0.083	-3.028	$\hat{\tau}$ = -4.810	S	$\hat{\tau}_\tau$ = -4.608	S
56	36	0.375	13.022	0.840	0.034	-1.436		NS		NS
57	36	0.991	14.117	0.856	0.076	-2.050		NS		NS
58	37	0.982	42.983	0.982	0.046	-1.669	$\hat{\tau}_\tau$ = -3.107	S		NS
59	37	0.843	26.227	0.953	0.053	-2.206		NS		NS
60	36	0.901	23.483	0.943	0.067	-1.640		NS		NS
61	36	0.642	9.317	0.716	0.078	-2.351		NS		NS

Table 2 (contd.)

Empirical Results

63	37	0.932	31.980	0.968	0.067	-1.705		NS		NS
64	26	2.421	9.522	0.795	0.101	-2.489		NS		NS
65	26	0.848	10.356	0.835	0.096	-4.220	$\hat{\tau}_\mu$ = -4.014	S	$\hat{\tau}_\tau$ = -4.135	S
66	26	2.224	14.121	0.894	0.108	-2.123	$\hat{\tau}_\tau$ = -3.923	S		NS
67	26	0.665	30.427	0.976	0.043	-1.844		NS	$\hat{\tau}_\tau$ = -2.648	S
68	35	0.128	1.081	0.049	0.040	-1.438	$\hat{\tau}_\tau$ = -3.899	S		NS
69	37	0.979	339.730	1.000	0.004	-1.015		NS		NS
70	37	0.975	231.097	0.999	0.005	-0.644		NS		NS
71	36	0.975	227.815	0.999	0.005	-0.475		NS		NS
72	36	0.988	238.750	0.999	0.005	-1.955	$\hat{\tau}_\tau$ = -3.400	S	$\hat{\tau}_\tau$ = -3.792	S
73	37	1.019	252.566	0.999	0.006	-4.384	$\hat{\tau}_\tau$ = -5.676	S	$\hat{\tau}_\tau$ = -5.612	S
74	12	†								
75	12	0.978	71.134	0.998	0.004	-1.808	$\hat{\tau}_\tau$ = -3.898	S		NS
76	35	0.411	2.086	0.166	0.061	-2.478	$\hat{\tau}_\tau$ = -4.721	S		NS
Quarterly data (mostly 1968:1-1997:1 or 1968:1-1993:1)										
1	105	0.284	16.373	0.723	0.042	-3.639	$\hat{\tau}$ = -3.403	S	$\hat{\tau}_\tau$ = -3.869	S
4	118	0.622	33.759	0.907	0.022	-3.244		NS	$\hat{\tau}_\tau$ = -2.309	S
49	118	0.863	9.065	0.408	0.054	-2.786	$\hat{\tau}_\tau$ = -3.522	S		NS
58	118	0.910	70.875	0.978	0.042	-1.881		NS		NS
69	118	0.968	482.150	1.000	0.003	-2.813	$\hat{\tau}_\mu$ = -5.343	S	$\hat{\tau}_\mu$ = -5.204	S
76	105	0.751	15.850	0.708	0.029	-3.310	$\hat{\tau}_\tau$ = -3.848	S		NS

Notes: The left-most column contains the sector number *S* from table 1. No. is the number of periods for which data on both employment and the wage restraint variable are available. The labels of the unit-root tests correspond to Fuller (1976). "S" and "NS" denote the conclusion of stationarity and non-stationarity. respectively. of the sequential test procedure.

† In the household sector imputed wages are – by definition – equal to value added. Hence the LHS and RHS are perfectly correlated.

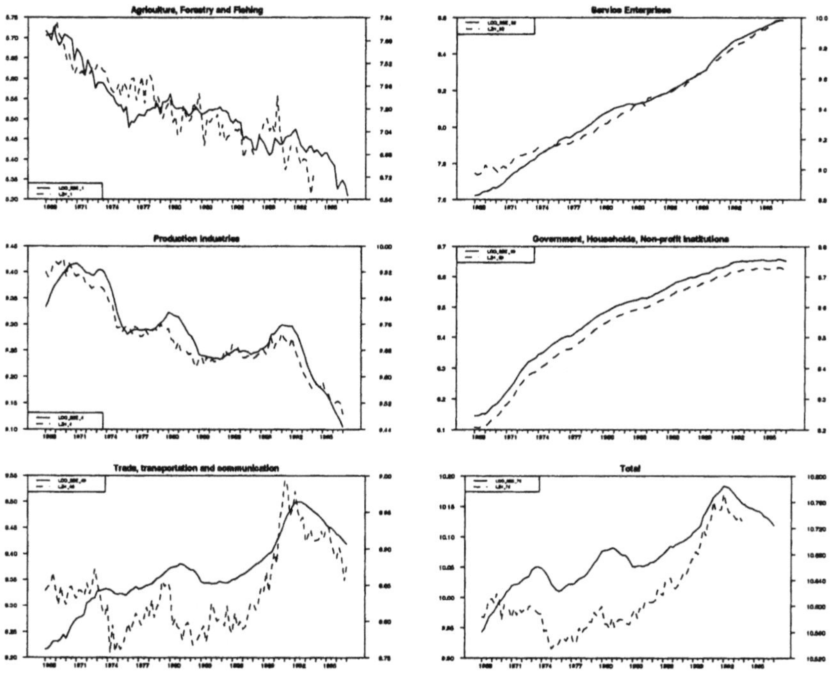

Figure 4: Sectoral Employment and Wage Restraint

The high relevance for the wage-restraint variable for sectoral employment is clearly visible in these figures in all cases, except for those already discussed above.

The next question to the data is whether and to which extent, a declining sector (i. e. with a declining share of value added) reacted to this by accepting a lower relative wage with the aim of (partly) securing employment in this sector. From the sectoral and aggregate employment equations, one can obtain the following relationship for relative employment in sector i:

$$(n_i - n) = [(y_i - p_i) - (y + p)] - [w_i - w] \qquad (11)$$

The first bracketed RHS-term is relative demand in sector i, the second the respective relative wage. In figure 5, I use two scatter-plot panels for each sector. In the upper panel, the relative wage and relative demand according to the above definition are plotted against each other. The figures show all sorts of correlation between these two variables. For the production industries, a declining relative demand was accompanied by a rising relative wage, and thus employment came under pressure from both sides stressed in this paper. On the other hand, the decreasing relative demand in the agricultural sector, for example, was answered by lower relative wages and thus employment could be partly restored.

The lower panel of fig. 5 depicts the LHS (relative employment) and RHS (relative wage restraint) of eq. (11) in order to check whether wage restraint (or aggressiveness) is associated with the expected employment effects. Theoretically, there should be a 1:1-relationship, which indeed can be observed, again with the exception of the trade sector.[21]

The first panels for each sector show that the sectoral wage response to a changing relative demand differs considerably both across sectors and over time. Whereas in agriculture, foresting and fishing, the declining relative demand was accompanied by a relative wage restraint, the opposite pattern can be observed in the production industries. In the services sector, on the other hand, both rising relative demand and declining relative wages contributed to the rising employment figures.

E. Conclusions

In this paper, I tried to model the relationship between nominal wages, nominal demand and the implied employment outcome both at the sectoral and the aggregate level. The result is simple enough to be potentially useful: Nominal wage increases in excess of nominal demand increases lower employment and vice versa. In addition, I could show that this result holds true, whether or not the labour income is included as an argument in the demand function, i. e. whether or not one takes into account the "purchasing power argument" of wages. A positive employment effect of rising nominal wages along the lines of the purchasing power argument is only conceivable under special circumstances as a transitory effect in a dynamic model in which both prices and quantities are sluggish. Although such rigidities of nominal and real variables exist and are analysed in great detail in the Neo-Keynesian literature (see e. g. Mankiw/Romer 1991), one also has to bear in mind that demand may adjust very slowly and feebly to sudden hikes of purchasing power. Indeed, a good deal of consumption theory after Keynes was concerned with the weak contemporaneous nexus between purchasing power (income) and consumption demand.

The discussion in this paper is cast in a very simple model that – for example – does not explicitely model labour supply, which may or may not be centralised by unions. Although current models of labour supply (either with or without unions) argue that the incumbent workers *want* high unemployment, no effort is made in this paper to tackle the question how this situation can be improved, i. e. how the adverse employment effects of these group-specific interests can be al-

[21] A full set of graphs for all sectors is available upon request.

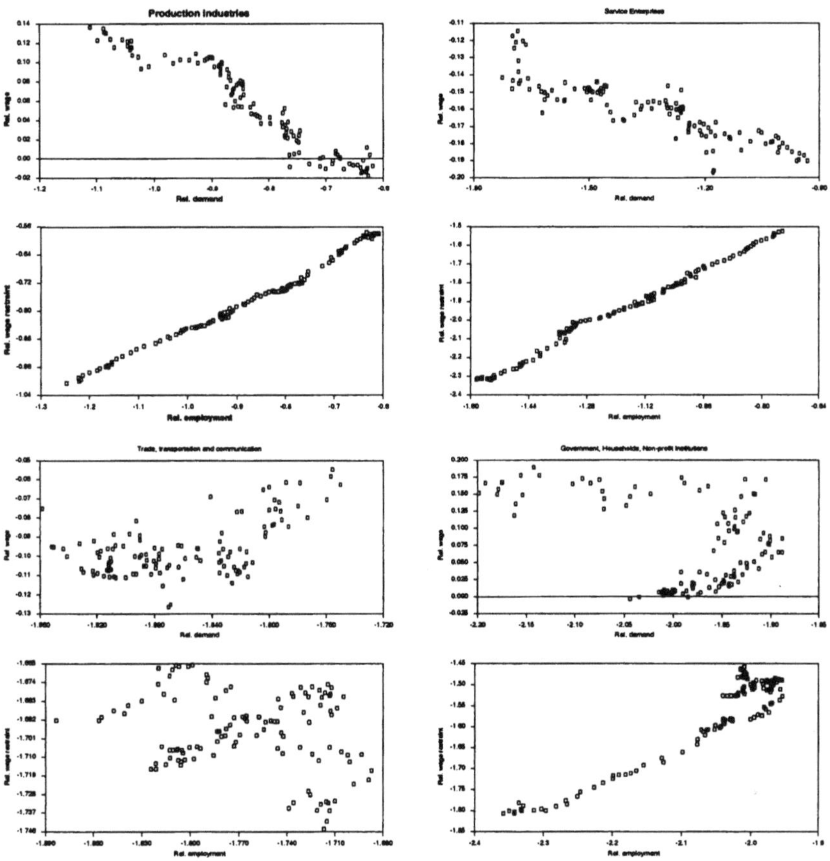

Figure 5: Relative Wages vs. Relative Demand and Relative Wage Restraint vs. Relative Employment

leviated (for recent surveys see Kirchgässner 1996 and Saint-Paul 1995). The possibility to give a well-founded estimate of the employment consequences of wage aspirations, however, could serve an important role in the political discussion of wage bargains.

References

Blanchard, O. J., and S. *Fischer* (1989): Lectures on Macroeconomics, Cambridge/Mass.: MIT-Press.

Boskin, M. J., and D. W. *Jorgenson* (1997): Implications of overstating inflation for indexing government programs and understanding economic progress, in: American Economic Review, Papers and Proceedings, Vol. 87, 1997, pp. 89–93.

Campbell, J. Y., and P. *Perron* (1991): Pitfalls and opportunities: What macroeconomists should know about unit roots, in: NBER Macroeconomics Annual, 1991, pp. 141–219.

Crafts, N. F. (1996): Endogenous growth: Lessons for and from economic history, CEPR Discussion Paper No. 1333, January.

Crafts, N. F., and G. *Toniolo* (eds.) (1996): Economic growth in Europe since 1945, Cambridge University Press.

Dixit, A., and J. E. *Stiglitz* (1977): Monopolistic competition and optimum product diversity, in: American Economic Review, Vol. 67, pp. 297–308

Enders, W. (1995): Applied econometric time series, New Work: John Wiley & Sons.

Europäische Kommission (1996): Europäische Wirtschaft, Nr. 61 (Jahreswirtschaftsbericht 1996).

Franz, W. (1996): Theoretische Ansätze zur Erklärung von Arbeitslosigkeit: Wo stehen wir 1995?, in: B. Gahlen et al. (eds.): Arbeitslosigkeit und Möglichkeiten ihrer Überwindung, Wirtschaftswissenschaftliches Seminar Ottobeuren, Bd. 25, Tübingen: J. C. B. Mohr (Paul Siebeck), pp. 3–45.

Fuller, W. (1976): Introduction to statistical time series, New York: John Wiley & Sons.

Jerger, J. (1993): Beschäftigung und Kapitalbildung – Eine theoretische Analyse mit einer Anwendung für BRD 1961–1989, Schriftenreihe des Instituts für allgemeine Wirtschaftsforschung, Bd. 44, Freiburg: Haufe-Verlag.

— (1996): Leitlinien für eine beschäftigungsorientierte Nominallohnpolitik, in: Külp, B. (ed.): Arbeitsmarkt und Arbeitslosigkeit, Freiburg: Haufe-Verlag, pp. 123–152.

Kirchgässner, G. (1996): Bewußt erzeugte und duldend hingenommene Arbeitslosigkeit: Zum Problem der Arbeitslosigkeit aus der Sicht der Neuen Politischen Ökonomie, in: B. Gahlen et al. (eds.): Arbeitslosigkeit und Möglichkeiten ihrer Überwindung, Wirtschaftswissenschaftliches Seminar Ottobeuren, Bd. 25, Tübingen: J. C. B. Mohr (Paul Siebeck), pp. 395–532.

Köddermann, R. (1996): Sind Löhne und Steuern zu hoch? Bemerkungen zur Standortdiskussion in Deutschland, in: ifo-Schnelldienst Nr. 20, Juli, pp. 6–15.

Koll, W. (1988): Geldmenge, Lohn und Beschäftigung. Gesamtwirtschaftliche Bedingungen für mehr Beschäftigung bei Stabilität, Walter-Eucken-Institut, Vorträge und Aufsätze 120, Tübingen: J. C. B. Mohr (Paul Siebeck).

Kromphardt, J. (1995): Nachfrageschocks, Preis-/Lohnbildung und Arbeitslosigkeit aus makroökonomischer Sicht, Beitrag zum 25. Wirtschaftswissenschaftlichen Seminar Ottobeuren vom 10.–14. September.

Landmann, O. (1989): Verteilungskonflikte, Kapitalbildung und Arbeitslosigkeit, in: Ramser, H.-J., and H. Riese (eds.): Beiträge zur angewandten Wirtschaftsforschung, Berlin: Springer-Verlag, pp. 59–85.

Landmann, O., and J. *Jerger* (1993): Unemployment and the real wage gap: A reappraisal of the German experience, in: Weltwirtschaftliches Archiv, Vol. 129, 1993, pp. 689–717.

Layard, R., et al. (1991): Unemployment, Oxford University Press.

Lehment, H. (1991): Lohnzurückhaltung, Arbeitszeitverkürzung und Beschäftigung. Eine empirische Untersuchung für die Bundesrepublik Deutschland 1973–1990, in: Die Weltwirtschaft, Heft 2, pp. 72–85.

Lehment, H. (1993): Bedingungen für einen kräftigen Beschäftigungsanstieg in der Bundesrepublik Deutschland – Zur Tarifpolitik der kommenden Jahre, in: Die Weltwirtschaft, Heft 3, pp. 302–310.

Lindbeck, A. (1993): Unemployment and Macroeconomics, Cambridge/Mass.: MIT Press.

Lindbeck, A., and D. J. *Snower* (1989): The insider-outsider theory of employment and unemployment, Cambridge/Mass.: MIT Press.

Mankiw, N. G., and D. *Romer* (eds.) (1991): New Keynesian economics, Vol. 1: Imperfect competition and sticky prices, Vol. 2: Coordination failures and real rigidities, Cambridge/Mass.: MIT Press.

Manning, A. (1990): Imperfect competition, multiple equilibria and unemployment policy, in: Economic Journal, Vol. 100, pp. 151–162.

OECD (1994): The OECD Jobs Study. Part II: The adjustment potential of the labour market, Paris: OECD.

OECD (1996): Employment Outlook, July 1996, Paris: OECD.

Perron, P. (1988): Trends and random walks in macroeconomic time series: Further evidence from a new approach, in: Journal of Economic Dynamics and Control, Vol. 12, pp. 297–332.

Rohwedder, J., and H. *Herberg* (1984): Effects of exogenous nominal wage increases: The purchasing power argument vs. the production cost argument, in: Zeitschrift für Wirtschafts- und Sozialwissenschaften, Bd. 103, pp. 585–601.

Sachverständigenrat zur Begutachtung der gesamtwirtschaftlichen Entwicklung (1965): Stabilisierung ohne Stagnation (Jahresgutachten 1964/65), Stuttgart/Mainz: Kohlhammer.

— (1977): Mehr Wachstum – mehr Beschäftigung (Jahresgutachten 1977/78), Stuttgart/ Mainz: Kohlhammer.

— (1995): Im Standortwettbeweb (Jahresgutachten 1995/96), Stuttgart/Mainz: Kohlhammer.

Saint-Paul, G. (1995): Some political aspects of unemployment, in: European Economic Review, Vol. 39, Nos. 3/4, pp. 575–582.

Schuster, H., and C. *Weiß* (1991): Lohnhöhe und Beschäftigung. Kaufkraft- und Kostenargument, in: Zeitschrift für Wirtschafts- und Sozialwissenschaften, Bd. 111, pp. 55–64.

Sinn, G., and H.-W. *Sinn* (1993): Kaltstart. Volkswirtschaftliche Aspekte der deutschen Vereinigung, 3. Auflage, München: dtv.

Solow, R. M. (1986): Unemployment – getting the question right, in: Economica Supplement, Vol. 53, pp. 23–34.

— (1990): The labor market as a social institution, Basil Blackwell.

Statistisches Bundesamt (jährlich): Fachserie 18: Volkswirtschaftliche Gesamtrechnungen (Hauptbericht), Stuttgart: Kohlhammer.

Job Creation in the Low-Wage Sector – The Role of Employment Subsidies

Alexander Spermann[1]

A. Introduction

The third industrial revolution is associated with information technologies that change our daily lives as well as our work lives. American authors like Jeremy Rifkin (1995) fear the "end of work", German journalists like Martin/Schumann (1996) identify a "globalisation trap" which threatens wealth and democracy. Pessimism about the "future of capitalism" (Thurow 1996) with a divided 20:80 winner-loser society is widespread. The future seems to be a capitalism without work (Beck 1996).

Economic trends in the nineties strengthen this view for most European countries: growth was largely without the creation of jobs. Many industry jobs disappeared, new jobs in the service sector were not created to a sufficient extent to overcompensate their loss. Therefore, unemployment rates as well as long-term unemployment have risen steadily in Europe (OECD 1996). Recent trends show that so far safe jobs in the banking and insurance sector will fall victim to automatisation and global competition. Industrial countries seem to transform into "informational" countries with far less jobs available to skilled but especially to unskilled workers.

Optimism comes from experiences in the United States Growth without inflation is associated with plenty of jobs for skilled and unskilled workers. Since 1993, more than 8 millions jobs have been created, mostly in the service sector, and the economy is close to full employment. A vast majority of the new jobs are full-time and high-skill with above-median wages (Council of Economic Advisers 1996). Critics of the American "job miracle" point out rising wage inequality:

[1] The author is grateful for comments by Jürgen Jerger, Jochen Michaelis, Michael P. Pflüger and seminar participants at Nagoya University (Japan). The usual disclaimer applies.

High-skilled workers have earned increasingly more than low-skilled workers in the nineties, because their wages improved while wages at the lower end worsened (Gottschalk 1997). As a consequence, employees who do not earn the subsistence level have become an important group called the "working poor". Wage inequality seems to be inevitable, but may be alleviated by life-long education and training (Topel 1997, Johnson 1997).

U.S. experiences indicate that new jobs will be uncertain and require high worker flexibility; part-time and short-time work will be widespread, low-skilled workers will be low-paid, but will find a job. Hence, the future of capitalism seems to be associated with the end of safe and life-long jobs, but not with the end of work.

Employment subsidies for low-wage jobs are proposed to boost European employment. In Germany, *employer subsidies* which are paid to employers dominate in practice. They are typically announced before elections as a means to reduce long-term unemployment. Theoretically, employer subsidies reduce labour costs for firms, boost employment and reduce structural unemployment due to increased labour demand. On the other hand, *employee subsidies* have been suggested as a means to make work pay for low-wage earners (e. g. OECD 1996). Low wages and part-time work may become attractive if wages are increased by personal transfers, so that the disposable income would be above the poverty threshold. Theoretically, employee subsidies increase after-transfer income of workers which makes work pay at lower levels of producer wages.

This paper provides a comparison of employer and employee subsidies with respect to equilibrium unemployment. The analytical framework – a one-sector model of equilibrium unemployment – is set up in chapter I. Employer and employee subsidies are introduced into the model in chapter II. The standard result suggests that employer and employee subsidies are equivalent with respect to both wages and employment. This result is challenged in chapter III. The discussion shows that important practical aspects such as transaction costs have to be considered for an adequate comparison. Chapter IV discusses employment subsidies in general with respect to problems like deadweight and displacement. It presents two proposals that largely avoid these problems by targeting the long-term unemployed. Chapter V concludes the paper.

B. The Analytical Framework

The Wage Setting (WS) – Price Setting (PS) model of the labour market which is now the standard one used to explain European unemployment shall be the analytical framework for the comparison of different kinds of employment subsidies (Carlin/Soskice 1990, Burda/Wyplosz 1997, Blanchard 1997).

The essence of this model is illustrated by the following diagram (see figure 1) which has the real wage on the vertical axis and the employment rate on the horizontal axis. Aggregate individual labour supply of households is given by the vertical N_s-curve. Aggregate labour demand by firms is given by the PS-curve. Firms set prices as mark-up on marginal costs in an imperfect product market. The PS-curve is assumed to be downward sloping due to decreasing returns to scale so that lower real wages are associated with higher employment similar to the ordinary labour demand curve. The WS-curve is the result of the bargaining process between utility-maximizing trade-unions and profit-maximizing firms. The WS-curve is often called the collective labour supply curve which lies left of the N_s-curve. It is upward sloping, because higher employment enables trade unions to enforce higher real wages in the bargaining process.

In this model, equilibrium employment is not determined by the intersection of labour demand and aggregated individual labour supply. However, this model explains involuntary unemployment which is prevalent in European labour markets. The labour market outcome is set by the intersection of the PS- and WS-curve. As a result of the bargaining process, real wages are higher and employment is lower. The resulting unemployment ($N_1 - N_2$) is involuntary for the affected individuals, but voluntary from the trade unions' point of view. Involuntary unemployment is explained by real wage rigidity caused by the bargaining process. The WS-PS model is interpreted as a one-sector model which illustrates the low-wage sector; spillovers to the high-wage sector are cut off. Furthermore, the low-wage sector is assumed to be small in comparison with the high-wage sector, so that the price level remains exogenous.

C. Employment Subsidies in a One-Sector Model of Equilibrium Unemployment

The effects of employment subsidies may be introduced into the one-sector WS-PS model. Here, we differentiate between employer subsidies and employee subsidies. The former are paid to employers, the latter to employees. Standard microeconomic theory tells us that in the long run – once wages and prices have adjusted fully to the subsidy – the real wage, net of subsidy, received by workers and that paid by the firms will be the same regardless of whether the subsidy is granted to the workers or to the firms.

Employer Subsidies reduce labour costs so that profit maximizing firms increase employment for a given real wage. Long-run equilibrium is assumed at the

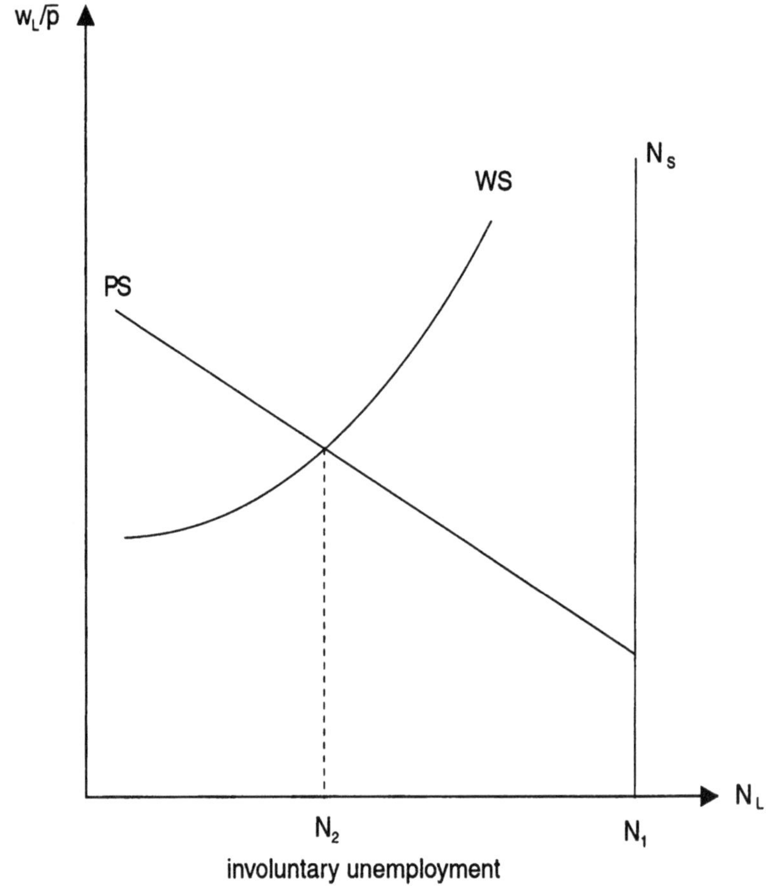

Figure 1: The One-Sector Wage Setting Price-Setting Model

intersection of the WS- and PS-curve at point A with the employment level N_0^* (see figure 2). At point A producer wage w^P and consumer wage w^c are identical. The introduction of an employer subsidy s drives a wedge between the producer and consumer wage. If the consumer wage is on the vertical axis, the PS-curve shifts to the right to PS' and results in a new long-run equilibrium at point C with the long-run employment level N_1^*. The WS-curve is assumed to remain unaffected. Notice that the consumer wage is observed in the market.

The introduction of *employee subsidies* allows for higher employment, because trade unions are interested in the consumer wage so that they accept a lower producer wage relative to a given real producer wage (Fehr 1990). Therefore, the WS-curve in figure 3 will shift to the right from WS to WS' by an employee sub-

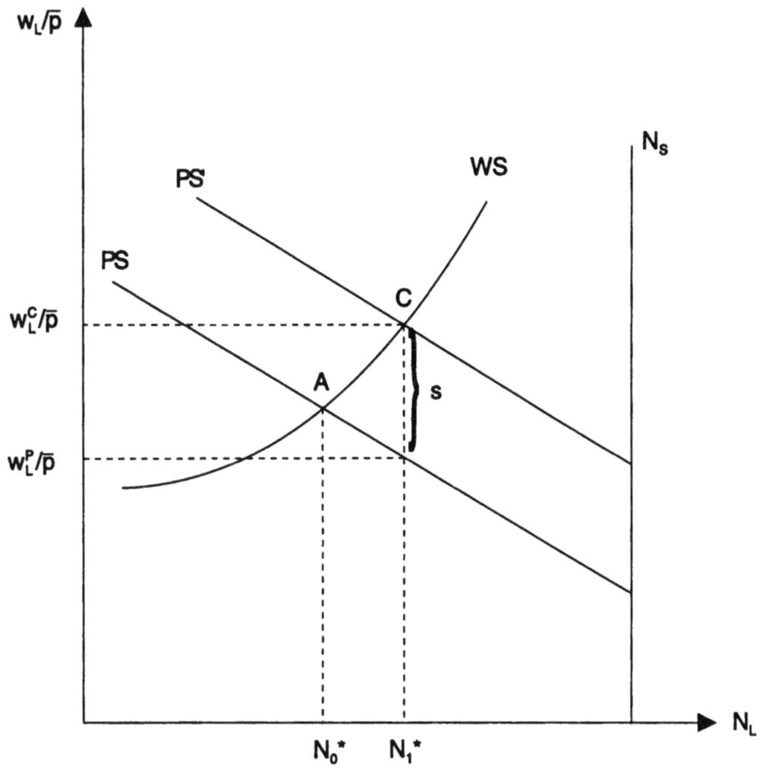

Figure 2: Employer Subsidies in the One-Sector WS-PS Model

sidy s, employment will increase from N_0^* to N_1^* (see figure 3). The new long-run equilibrium is at point D. The PS-curve is assumed to remain unaffectul. Notice that the producer wage is observed in the market.

Both employer and employee subsidies yield equivalent employment effects. But observed market wages are different. If employer subsidies are introduced, the higher consumer wage is observed in the market, whereas with employee subsidies the lower producer wage is the market wage.

D. Discussion of the Standard Result

The equivalence of employer and employee subsidies with respect to employment is in dispute. The introduction of transaction costs and experiences with experimental studies shed new light on the comparison of different kinds of employment subsidies. Former work on this comparison is related to competitive

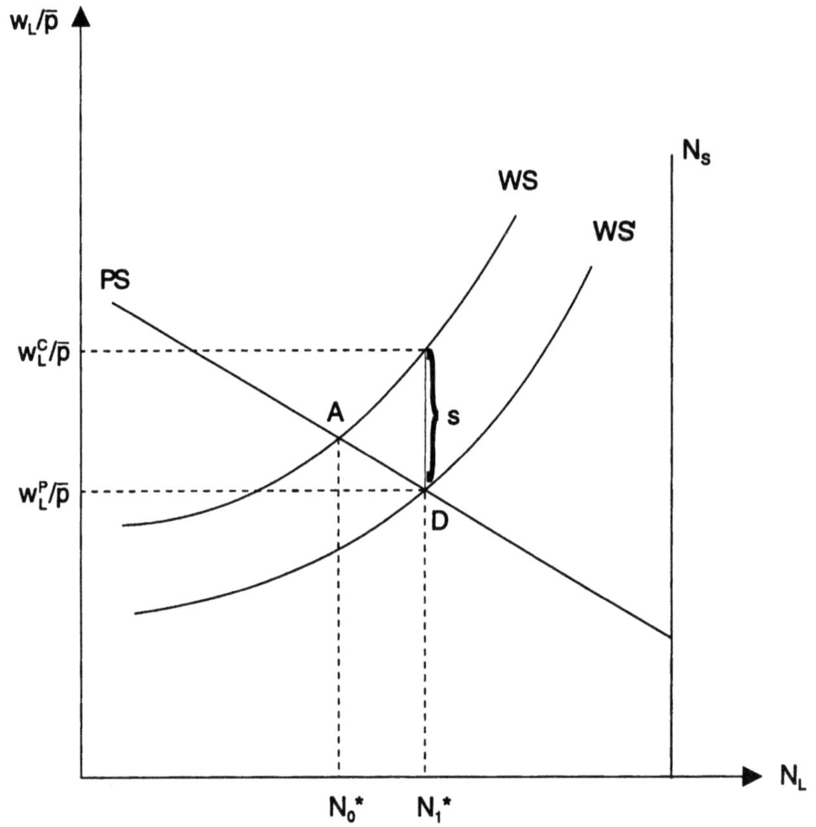

Figure 3: Employee Subsidies in the One-Sector WS-PS Model

models of unemployment rather than models of equilibrium unemployment (Lerman 1982, Perloff 1982).

(1) Transaction Costs

Employer subsidies are in practice associated with transaction costs such as hiring and firing costs. In reality, high *hiring costs* for employers make recruitments of the disadvantaged unemployed unattractive. This is true especially for small and medium-sized firms which need a relatively large portion of manpower to keep informed about existing employer subsidy programs; in Germany, almost a dozen programs exist for the disadvantaged unemployed. U.S. experiences confirm this view. Bishop/Kang (1991) analysed the causes for the low participation rates of the Targeted Jobs Tax Credit (TJTC) between 1979 and 1985; the TJTC has been the major U.S. employer subsidy program offered to firms that hired certain disadvantaged individuals since 1979. Information costs are found to be

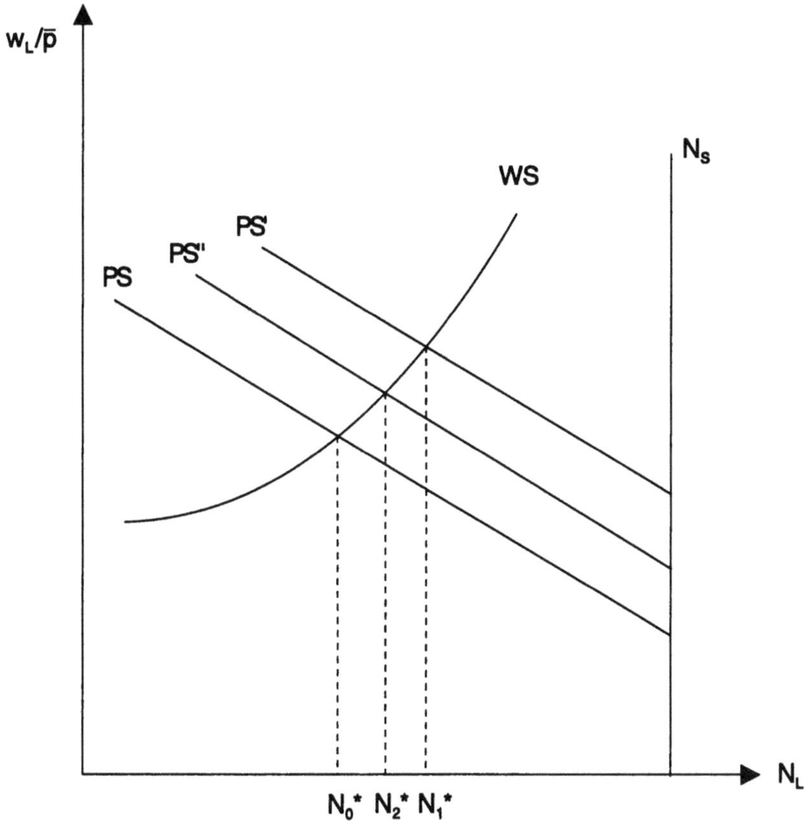

Figure 4: Employer Subsidies with Transaction Cost

the key barrier to TJTC participation. The cost-effectiveness of TJTC is low because of the very high recruitment cost of hiring additional TJTC-eligibles.

Another problem with time-restricted employer subsidies is churning. Employers fire subsidized workers as soon as the subsidy has run out. Thus, churning is associated with *firing costs*. Churning is observed in practice, but, to the best of my knowledge, there is no empirical study in this field.

Transaction costs may be introduced to the WS-PS model as an additional cost parameter which dampens the rightward shift of the PS-curve. The new PS''-curve typically lies left of the PS'-curve. Hence, employer subsidies are associated with a lower increase of employment relative to a situation without transaction costs. The new long-run equilibrium will be N_2^* rather than N_1^* in figure 4.

Employee subsidies impose transaction costs on employees rather than employers because employees have to care about the employee subsidy. At first glance, employment effects of employment subsidies should not differ because of the introduction of transaction costs. However, a closer inspection reveals two differences. First, additional transaction costs imposed on employees should not dampen their search activities if unemployment is high. Second, firing costs caused by time-restricted employer subsidies do not exist anymore, because churning is irrelevant in the case of employee subsidies. There is no reason for employers to fire subsidized workers because producer wages do not change if time-restricted employee subsidies run out. But work will no longer pay for employees. Nevertheless, employees may continue to work if job perspectives exist. Hence, transaction costs seem to be lower with employee subsidies.

Therefore, employment effects associated with employee subsidies are higher than with employer subsidies, due to the different importance of transaction costs.

(2) Experimental Studies

Woodbury/Spiegelman (1987) provide evidence for higher employment effects of employee subsidies from two controlled social experiments in Illinois 1984/85. In one of the experiments (the Employer Bonus Experiment), a random sample of Unemployment Insurance (UI) claimants were told that their next employer would qualify for a cash bonus of $500 if they, the claimants, found a job within eleven weeks of filing the UI claim, and if they retained that job for four months. In the other experiment (the Claimant Bonus Experiment), claimants were instructed that they would qualify for a cash bonus of $500 if they found a job within the same time period and held it for the same time period. The authors report that employer subsidies had a far smaller effect on employment than employee subsidies. But they do not explain why the experimental treatments influenced the participants' behaviour differently.

Decker/O'Leary (1995) evaluate pooled evidence from Re-Employment Bonus Experiments in Pennsylvania and Washington 1988/89 which were inspired by the positive experiences of the Illinois Bonus Experiments. Evaluations of the two experiments indicated that re-employment bonuses reduced the amount of time spent on UI, thereby reducing benefit payments. But the amount of bonus payments plus the administrative costs associated with making the offers exceeded the savings in UI payments. The authors conclude that a re-employment bonus is not a cost-effective method of accelerating the re-employment of UI claimants.

Greenberg et al. (1995) use a microsimulation model to predict the impacts of the five new welfare reform programs being tested in six areas of the United States and Canada. All programs make work pay for welfare recipients by employee subsidies. The simulation results suggest that the Canadian Self-Sufficiency Project (SSP) and the Minnesota Family Program (MFIP) will modestly increase the number of welfare recipients who work.

Meyer (1995, 1996) argues that the permanent adoption of a re-employment bonus could have important unintended negative effects because of behavioural responses. First, the currently unemployed who do not file could respond to the increased incentives to file for UI benefits. Second, those currently not unemployed but changing jobs could start work slightly later and file for UI benefits. And third, higher compensation for short UI spells will make layoffs more attractive to firms. All of these effects would tend to increase unemployment as well as increase UI payments.

Keane (1995) uses a simulation model of the labour force participation behaviour of low-income single mothers to show that an employee subsidy can substantially increase the number of single mothers who work, reduce their reliance on welfare, and save the government money while at the same time actually making single mothers better off.

Card/Robins (1996) present early findings from an experimental evaluation of the Canadian SSP. They emphasize that SSP is a unique social experiment being conducted at two different sites in Canada that offers a generous financial incentive for long-term welfare recipients to find a full-time job and leave welfare. The authors report a significant increase in full-time employment, but it appears that recipients are taking jobs that pay relatively low wages – within $1.00 to $3.00 per hour above the minimum wage.

Experimental studies and simulation models indicate that employee subsidies boost employment. Some experimental studies support the view that employee subsidies may be associated with higher employment effects than employer subsidies.

E. General Problems of Employment Subsidies

Employment subsidies are often criticized as an inappropriate method to fight long-term unemployment. Two main arguments stand out. First, employment subsidies are said to provide subsidies to some workers who would have found jobs anyway (deadweight). Second, subsidized workers are said to crowd out non-subsidized workers (displacement). Both problems exist in reality, but could be alleviated by targeting the long-term unemployed. These workers have relatively low chances of finding jobs and they are often very imperfect substitutes for incumbent employees, particularly in jobs that require experience and skill (Snower 1994a, b).

Two proposals which use transfer payments to the long-term unemployed as employment subsidies are presently discussed. Snower (1994a, b) suggests a self-financing employer subsidy scheme called "Benefit Transfer Program (BTP)". The basic idea is to give the long-term unemployed a new option: to use a portion of their unemployment benefits as vouchers for employers that hire them. Jerger/Spermann (1997) suggest a self-financing employee subsidy scheme called "Targeted Negative Income Tax (TNIT)". The basic notion is that own earnings of the means-tested long-term unemployed shall reduce benefits only by half. Both proposals do not require additional state expenditures like ordinary subsidy programs. Their employment effects are subject to further research.

F. Conclusions

Employment subsidies are often recommended to tackle structural employment problems. At first glance it does not matter if subsidies are paid to employers or employees. A closer inspection of this theoretical standard result sheds new light on the comparison between these two kinds of employment subsidies. Highly aggregated models ignore transaction costs as a microeconomic disincentive for employers to accept employer subsidies. Experimental studies suggest that employee subsidies may be associated with higher employment effects than employer subsidies. In general, employment subsidies are associated with deadweight and displacement effects. Targeting employment subsidies to the long-term unemployed may alleviate these problems.

References

Beck, U. (1996): Kapitalismus ohne Arbeit, Der Spiegel No. 20/1996, pp. 140–146.

Blanchard, O. (1997): Macroeconomics, New Jersey.

Bishop, J. H., and S. *Kang* (1991): Applying for Entitlements: Employers and the Targeted Jobs Tax Credit, Journal of Policy Analysis and Management, 10, pp. 24–45.

Burda, M., and C. *Wyplosz* (1997): Macroeconomics, A European Text, 2nd ed., Oxford.

Card, D., and P. K. *Robins* (1996): Do Financial Incentives Encourage Welfare Recipients to Work? Evidence from a Randomized Evaluation of the Self-Sufficiency Project, NBER Working Paper No. 5701.

Carlin, W., and D. *Soskice* (1990): Macroeconomics and the Wage Bargain, New York.

Council of Economic Advisers (1996): Job Creation and Employment Opportunities: The United States Labor Market, 1993–1996, Washington.

Decker, P. T., and C. J. *O'Leary* (1995): Evaluating Pooled Evidence from the Reemployment Bonus Experiments, Journal of Human Resources, 30, pp. 534–550.

Fehr, E. (1990): Fiscal Incentives in a Model of Equilibrium Unemployment, Journal of Institutional and Theoretical Economics, 146, pp. 617–639.

Gottschalk, P. (1997): Inequality, Income Growth, and Mobility: The Basic Facts, Journal of Economic Perspectives, 11, pp. 21–40.

Greenberg, D. H., and C. *Michalopoulos* and P. K. *Robins* and R. *Wood* (1995): Making Work Pay for Welfare Recipients, Contemporary Economic Policy, 13, pp. 39–52.

Jerger, J., and A. *Spermann* (1997): Promoting Low-Wage Employment: The Case for a targeted negative income tax, Jahrbuch für Wirtschaftswissenschaften, Revue of Economics, 48, pp. 269–287.

Johnson, G. F. (1997): Changes in Earnings Inequality: The Role of Demand Shifts, Journal of Economic Perspectives, 11, pp. 41–54.

Keane, M. P. (1995): A New Idea for Welfare Reform, in: Federal Reserve Bank of Minneapolis, Quarterly Review, Spring, pp. 2–28.

Layard, R., S. Nickell and R. Jackman (1991): Unemployment, Oxford University Press.

Lerman, R. I. (1982): A Comparison of Employer and Worker Wage Subsidies, in: Haveman, R. H. and J. L. Palmer (ed.): Jobs for Disadvantaged Workers: The Economics of Employment Subsidies, Washington, pp. 159–180.

Martin, H.-P., and H. *Schumann* (1996): Die Globalisierungsfalle, Hamburg.

Meyer, B. D. (1995): Lessons from the U.S. Unemployment Insurance Experiments, Journal of Economic Literature, 33, pp. 91–131.

Meyer, B. D. (1996): What Have We Learned from the Illinois Reemployment Bonus Experiment?, Journal of Labor Economics, 14, pp. 26–51.

OECD (1996): Employment Outlook, Paris.

Perloff, J. M. (1982): Micro- and Macroeconomic Effects, in: Haveman, R. H., and J. L. Palmer (eds.): Jobs for Disadvantaged Workers: The Economics of Employment Subsidies, Washington, pp. 95–123.

Rifkin, J. (1995): The End of Work, New York.

Snower, D. J. (1994a): Converting Unemployment Benefits into Employment Subsidies, American Economic Review, Papers and Proceedings, 84, pp. 65–70.

Snower, D. J. (1994b): The Simple Economics of Benefit Transfers, CEPR Discussion Paper No. 1086, London.

Thurow, L. (1996): The Future of Capitalism.

Topel, R. H. (1997): Factor Proportions and Relative Wages: The Supply-Side Determinants of Wage Inequality, Journal of Economic Perspectives, 11, pp. 55–74.

Woodbury, S. A., and R. G. *Spiegelman* (1987): Bonuses to Workers and Employers to Reduce Unemployment: Randomized Trials in Illinois, American Economic Review, 77, pp. 513–530.

The Hierarchical Market-Firm Nexus and the Institutional Analysis of the Recent Japanese Economy

Hiroyasu Uemura, Akinori Isogai, and Akira Ebizuka

Introduction

What are the main characteristics of the Japanese economic system? How are they changing in the recession in the 1990s? In order to answer these questions, we have to investigate in detail the structures of the Japanese economic system which have been developing and evolving in the post-war period. The institutional analysis of the Japanese economic system has been developed recently by many researchers who are interested in the economics of institutions. Above all, many Japanese régulationists have contributed to the analysis, and they emphasise that the mode of régulation[1] of the post-war Japanese economy is that of "Company-ism". As far as we understand, the core argument of the "Company-ism" hypothesis is that large firms have a strong power to promote social integration in Japanese society. However, with this hypothesis, only the organisation of large firm has been discussed so far.

The purpose of our proposing the hypothesis of "the Hierarchical Market-Firm Nexus" is to develop the "Company-ism" hypothesis in the much larger framework of the Japanese socio-economic system which includes the structures of the labour market and inter-firm relations. The messages of our hypothesis can be summarised as follows. First, it is necessary to understand the specific "mode of régulation" of the Japanese economy as the ensemble which is composed of various institutions articulated with one another establishing "structural compatibility" in the socio-economic system. Second, the ensemble of institutions is hierarchically structured over firm organisation, the labour market and inter-firm relations. Third, the "Hierarchical Market-Firm Nexus" has produced some specific "structural effects" in the Japanese socio-economic system, and has determined the dynamics of the economy since the 1970s.

---

[1] The French spelling of "régulation" tries to emphasize the particular meaning of this term in the French socio-economic literature.

In this paper, we will explain our theoretical framework, taking into account the recent development of the economics of institutions, and then, we will develop our argument so as to include the analysis of the Japanese economy in the recession in the 1990s. We will present our tentative conclusion regarding the question, whether the Hierarchical Market-Firm Nexus is experiencing structural shifts, facing the recession and the appreciation of the Yen in the 1990s.

A. Institutional Analysis of "the Hierarchical Market-Firm Nexus"

I. Institutional Analysis and the Régulation Approach

To develop our analysis of institutions and economic dynamics in the Japanese economy, the concept of "the mode of régulation" is very suggestive. How can capitalist society reproduce itself perpetually, though it is full of contradictions, conflicts, antagonism, and violence? This is the fundamental problem of the régulation theory. Capitalist society reproduces itself not only through the market mechanism but also through various institutions which are "embedded" in the socio-economic system (Hollongsworth and Boyer 1997). The mode of régulation is usually understood to refer to a set of rules of the social game which the principal forms of institutions produce to establish social regularity. Therefore, the important point for analysing "the mode of régulation" is to investigate how principal institutions are articulated with one another and to make clear what structural effects the articulation produces socially and economically. In other words, an institution can have its proper significance only within the social arrangements of institutions in the socio-economic system. Therefore, we call this kind of approach "the institutional analysis of the socio-economic system".

In this approach, we understand 'institution' as follows. On the one hand, it is a social apparatus with rules and conventions which makes individuals behave along a definite social regularity, on the other hand, it is reproduced through the behaviours of individuals, even with the possibility of a disposition towards social disorder caused by the conflicting and contradicting nature of society. When the ensemble of institutions makes the socio-economic system reproduce itself continuously with structural stability in a dynamic process, we think that those institutions have "structural compatibility" with one another. The articulation of institutions has not only the possibility of being compatible or complementary with one another but also that of evolution and structural change with social conflicts in a cumulative process. Therefore, in "the institutional analysis of the socio-economic system", the mode of articulating institutions and the co-ordinating mechanisms they produce must be investigated in a particular context in the socio-economic system as well as a particular stage of historical development with so-called "path-dependency".

II. "Wage-Labour Nexus" and "Market-Firm Nexus"

We focus on the "wage-labour nexus" ("rapport salarial") among other institutional forms, as does the régulation school. The wage-labour nexus is defined as "the ensemble of conditions governing the use and reproduction of the work force" (Boyer 1981). Therefore, not only micro-economic factors but also macro-economic ones should be considered in the analysis of the wage-labour nexus, as far as they govern the use and reproduction of the work force. In the analysis of the Japanese economy, unfortunately, the organisation of large firms has been exclusively focused on. However, a firm organisation can exist only if it is supported by the network of institutions which are compatible with it. Therefore, the analysis of firm organisation must be complemented by the analysis of the network of articulated institutional forms. We think that only by doing so is it possible to provide a bridge connecting the micro-economic analysis of institutions and individual behaviours with the macro-economic analysis of economic dynamics and to establish the analytical framework of the so-called "micro-macro loop".

From this understanding, we will analyse the contemporary Japanese economy from three aspects, that is, (1) firm organisation, (2) the labour market, and (3) inter-firm relations. This framework of analysis is based on our view that the labour market is one important component of the wage-labour nexus, but particular arrangements in the labour market are reproduced together with arrangements based on firm's strategies (both within a firm and between firms). For example, the hierarchical segmentation in the labour market makes inter-firm relations more hierarchical according to the kind of workers a firm employs, and in turn, the inter-firm relations reinforce segmentation in the labour market. In short, we should consider the particular arrangements in the wage-labour nexus from the perspective of the relationship between firm organisation, the labour market, and inter-firm relations in the socio-economic system.

Here, we think that, when these three components are structurally compatible, a particular wage-labour nexus is also stable. We call this framework of analysis "the Market-Firm Nexus" (MFN). This is a framework with which we can analyse the relationship between a firm organisation at micro-economic level and macro-economic dynamics, because it highlights a set of co-ordinating mechanisms produced by institutions embedded in it. Analytically, the important point is how the three components are structurally compatible and what kind of "structural effect" they produce through the co-ordinating mechanisms.

III. The Hypothesis of "the Hierarchical Market-Firm Nexus"

We will analyse the Japanese economic system from the viewpoint of the Market-Firm Nexus. The institutional arrangement of labour relations in the post-war Japanese economy is often characterised as "micro-corporatism". It usually means a regime in which there is a capital-labour accord at the firm level. The core ingredient in the capital-labour accord is said to be the exchange of job security for the active commitment of workers to their company.

However, we think that the following conditions are necessary for job security to produce efficiency rather than inefficiency with idleness and inflexibility in the framework of the Market-Firm Nexus.

(1) Firm organisation: There must be an incentive mechanism to promote the work effort of employees in a firm as a place to achieve a productive combination. We think that the promotion system, the seniority wage system, the retirement pay system, and the company based welfare in the "ranking hierarchy" (Aoki 1988) as the incentive mechanism is embedded well within the Japanese firm. At the same time, competition to get a larger market share is pursued to ensure the growth of firms so that there will be enough positions for their employees. In these circumstances, it is quite likely that the number of core workers in the life-time employment system is reduced so as to lower overhead costs, and also that workers are made multi-skilled in order to utilise them effectively, as they cannot be laid off.

(2) Labour market: A penalty at the time of quitting a company is needed in order to firmly integrate workers into their firm with life-time employment. In other words, the potential threat of bankruptcy must be reinforced by a financial penalty for changing jobs. In the Japanese economy, this is brought about by downward mobility in the hierarchically segmented labour market which has differentials in the various conditions of employment.

As for wages, even if we control such factors as education and experience, there still exist definite firm-size wage differentials in the Japanese labour market (Rebick 1993). In addition, there are large differentials in company-based welfare between large firms and small and medium-size firms (Miyajima 1992). Therefore, the differential of life-time incomes is quite large, and this makes the financial penalty of mid-career job change much more severe, together with downward mobility in the labour market (Figure 1).

In this way, the seniority wages with firm-size differentials and the hierarchical labour market only with downward mobility produce the enormous costs of changing a job in mid-career. As is known well, the Social Structures of Accumulation (SSA) School in the U.S. calls the difference between worker's current incomes and a weighted average of income prospects at the time of separation

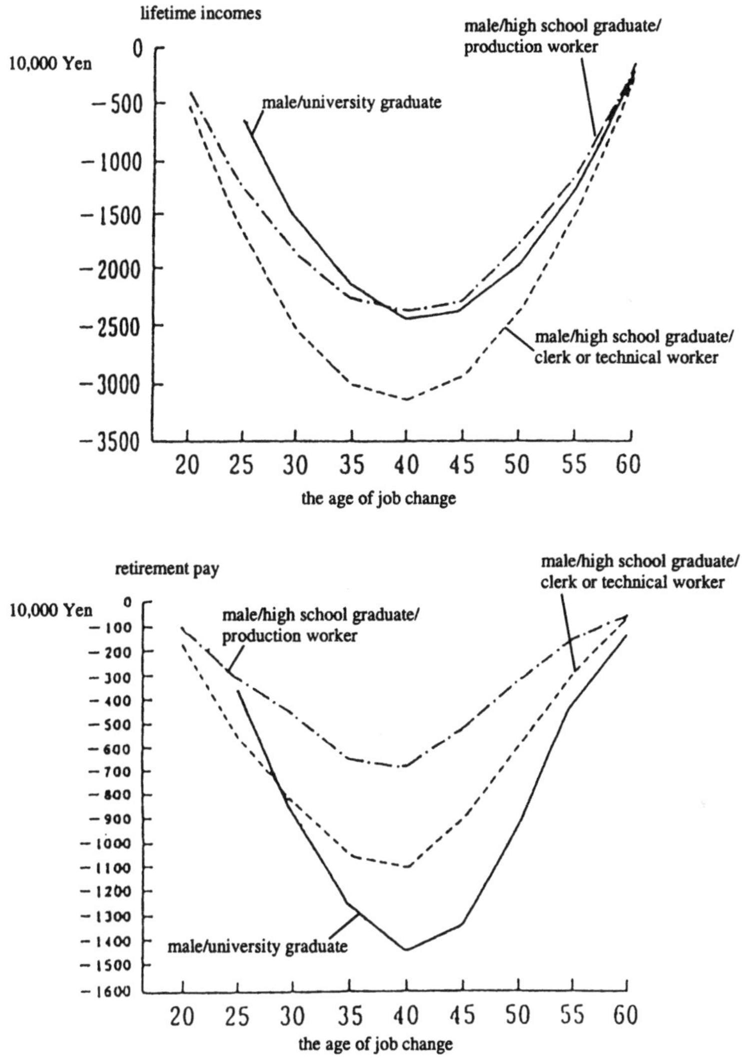

Source: White Paper of Labour (1993)

Figure 1: The Cost of Mid-Career Job Change

"job-loss costs" (Bowles 1985, Bowles and Boyer 1990). They argue that the larger the costs of job loss are, the bigger the work effort is. In this argument, they assume that job-loss costs are mainly affected by conditions in the external labour market. In the case of the Japanese economy, however, the possibility of unemployment is quite low, and workers are actually unlikely to be laid off. Therefore, we should modify this framework of analysis to be able to explain the hierarchically structured socio-economic system in Japan. In this paper, we will call the costs of mid-career job change in terms of life-time incomes "institutionalised job-loss costs". This can be understood as a "functional equivalent" of the threat of unemployment.

(3) Inter-firm relations: Co-ordinating mechanisms to satisfy the following three conditions are needed in order to retain the system of life-time employment in the capitalist market economy, in which uncertainty dominates and fluctuations occur unexpectedly all the time. First, it must be easy to adjust wages to economic fluctuations. Second, a buffer must exist to protect the employment of core workers, when their firm is facing economic fluctuations. Third, there must be no drastic change that might destroy the structures which function as a core and its buffer. What attracts attention in the Japanese inter-firm relations are the widely existing subcontractor systems. In fact, more than 60 percent of small and medium-size firms are integrated into subcontractor systems. Furthermore, the subcontractor systems have the hierarchical structures of firms according to the scale of capital and the number of employees. The subcontractor systems play the role of 'buffer' in the following ways.

First, there is a pressure to reduce the number of employees with life-time employment in large firms. Then, this causes another pressure to externalise labour intensive production processes and to purchase externally products which are produced in small and medium-size firms. These pressures promote the formation of the subcontractor system. In this way, the subcontractor systems play a role as a buffer. In addition, the smaller the firm-size is, the higher the relative share of part-time workers (Table 1).

Second, we have to emphasise here that there is an asymmetry between a parent company and its subcontractors in their terms of trade. Namely, the pressure of competition on a large number of subcontractors worsens their terms of trade, and it makes the value-added productivity of a parent firm increase intensively by lowering its costs. As a result, it contributes to the increase in profits of the parent company. Furthermore, another important aspect of the competition among subcontractors and the organic inter-firm relations is the fact that it promotes improvement in the quality of their products.

Third, in addition to this, it is very interesting that the subcontractor systems have been functioning as a social buffer or an apparatus for stabilising society in such a way that, even in a period of recession, small and medium-size firms absorb workers, minimising the unemployment rate (Muramatsu 1994).

To summarise the above discussions, it can be concluded that the "micro-corporatism" which is organised on the basis of job security in a large firm is quite

Table 1

Ratio of Employees According to Forms of Working, Firm-Sizes and Sex

	Total	Regular worker	Part-timer	Other
Male and Female				
Total	(100.0) 100.0	77.2	13.7	9.1
Over 1000 employees	(26.0) 100.0	83.0	9.9	7.1
300 ~ 999	(14.6) 100.0	81.2	11.5	7.3
100 ~ 299	(15.0) 100.0	76.8	14.1	9.1
30 ~ 99	(17.4) 100.0	73.9	14.6	11.5
5 ~ 29	(27.1) 100.0	71.7	17.6	10.7
Male				
Total	(100.0) 100.0	86.9	4.4	8.7
Over 1000 employees	(28.1) 100.0	92.1	3.2	4.7
300 ~ 999	(15.2) 100.0	90.6	2.5	6.9
100 ~ 299	(15.0) 100.0	85.5	5.1	9.4
30 ~ 99	(16.4) 100.0	84.2	4.9	10.9
5 ~ 29	(25.2) 100.0	81.6	6.2	12.2
Female				
Total	(100.0) 100.0	61.4	28.6	10.0
Over 1000 employees	(22.6) 100.0	64.6	23.5	11.9
300 ~ 999	(13.5) 100.0	64.1	28.0	7.9
100 ~ 299	(14.9) 100.0	62.8	28.6	8.6
30 ~ 99	(18.8) 100.0	59.4	28.2	12.4
5 ~ 29	(30.1) 100.0	58.4	32.9	8.7

Source: Ministry of Labour, Labour Policy Bureau, Report of the Research on Diversifying Firm-Workers, 1996, pp. 39–41.

limited in scope in the national economy as a whole, and that it is necessarily complemented by a specific Market-Firm Nexus consisting of the ranking hierarchy within a firm, the hierarchically segmented labour market only with downward mobility, and hierarchical inter-firm relations containing different types of flexibility. Now, we call such an hierarchically structured Market-Firm Nexus in the socio-economic system "the Hierarchical Market-Firm Nexus", which is shown in the following triangle.

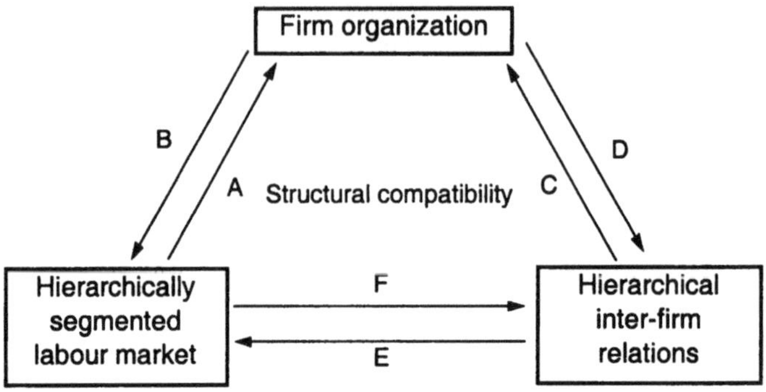

Each arrow has the following meanings and contents. A: Institutionalised job-loss costs as an incentive mechanism and the flexibility of employment. B: Segmentation as a result of the firm's strategy. C: Buffer (or external flexibility) to cope with external shocks and productivity-enhancing effects in the inter-firm network of productive system. D: Externalisation and control of the productive activities. E: Segmented demand of labour F: Stratified labour supply by segmented workers.

B. "The Hierarchical Market-Firm Nexus" as a Set of Coordinating Mechanisms in Economic Dynamics

In this section, we will analyse the functional role of the Hierarchical Market-Firm Nexus as a set of co-ordinating mechanisms in the dynamics of the Japanese economy. Here, we will consider the three dynamic structural effects of the Hierarchical Market-Firm Nexus, that is, the incentive mechanism, the flexibility of wages and employment, and the productivity-enhancing effect.

I. Structures of the Incentive Mechanism

The active commitment of workers to their company through long and hard work can be regarded as a quite specific "structural effect" of the Hierarchical Market-Firm Nexus as a whole in Japan. Figure 2 shows the structures of this incentive mechanism. The structures must be analysed under two aspects. One is the difference between internal factors existing within firm organisation and external factors which constitute the socio-economic environment of firm organisation, and the other is that between regular and non-regular workers. Sticks and carrots are embedded very well in those socio-economic structures.

Here we will mainly focus on the factors influencing regular workers. They are situated in "the ranking hierarchy" within a firm organisation. Their wages rise at regular intervals, and at the time of promotion to higher ranks on the basis of age and tenure. Their wages are decided on the basis of a "job grade wage rate" rather than being attached to a particular job. The most crucial factor in deciding their wages and promotion is the assessment by a direct supervisor (which is called 'SATEI'). In this context, the important thing for explaining the integration of workers into a company is the fact that it is not only the assessment of the employee's performance but also that of his potential ability such as adaptability to technical changes, versatility, loyalty to his company, and so on. Under these conditions, employees are forced to be interested in mastering even more skills than those concerning their present jobs. Furthermore, the merit assessment results in the differentials of promotion in their company in the long term. Thus, it causes the differentials of the life-time incomes. In the promotion system based on the merit assessment and the wage determination system in conformity with ranks, these differentials have incentive effects on employees and make them compete with one another in their company.

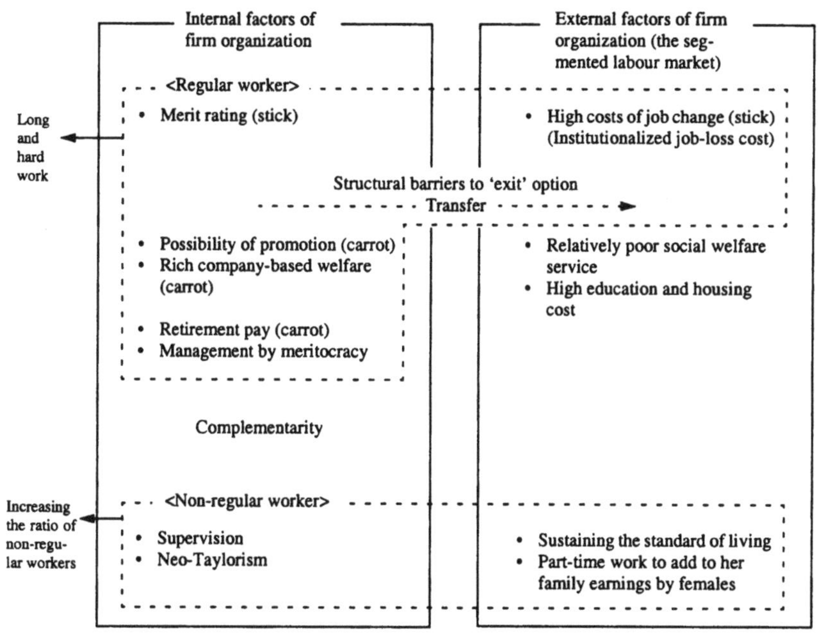

Figure 2: The Structures of Incentive Mechanism in the Hierarchical Market-Firm Nexus

II. Cost of Job Change and "Institutionalized Job-Loss Costs"

In the Hierarchical Market-Firm Nexus, an employee who quits his company in mid-career must expect a large financial and social penalty in the Japanese socio-economic system. In fact, the costs of job change are quite large for regular male workers in a large company. Their former wage level cannot be kept after their job change, and their wage growth will decelerate. From the estimation of wage functions in both Japan and the U.S., Higuchi (1991) draws the conclusion that the effect of the length of service years on wages is larger in Japan than in the U.S. We can also see the high evaluation given to the length of service years concerning the different categories of workers in a few very simple but interesting graphs in figures 3 and 4. When a worker changes his job, his wages may go down to the level of zero service years. Furthermore, he has usually to be re-employed in a firm of lower rank in the hierarchy of firms. He must also expect a considerable decrease in his retirement pay. With these high costs of job change, workers are enforced not to quit their company and to devote themselves to their hard work.

What has to be noticed is the fact that the incentive effect of the costs of job change cannot be explained only by the upward-sloping wage profile. The point to be stressed here is that this kind of incentive effect is a very specific structural effect of the hierarchical structures. The costs of job change increase sharply due to the complementarity between two kinds of factors, that is, one concerning the inside-firm factors such as retirement pay, mandatory retirement and the exclu-

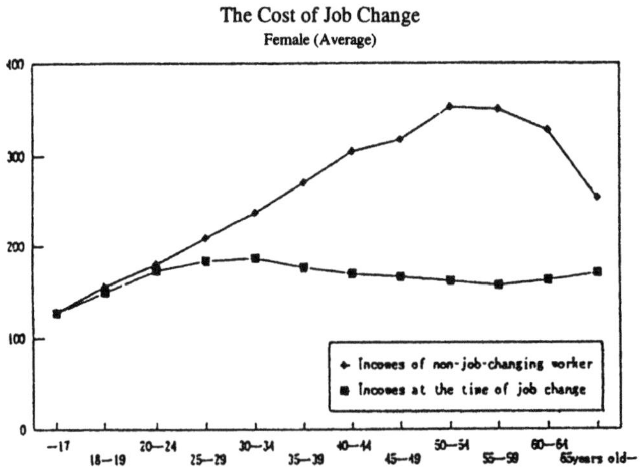

Source: Ministry of Labour, Basic Survey on Wages, 1995

Figure 3: Wage Profile and the Cost of Job Change (Female Worker)

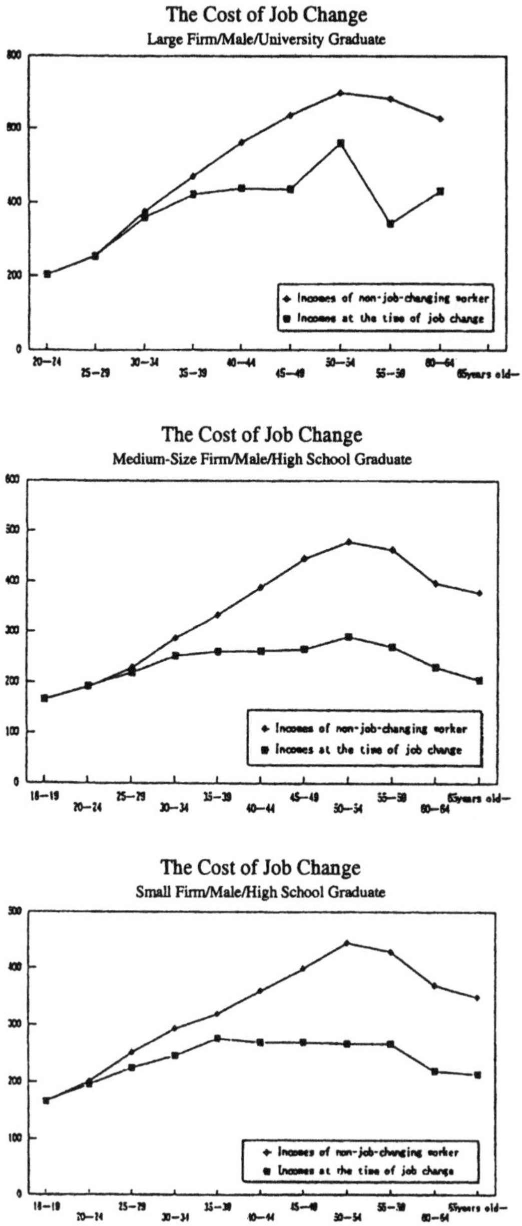

Source: Ministry of Labour, Basic Survey on Labour, 1995

Figure 4: Wage Profile and the Cost of Job Change (Male Worker) sive recruitment of new graduates, and the other concerning the outside-firm factors such as the hierarchical inter-firm structures, poor social welfare services, high education costs, and high housing expenses. Furthermore, given the segmented labour market and the hierarchical inter-firm relations, it must be a commonly accepted idea that the mid-career job change brings about downward movement in a social context.

This structural effect which the total structure of the Hierarchical Market-Firm Nexus and the complementarity of its sub-systems produce is what we call "institutionalised job-loss costs". We think that this is a functional equivalent of the threat of unemployment in the competitive labour market. This plays a crucial role in stimulating the work efforts of male employees in a large company. It is perpetually effective through economic fluctuations, as it is highly institutionalised. In other words, the incentive effect of institutionalised job-loss costs keeps regulating workers' efforts even in a quasi-full employment situation.

III. Flexibility of Wages and Employment

In the Japanese economy, wages are sufficiently flexible to cope with different economic conditions. This does not, however, mean that the labour market is arranged like the perfectly competitive market. It is quite segmented and institutionalised in the Hierarchical Market-Firm Nexus.

To investigate wage determination for different categories of workers (firm-size, male/female), we used regression analysis, setting the following equation.

$$\hat{W}_t = a \cdot \hat{PROF}_t + b \cdot U_{t-1} + c \cdot \hat{P}_{t-1} + d \text{ or}$$
$$\hat{W}_t = a \cdot \hat{PROF}_t + b \cdot RJOA_t + c \cdot \hat{P}_{t-1} + d$$

where $\hat{W}_t$ is the growth rate of nominal wages, $\hat{PROF}_t$ is the growth rate of the total ordinary profits of corporations, U_t is the unemployment rate at the end of a year (U_{mt} is that of male workers and U_{ft} is that of female workers), $RJOA_t$ is the ratio of job offers to applicants, and $\hat{P}_{t-1}$ is the growth rate of the consumer price index. We obtained the results as shown in Table 2.

The result can be explained as follows. As for male workers in a large firm (with over 1000 employees), nominal wages are sensitive to the total ordinary profits of corporation, the unemployment rate at the end of the previous year (rather than the current ratio of job offers to applicants), and the consumer price index in the previous year. This suggests that nominal wages are determined by a kind of profit-sharing mechanism (Hirano 1992) and a formal wage bargaining procedure taking into account the unemployment rate and inflation, which seems

Table 2

Dualistic Wage Determination (Firm-Size; Male/Female) (1977–1990)

Wage equation:

$$\hat{W}_t = a \cdot P\hat{R}OF_t + b \cdot U_{t-1} + c \cdot \hat{P}_{t-1} + d + e_t \text{ or}$$

$$\hat{W}_t = a \cdot P\hat{R}OF_t + b \cdot RJOA_t + c \cdot \hat{P}_{t-1} + d + e_t$$

e_t : stochastic term

	$P\hat{R}OF_t$	$U_{m,t-1}$	$\hat{P}_{t-1}$	d	$\bar{R}^2$	DW
$\hat{W}_m(L)_t$	0.014*	−3.304**	0.497**	12.06**	0.9131	2.380
	(2.40)	(−4.26)	(6.33)	(5.32)		
$\hat{W}_m(S)_t$	0.000	−3.069**	0.444**	11.38**	0.9037	0.967
	(0.01)	(−3.99)	(5.70)	(5.07)		
	$P\hat{R}OF_t$	$U_{f,t-1}$	$\hat{P}_{t-1}$	d	$\bar{R}^2$	DW
$\hat{W}_f(L)_t$	0.006	0.752	0.713**	0.6057	0.6752	2.545
	(0.51)	(0.51)	(3.88)	(0.13)		
$\hat{W}_f(S)_t$	0.006	−3.414*	0.296*	12.37**	0.8218	2.434
	(0.73)	(−3.01)	(2.27)	(3.87)		
	$P\hat{R}OF_t$	$RJOA_t$	$\hat{P}_{t-1}$	d	$\bar{R}^2$	DW
$\hat{W}_m(L)_t$	0.016	2.802	0.816**	−0.1534	0.8242	3.032
	(1.58)	(1.98)	(7.52)	(−0.11)		
$\hat{W}_m(S)_t$	0.009	4.052**	0.803**	1.322	0.9123	2.376
	(1.27)	(4.30)	(11.12)	(−1.43)		
$\hat{W}_f(L)_t$	0.011	0.133	0.646**	4.767	0.6669	2.249
	(0.78)	(0.07)	(4.48)	(1.49)		
$\hat{W}_f(S)_t$	0.004	2.705	0.713**	0.2699	0.7351	2.774
	(0.36)	(1.67)	(5.77)	(0.17)		

Note: Numbers in brackets are t-statistics. ** (*) denotes significance at the 1% (5%) level on a t-test.
$\hat{W}_m(L)$: the growth rate of male workers' nominal wages in firms with over 1000 employees. $\hat{W}_m(S)$: the growth rate of male workers' nominal wages in firms with 10–99 employees. $\hat{W}_f(L)$: the growth rate of male workers' nominal wages in firms with over 1000 employees. $\hat{W}_f(S)$: the growth rate of male workers' nominal wages in firms with 10–99 employees. *PROF*: the growth rate of ordinary profits of corporations. U_m: the unemployment rate of male workers at the end of the year. U_f: the unemployment rate of female workers at the end of the year. *RJOA*: the ratio of job offers to applicants. $\hat{P}$: the growth rate of consumer price index (1985=100)

Source: Japanese Wage Census, Ministry of Labour, and Annual Report on the Labour Force Survey, Statistics Bureau, and Corporation Statistics, Ministry of Finance.

to be partly ensured by the spring offensive system (SHUNTO) in spite of its diminishing influence in the 1980s (Tsuru 1992). On the contrary, for male workers in small firms, nominal wages are not sensitive to the total ordinary profits of corporations, while they are very sensitive to the ratio of job offers to applicants in the same year and the consumer price index in the previous year. Therefore, the wage determination of male workers in small firms is influenced very much by conditions in the spot labour market. As for the wages of female workers, only those in small firms are sensitive to the unemployment rate and inflation, while those in large firms cannot be explained by this kind of wage equation. It seems that these different wage determination mechanisms are coexisting in the Japanese employment system.

With these different wage determination mechanisms, firm-size wage differentials are brought about on the basis of value-added productivity differentials and the segmentation of workers into regular workers and non-regular workers in large firms. The wage determination of male workers in large firms is highly institutionalised and that of male workers in small firms is rather competitive, so wage differentials between workers in these two categories fluctuate counter-cyclically. In the Hierarchical Market-Firm Nexus, wage moderation may also be ensured in the following way. On the one hand, the increase in wages is moderated by the profit-sharing mechanism and the spring offensive system in large firms, on the other hand, the increase in wages is also limited by low value-added productivity in small firms. This set of co-ordination mechanisms may account for the striking fact that the Japanese economy did not experience a wage explosion even in the situation of quasi-full employment in the late 1980s.

To understand precisely the co-ordination mechanism of employment in the Japanese economy, it is important to pay attention to the hierarchical inter-firm relations and the existence of non-regular workers in various forms whose employment is very sensitive to economic fluctuations. In short, we can conclude two things. First, the flexibility of employment of non-regular workers makes possible the long-term employment relation of regular workers by reducing wage costs. Second, from the macro-economic point of view, the transfer of workers from a parent company to its subcontractors and the absorption of employment by small and medium-size firms plays a role as a co-ordinating mechanism to keep total employment even in recession periods. Therefore, the stability of employment, that of regular workers, is ensured not only by implicit compromise in large firms, but also by the inter-firm co-ordinating mechanism and the segmented labour market in the Hierarchical Market-Firm Nexus. We can depict the structures of employment in the Hierarchical Market-Firm Nexus, paying attention to the life-cycle of both male and female worker in Figure 5.

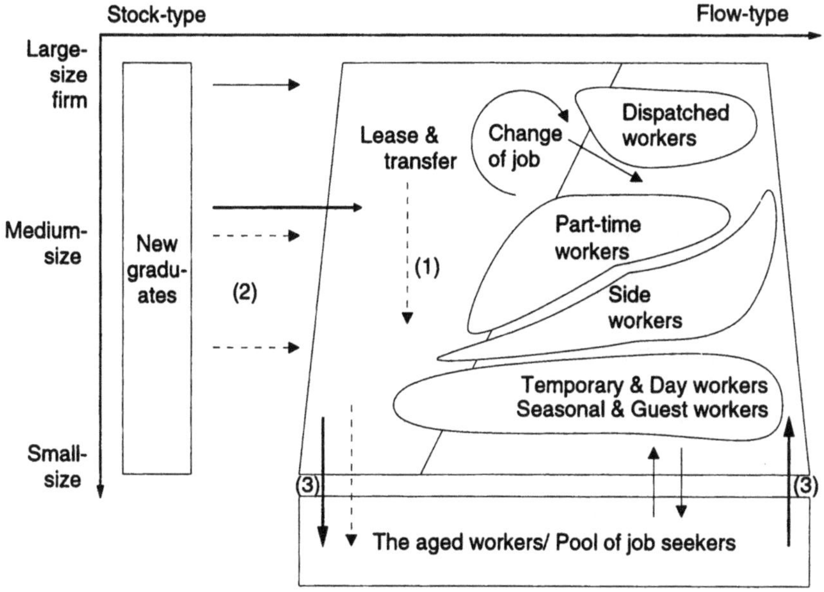

Notes: 1) The 'stock-type labour market' consists of regular workers who work for one firm only and accumulate their abilities for work on the basis of long-term employment practice, while the 'flow-type labour market' consists of various non-regular workers. This distinction is from Tsuda (1987).
2) Arrows of (1) and (2) indicate that small and medium-size firms play a role as the 'sponge' of employment during severe recession.
3) Arrows at (3) indicate the life-cycle in the supply of female workers.

Figure 5: The Structures of Employment in the Hierarchical Market-Firm Nexus

In this way, these kinds of co-ordinating mechanisms of wages and employment determine the fluctuations of wages and wage share at aggregate level. The growth rates of nominal wages became almost the same in the different sizes of firm in the late 1970s, and was moderate even in the boom period in the late 1980s (see Figure 6 and Figure 7). This effect of wage moderation played really a crucial role in retaining the stable trend of wage share during the 1980s. The growth rates of nominal wages by industry have shown dispersion and diversification according to earnings conditions in each industry since the late 1970s (Okina, Takeuchi and Yoshikawa 1989). In short, we can observe that, since the late 1970s when the Hierarchical Market-Firm Nexus was established, the growth rates of nominal wages have been equalised with one another within each industry, and that the equalisation mechanism of wages has been declining between the different industries.

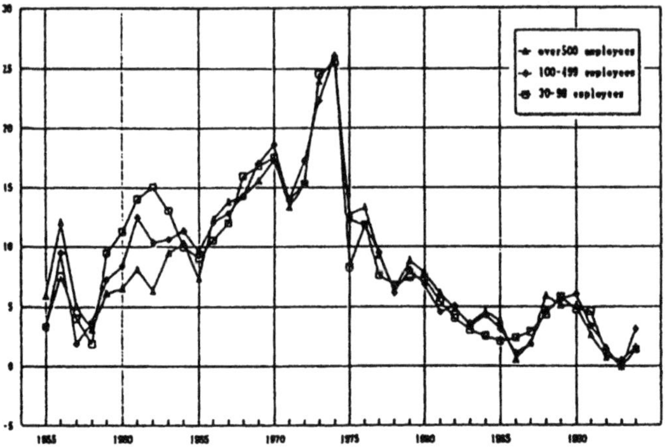

Source: Ministry of Labour, Monthly Labour Statistics

Figure 6: Nominal Wage Growth in the Different Sizes of Firm (Manufacturing)
Annual Growth Rate

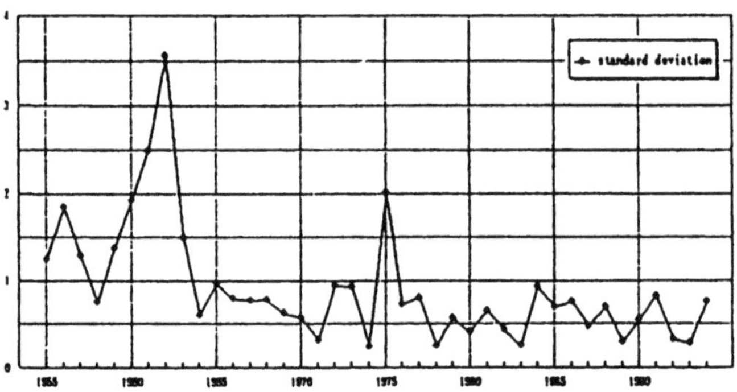

Source: Ministry of Labour, Monthly Labour Statistics

Figure 7: The Standard Deviation of the Growth of Nominal Wages

IV. Structural Compatibility and Productivity-Enhancing Mechanism in the "Hierarchical Market-Firm Nexus"

One of the remarkable features of the Japanese economic system is its flexibility in coping with economic fluctuations and structural changes. Flexibility in the Japanese economy system is very complex in its structures, and it should be characterised by "the structural compatibility of internal and external flexibility". The following table summarises our discussion from this perspective, showing the different types of flexibility with regard to the different types of workers.

Table 3
Flexibility of Regular and Non-Regular Workers

	Large firm		Small firm	
	Regular	Non-regular	Regular	Non-regular
Working hours	Overtime work	Flexible	Overtime work	Flexible
Skill formation	High level		Relatively low level	
Commitment	Active		Active	
Innovation	Promotion	Acceptance	Promotion	Acceptance
Employment	No flexibility, life-time employment	Flexible	Relatively high separation rate	
Wage determination	Flexible, profit-sharing SHUNTO	Competitive, very low wages	Flexible, sensitive to the local market	Competitive, very low wages

As we can see in table 3, the internal flexibility of regular workers in large firms, that is, flexibly extended working hours, the active commitment of workers to their company, the high level of skill formation in on-the-job training, and the promotion of innovation, is complemented well by the external flexibility of wages and the employment of non-regular workers in large firms and both regular and non-regular workers in small (and medium-size) firms. Therefore, it is necessary to investigate the structural characteristics of flexibility especially from the viewpoint of the structural compatibility of internal and external flexibility based on the Hierarchical Market-Firm Nexus.

Of course, from a much more dynamic perspective, we should not deny the quite 'offensive' character of such internal flexibility as organisational innovation with a longer time horizon, the organisational planning to respond effectively to demand in the market (like the just-in-time system), the long-term skill formation in on-the-job training, and the reallocation of workers within a firm in a longer term perspective (Boyer 1995). These must be the source of the dynamic efficiency of the Japanese firm organisation. Moreover, not only the effect of the division of labour within the subcontractor system but also the competitive pressure on subcontractors to introduce new technologies into their production process plays a very important role to enhance productivity in the long run. However, this dynamic efficiency is brought about on the basis of the existence of non-regular workers and the hierarchical inter-firm relations in the Hierarchical Market-Firm Nexus. As for the incentive mechanism to promote internal flexibility for regular workers, especially that in a large firm, we can see that it is complemented by the existence of the costs of job change in the Hierarchical Market-Firm Nexus. Therefore, the strength of the Japanese economy is its very ability to produce the "structural compatibility" of internal and external flexibility on the basis of the Hierarchical Market-Firm Nexus.

V. Socio-economic Reproduction of the Hierarchical Market-Firm Nexus

To summarise the above discussions, we analyse here the reproduction mechanism of the Hierarchical Market-Firm Nexus in the Japanese socio-economic context, because we think that the complementarity between different institutions should be discussed not only within the economic system but also in the reproduction process of the socio-economic system as a whole. The reproduction of the Hierarchical Market-Firm Nexus is illustrated from the viewpoint of "circular and cumulative causation" in Figure 8.

This is a kind of "productivity regime", because we take demand formation as given. As we explained before, the Hierarchical Market-Firm Nexus consists of a ranking hierarchy within a firm organisation, the segmented labour market, and hierarchical inter-firm relations. In the hierarchical nexus, job-loss costs are institutionalised in a very Japanese manner and play a role as an incentive mechanism together with the promotion scheme within a firm and poor social welfare services. This makes workers compete with one another and work very hard. On the basis of the hierarchical nexus having "structural compatibility", internal and external flexibility complement each other, and this enables the Japanese economic system to cope well with economic fluctuations and changes in the terms of international trade. Namely, wages and employment are co-ordinated in different ways between large firms and small firms as well as between regular and non-regular workers. The internal flexibility concerning regular workers, that is, the promotion of innovation, skill formation, and the reallocation of employees coupled with job security, is complemented by the external flexibility of wages and employment of non-regular workers and subcontractors. This leads to high, but differential productivity growth between the different sizes of firms, on the one hand, and it also leads to wage differentials and wage moderation, on the other. Next, productivity differentials and wage differentials produce firm-size profitability differentials and reinforce differential and hierarchical structures among firms.

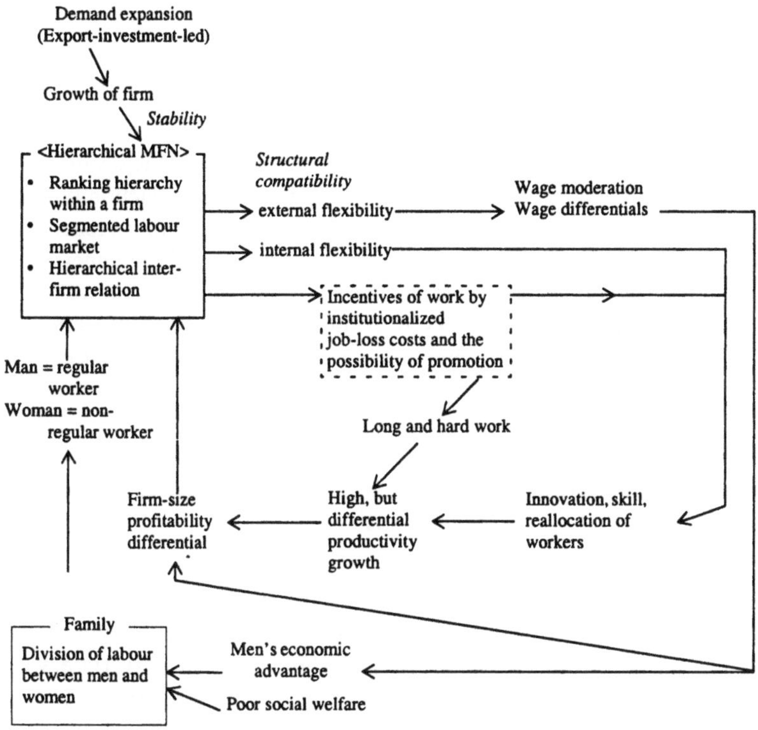

Figure 8: The Schema of Social Reproduction of the Hierarchical Market-firm Nexus

Looking at the Japanese family, we have to recognise that a kind of "patriarchy" still exists there. This is, however, not only a cultural phenomenon but also a socio-economic one which is determined by the economic and social reproduction of the Japanese society. In other words, it is the specific division of labour between men and women which reproduces, and is reproduced by, the Hierarchical Market-Firm Nexus (the same kind of argument is seen in Ohsawa 1993). Namely, wage differentials between regular and non-regular workers lead to earnings differentials between male and female workers. Thus, male workers have an economic advantage, because a woman will be in charge of child care, household affairs and taking care of elderly people in most cases in the Japanese socio-economic system. As social welfare services are relatively poor in Japan, the family must be the basis of the social reproduction of labour power. Therefore, in this context, it is "rational" from the economic point of view that a man becomes a regular worker working many hours, while a woman retires very early and becomes a non-regular worker after taking charge of the social reproduction. In these circumstances, companies do not provide a sufficient scheme of skill formation for female workers. This must indeed be a "vicious circle" for women, which is, in a sense, the other side of the coin of the "virtuous cycle" of the efficient economic system which realises the flexibility of employment.

In short, we want to emphasise here two points as follows. First, structural compatibility which the Hierarchical Market-Firm Nexus produces can be maintained in the very dynamic social process. Second, the reproduction process of the Hierarchical Market-Firm Nexus involves not only economic agents such as workers belonging to a firm organisation but also their family members. In this sense, the framework we have presented here is quite helpful, when we consider the influences of such social changes as the increasing number of working women, the ageing society, and the interaction between the conditions of economic growth and the environmental factors of social reproduction.

C. Japanese Economy in the 1990s and Structural Shifts in the Hierarchical Market-Firm Nexus

The purpose of this section is to discuss changes in the Hierarchical Market-Firm Nexus in the present serious recession (the so-called "Heisei Recession") which started with the collapse of the Bubble Boom in 1991. Here, we will provide some materials and data for the investigation of the question, "Is the Hierarchical Market-Firm Nexus reaching its limit, or newly evolving, in the 1990s?", and we will also draw our own tentative conclusion. We have already discussed the macro-economic structures and the dynamics of capital accumulation which are coordinated on the basis of the Hierarchical Market-Firm Nexus (Uemura, Isogai and Ebizuka 1996, and Ebizuka, Isogai and Uemura 1996), so we will begin by summarising our analysis of the problem, how a demand regime has been established as a stable pattern of demand formation on the basis of the Hierarchical Market-Firm Nexus, and then, we will proceed to analyse the possibility of its structural shifts in the Heisei Recession.

I. The Hierarchical Market-Firm Nexus and the Demand Regime

We will introduce a framework for considering the demand regime established on the basis of the Hierarchical Market-Firm Nexus in Figure 9. In this Figure, two problems should be paid attention to. The one is the transformation of the growth pattern into export-investment-led growth on the basis of the Hierarchical Market-Firm Nexus, and the other is how the domestic demand structures have evolved, as the Hierarchical Market-Firm Nexus has been fully developed.

First of all, we will mainly focus on the discussion about the transformation of the demand regime into export-investment-led growth. We can see the transformation of the growth regime in Table 4 and Table 5. Namely, the causality from export to GDP, which had not been significant in the period of high economic growth in the 1960s, became significant in the 1970s. The effect of export on GDP was strengthened in the 1970s, while that of investment on GDP was weakened. Moreover, needless to say, the Dollar appreciation (= the Yen depreciation), which was caused by Reaganomics, was very advantageous to the export-investment-led growth of the Japanese economy in the first half of the 1980s. This depreciation of the Yen did not really reflect the productivity growth differential between the export-goods sector of Japan and that of the U.S. This must have been a great divergence from the so-called "equilibrium exchange rate" which is defined as the exchange rate corresponding to the Purchasing Power Parity (PPP) of the export goods sector. The Japanese export goods industries took a harsh export offensive to other countries by taking advantage of the depreciation of the Yen, and the Japanese economy realised the very dynamic export-led growth. Furthermore, it was the full establishment of the Hierarchical Market-Firm Nexus that sustained the expansion of export by establishing the "structural compatibility" in such a way that it integrated workers into firm organisations, co-ordinated wages flexibly corresponding to changes in the terms of trade, and promoted vigorous investment.

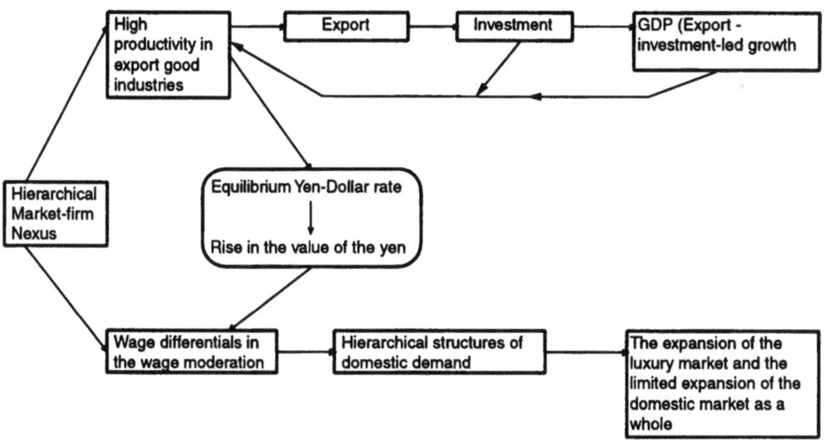

Figure 9: Demand Regime in the Hierarchical Market-Firm Nexus

However, the appreciation of the Yen was accelerated very rapidly after the Plaza Agreement, so Japanese economic growth could not easily depend on the demand of other countries, and it had to depend much more on domestic demand.

Table 4

Granger Causality Test Concerning Each Component of Aggregate Demand and GDP

			F-statistics	
			1957–73	1974–92
Private investment	→	GDP	2.28**	1.83*
GDP	→	Private investment	0.88	3.11**
Private final consumption	→	GDP	1.39	0.99
GDP	→	Private final consumption	1.44	1.49
Private investment	→	Private final consumption	2.40**	1.58
Private final consumption	→	Private investment	1.51	1.11
Export	→	GDP	1.52	4.01**
GDP	→	Export	0.89	1.90*

Note: * (**) denotes significance at 10 % (5 %) level.
Source: Economic Survey of Japan (Economic White Paper), 1993, p. 96

Table 5

VAR Analysis on GDP, Private Investment and GDP

	S. E.	Private Investment	Export	GDP
Private Investment	0.014	87.3	12.4	0.4
	0.007	38.6	40.0	21.3
Export	0.039	63.1	34.4	2.5
	0.015	16.0	57.2	26.8
GDP	0.037	56.5	3.3	40.2
	0.026	8.3	8.7	83.1

Note: The upper numbers of each cell denote 1956–73, and the lower numbers denote 1974–92
Source: The Economic White Paper, 1993, p. 97

In fact, the contribution rate of foreign demand to economic growth became negative, on the one hand, that of domestic demand became more than 5 % on the other. This was made possible by a super-easy money policy pursued by the Bank of Japan intending to overcome the "Yendaka Recession". This super monetary relaxation caused assets inflation and the expansion of consumption by "assets effect", and it promoted investment by lowering the costs of finance. Japanese companies focused on the domestic market in their strategies, and made an effort to shift their target to the domestic demand. The "Bubble Boom" promoted this change very much. At that time, the rapid increase in land and stock prices was widening "assets differentials" between households. Consequently, the Japanese economy experienced the phenomenon of high-grade consumption which was mainly supported by consumers who came to have an increasing amount of assets. Companies coped with these changes by making their commodities more luxury and multi-functioning and extending their sales networks. Then, they also promoted vigorous investment.

Therefore, it might be quite reasonable to think that economic growth was sustained well by the phenomenon of high-grade consumption and the rapid increase in investment in the second half of the 1980s. However, we realised that this growth pattern could not be sustained in the long run, after we experienced the collapse of the "Bubble Boom" and the present long-lasting recession. The excess capital which was accumulated in the 1980s needs to be adjusted in this recession. What we have to emphasise here is the fact that the rapid increase in investment started not typically in the "Bubble Boom" but in the first half of the 1980s (Figure 10). In other words, the "excess capacity", which would not have been sustained with the "proper" exchange rate, was formed in the export-investment-led growth in the special circumstances of the over-appreciation of the Yen in the first half of the 1980s (Ariizumi 1995). Then, this excess capacity increased much more in the period of the "Bubble Boom". Therefore, the adjustment of capital stock in this recession can be characterised as that of capital stock piled up in the Bubble Boom as well as the "prolonged" adjustment of excess capital which was accumulated under the conditions of the over-depreciation of the Yen before 1985. In fact, the rate of profit of private corporations started to fall considerably even in the period of the "Bubble Boom" in the late 1980s as shown in Figure 11. The rate of profit is expressed in the following equation.

$$r = \frac{\Pi}{K} = \frac{\Pi}{Y} \cdot \frac{Y}{K}$$

where r is the rate of profit, Π is profit, K is real capital stock, Y is real output (real national incomes).

In the second half of the 1980s, the wage share $(1 - \Pi)/Y$ was quite stable, so that the decrease in the rate of profit mainly reflected the decrease in output/capital ratio (Y/K) which was caused by the over-accumulation of capital.

The adjustment of the "excess capacity" is being accomplished in several ways. First, it is being accomplished in the form of increasing foreign direct investment

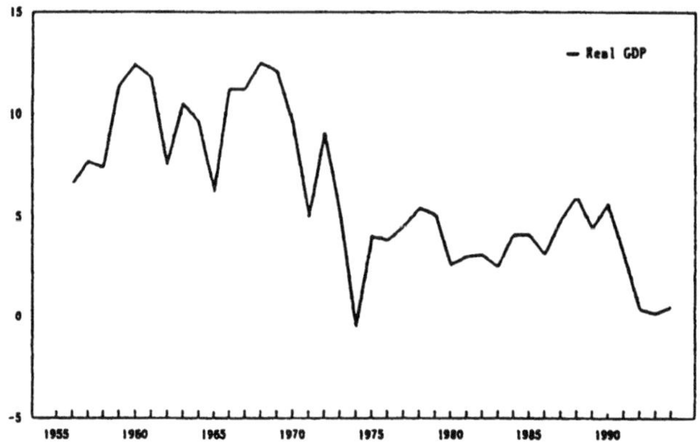

Source: Economic Planning Agency, Annual Report on National Accounts

Figure 10a: Real GDP (Annual Growth Rate), 1956–1994

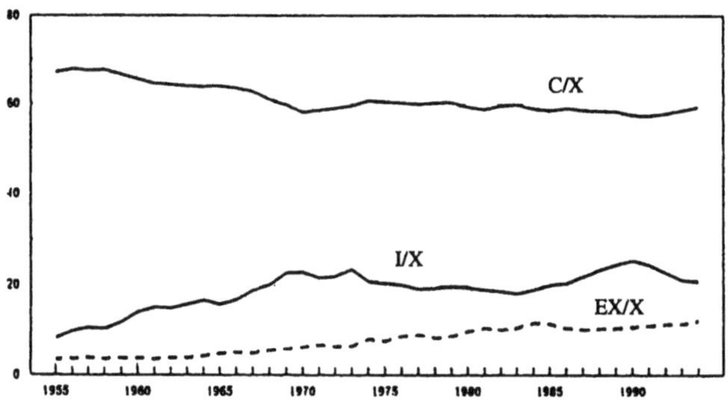

Source: Economic Planning Agency, Annual Report on National Accounts

Figure 10b: The Percentage Distribution of C, I and EX (at constant prices)
X: GDP, C: Consumption, I: Investment, EX: Export

in Asian countries. Second, it is also done by scrapping capital stocks at the cost of employment. In fact, a sharp fall in employment is observed in the manufacturing sector in this recession. This is caused by a reduction in the employment not only of non-regular but also of regular workers in the sector.

Now, we will investigate in detail the Japanese economy with both macro and micro-economic data in order to understand what kinds of changes are occurring in this "Heisei Recession".

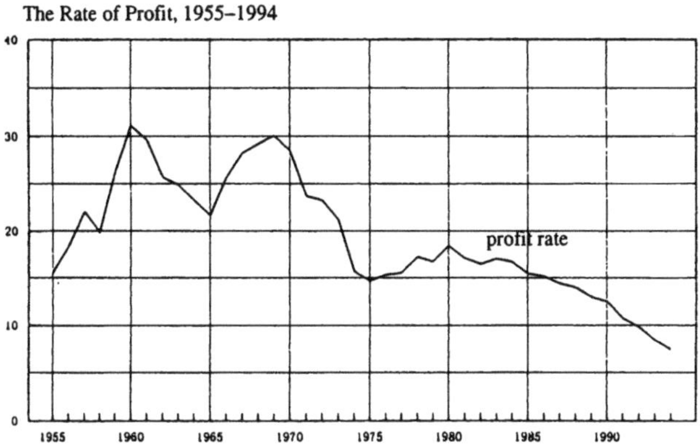

Source: Economic Planning Agency, Annual Report on National Accounts, and Gross Capital Stock of Private Enterprises

Note: Profit Rate = (corporate incomes + interest + dividents) / corporates' capital stock

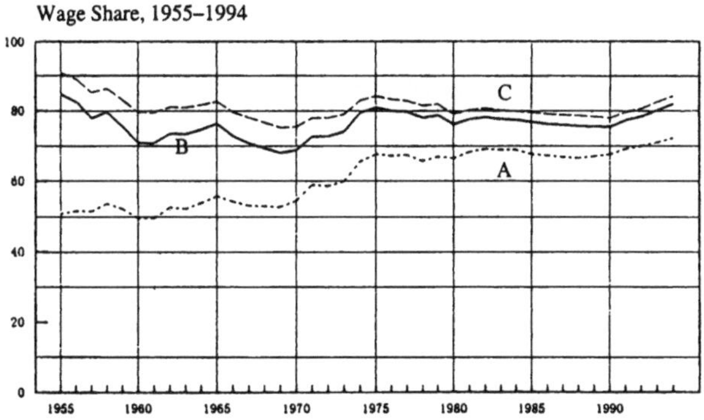

Source: Economic Planning Agency, Annual Report on National Accounts, and Gross Capital Stock of Private Enterprises

Note: A = (wages + self-employees' incomes) / national incomes,
B = wages / (national incomes – self employees' incomes), C = wages / national incomes

Figure 11: The Rate of Profit and Wage Share

II. The "Heisei Recession" Compared with Previous Ones

First of all, we will see the characteristics of the macro-economic pattern in this recession by checking macro-economic indicators. Figure 12 shows a comparison of the process of recession after the peak of the cycle (it is depicted as Time 0) of the "Heisei Recession" with that of the recession after the first oil shock. We can see several important characteristics.

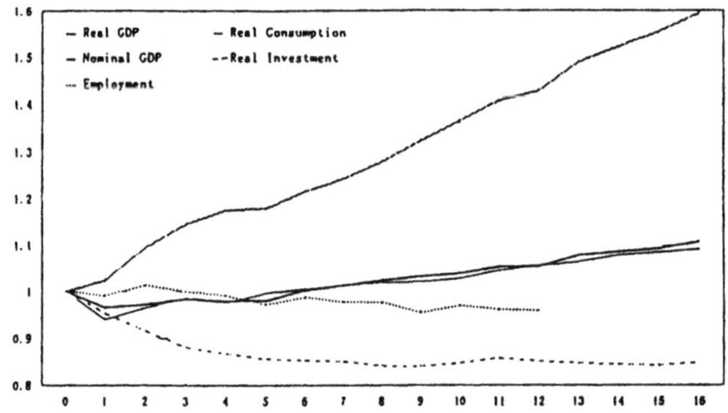

Note: The peak is the 4th quarter of 1973.

Figure 12a: Relative Changes in Real GDP, Nominal GDP and Employment after the Oil Shock

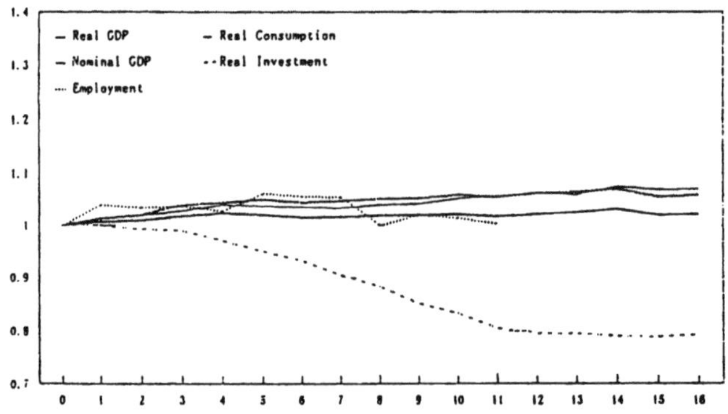

Note: The peak is the 1st quarter of 1991.

Figure 12b: Relative Changes in Real GDP, Nominal GDP and Employment in the Heisei Recession

GDP: There is a big difference in the movement of Nominal GDP between the recession after the first oil shock and the "Heisei Recession". There was a sharp fall in Real GDP at first, but the recovery was accelerated one year and a half after the recession induced by the oil shock. In the present recession there is, in contrast, stagnation, although the decline is relatively modest. We experienced high inflation in the recession after the oil shock, so the recession was a typical stagflation. The "Heisei Recession", on the contrary, is a deflationary one.

Consumption: We can also observe a long-lasting stagnation in consumption in this recession. Real consumption dropped sharply just after the oil shock, but it started to recover one year and a half after it. In this recession, on the contrary, it is not likely to recover well even two years after the collapse of the "Bubble Boom", and it threatens to become worse.

Investment: The decrease in investment in this recession is much greater than that in the recession after the oil shock, and it takes the economy more time to reach the bottom. This is caused by the drastic adjustment of excess capacity which was piled up in the period of the "Bubble Boom". Generally speaking, there is a pressure to adjust excess capital stock to a much lower level in a recession as a phase of the business cycle, so it may usually cause a downward spiral because of the decrease in investment as a component of aggregate demand. How should we understand the long duration of stagnant investment in this recession? Is it a usual adjustment process of capital stock, or are there more profound structural factors behind the cyclical adjustments in the recession as well as the sequel of the financial disturbances in the collapse of the "Bubble"? According to our understanding, structural factors are strongly influencing adjustment processes in this recession, as is shown in the data of different sizes of firm, especially that of small and medium-size firms.

Employment: In the recession after the first oil shock, employment decreased slightly, because large firms especially promoted a belt-tightening management to cope with the recession. In this recession, on the contrary, a decrease in employment is not seen, and it is maintained, at least, at the macro-economic level.

Summarising these characteristics, we can say the following in general: although the decrease in indicators (except investment) is rather mild, the economy experiences long-lasting stagnation and lacks the power to recover in this recession. Furthermore, judging form the business outlook DI in Enterprise *Short-term Economic Forecasting Investigation* of the Bank of Japan (May, 1995), the decrease in DI is not less than that in the recession after the first oil shock. Especially, non-manufacturing activities are not "recession-proof" in this recession, and they are much more stagnant than in the recession after the first oil shock. Therefore, as far as the diffusion of recession is concerned, this recession is much larger than any other recession we have experienced.

Now, we will compare this recession with previous ones by investigating the data of the different sizes of firm. We can see the comparison of recovery process in output and investment in Figure 13 and Figure 14. As for output, both large firms and small and medium-size ones experience a longer-lasting stagnation in

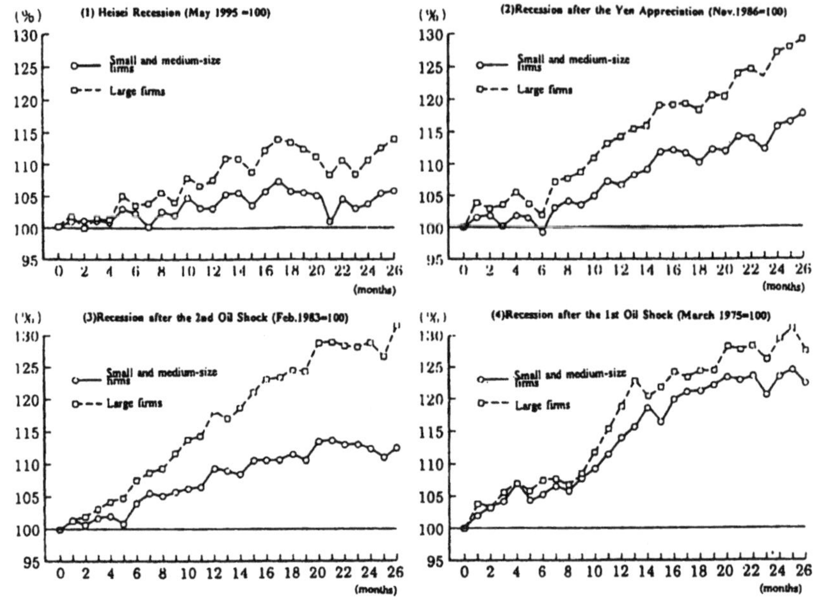

Figure 13: The Comparison of Recoveries of Production from the Bottom

this recession than in previous ones. Especially, small and medium-size firms experience the severest stagnation in output. Investment in small and medium-size firms has been very stagnant, and a delay of recovery in investment can be observed in small and medium-size firms. In other words, we cannot see the leading recovery in small and medium size firms which we have seen in previous recessions (Figure 15). This is because the process is influenced not only by such a "cyclical" factor as the adjustment of capital stock but also by deeply seated "structural" factors. What especially suggests the existence of "structural" factors is the fact that we cannot see the leading recovery in small and medium-size firms in the transport machinery sector, which was typically seen before. Especially, in the car industry which has large-scale hierarchical subcontractor systems, the extension of overseas businesses of parent companies, the production by in-house plants, and the use of common standards of parts put a lot of pressure on the activities of small and medium-size firms, and this prevents investment from recovering. As we will explain in detail later, this is caused by the "increasing fluidity" of subcontractor structures. Another factor is profitability differentials between large firms and small and medium-size ones. As the ordinary profit/total capital ratio in Figure 16 shows, it has been lower in small and medium-size firms than large ones, and the differential has been widening since 1994. When we see the turnover rate of total capital and the ordinary profit/sales ratio which are the components of the ordinary profit/total capital ratio, the profitability differential is

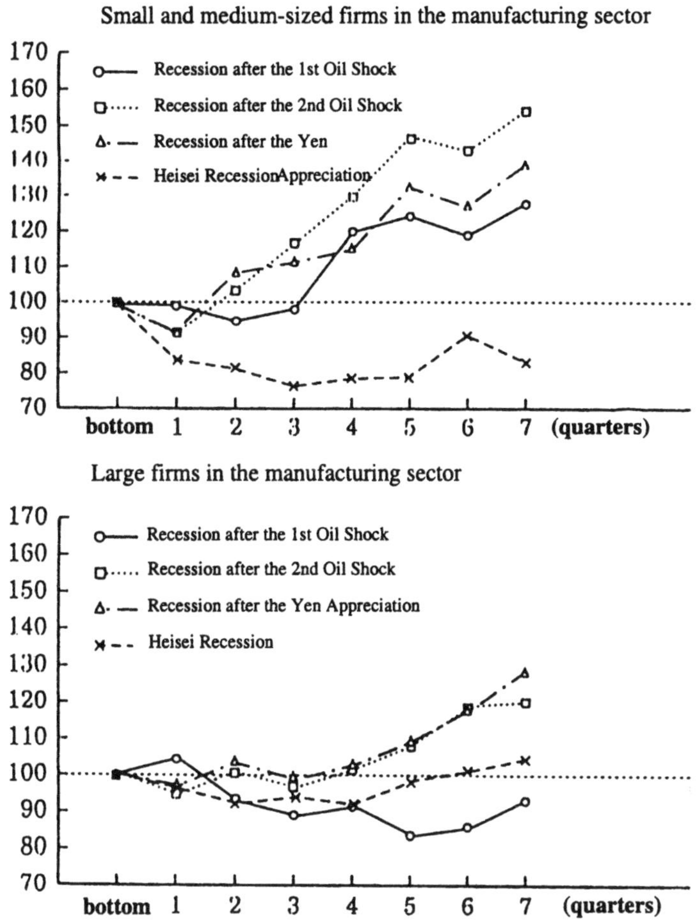

Source: White Paper of Small and Medium-size Firm, 1996, Fig. 1-2-11

Figure 14: The Movement of Investment in Recoveries

mainly due to the decrease in the ordinary profit/sales ratio in small and medium-size firms. This may be related to such recent changes in the subcontractor system as the decrease not only in the number of orders but also in the unit prices offered by parent companies.

Next, we will check the trends of employment in the different sizes of firm. As shown in Figure 17, the decrease in employment is very sharp in large firms with over 500 employees, while employment is maintained in small and medium-size firms. Therefore, small and medium-size firms still play a role as the "sponge" of

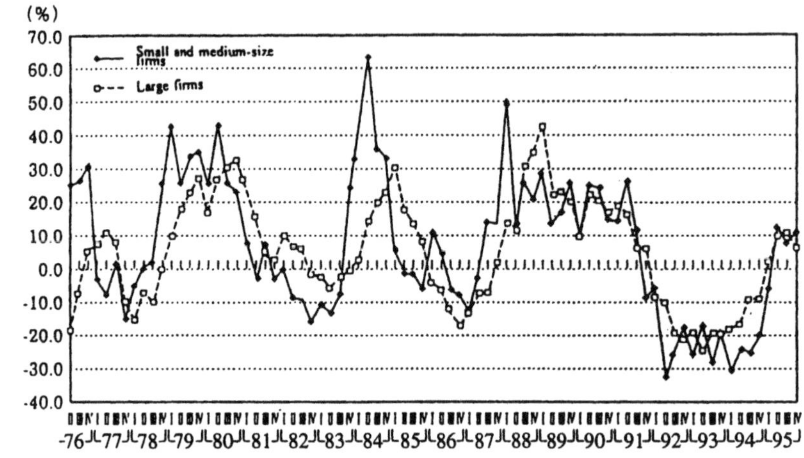

Source: White Paper of Small and Medium-size Firm, 1996, Fig. 1-2-21

Figure 15: Changes in Investment in the Manufacturing Sector
(Annual Growth Rate)

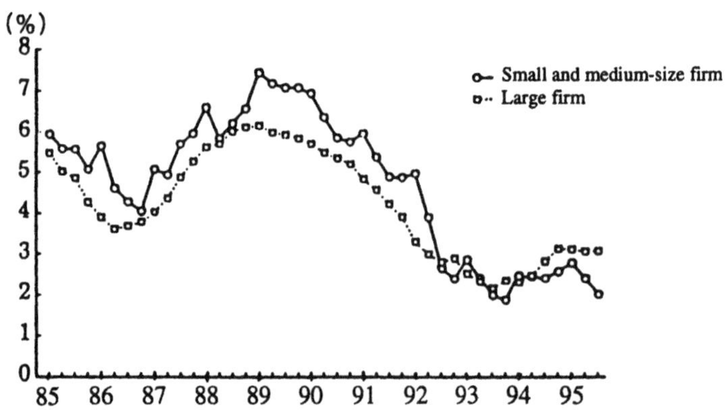

Source: White Paper of Small and Medium-size Firm, 1996, Fig. 1-2-19

Figure 16: Ordinary Profit/Total Capital Ratio in the Manufacturing Sector

employment, even in this recession. If we investigate the different trends of employment between the manufacturing and non-manufacturing sectors, we can see a quite interesting structural shift in employment in this recession. Namely, workers who have been dismissed in the manufacturing sector are partly absorbed in the service sector (Figure 18). Therefore, we can conclude that the employment is maintained at the macro-economic level in this recession, because small and medium-size firms in the manufacturing sector as well as the service

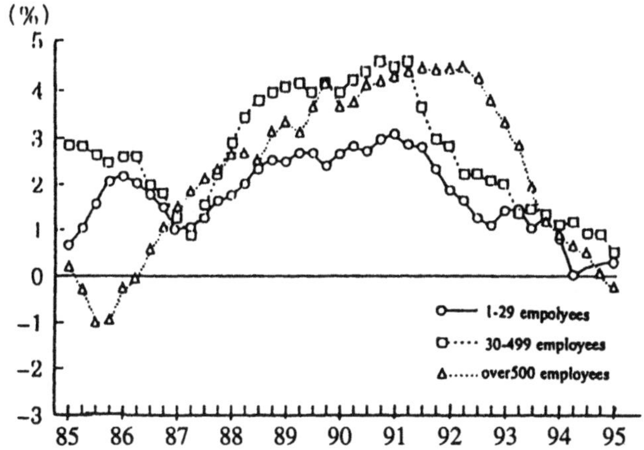

Source: White Paper of Small and Medium-size Firm, 1996, Fig. 1-3-1

Figure 17: Changes in Employment in the Different Sizes of Firms

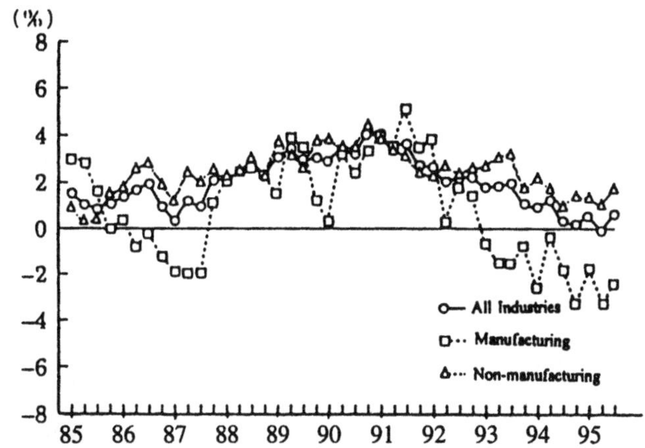

Source: White Paper of Small and Medium-size Firm, 1996, Fig. 1-3-1

Figure 18: Changes in Employment in Different Sectors
(Annual Growth Rate)

sector in general absorb employment in spite of the decrease in employment in large firms in the manufacturing sector. We can see this in the typical framework of the structural shift in output, productivity and employment in Figure 19.

The relationship between the variables which are depicted in Figure 19 is formalised in the following equations.

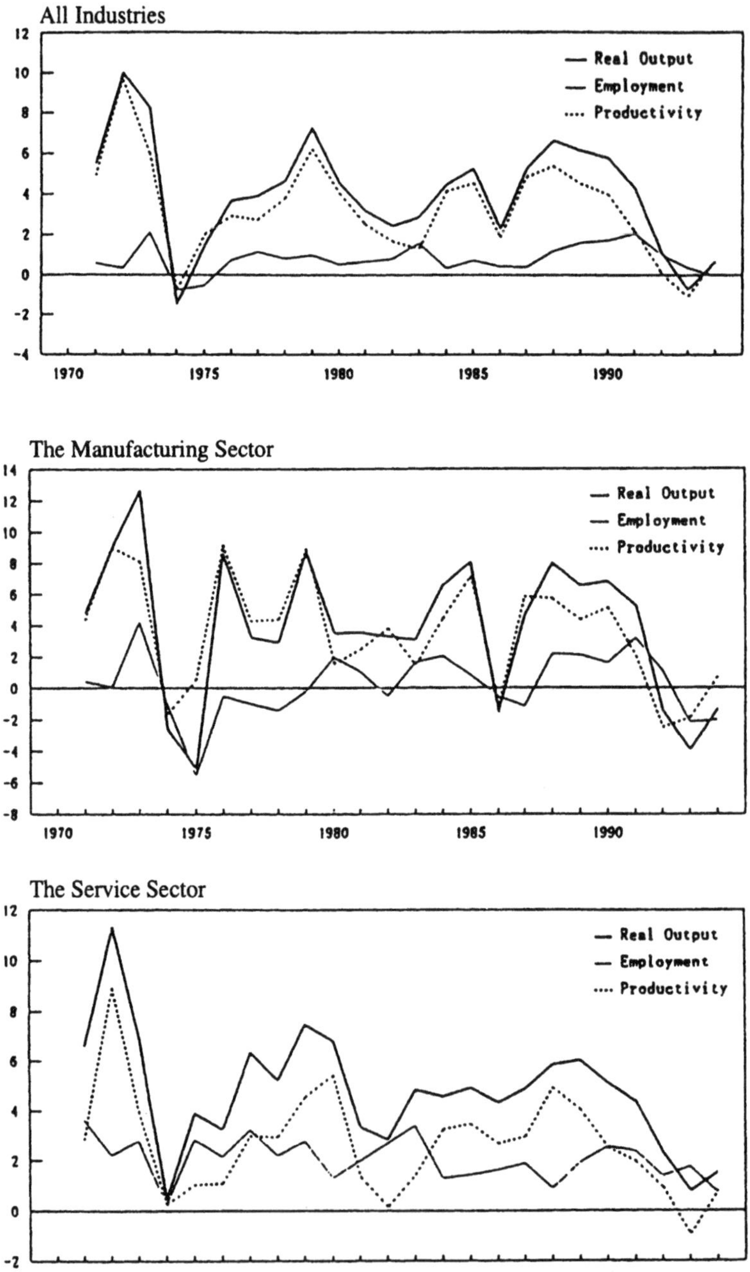

Figure 19: The Structural Shift in Output, Productivity and Employment

$$\hat{N}m = \hat{X}m - \hat{\lambda}m, \quad \hat{N}s = \hat{X}s - \hat{\lambda}s$$

where $\hat{N}$ is the growth rate of employment, $\hat{X}$ is the growth rate of real output, and $\hat{\lambda}$ is the growth rate of labour productivity. Suffixes *m* and *s* denote the manufacturing sector and the service sector respectively. This structural shift can be said to be a kind of "negative de-industrialisation" (Rowthorn and Wells 1987, Petit 1988), because it is brought about by the stagnant manufacturing output in the recession.

III. The Hierarchical Market-Firm Nexus in the "Heisei Recession"

In the following, we will investigate how long-lasting recession influences the structures and co-ordinating mechanisms of the Hierarchical Market-firm Nexus in the 1990s. Here, we will focus especially on two problems. First, we will investigate whether the incentive mechanism is changing, both within firm organisation and in the Hierarchical Market-Firm Nexus, under the pressure of this recession. Second, we will also investigate whether this recession will bring about changes in the "structural compatibility" of the Hierarchical Market-Firm Nexus.

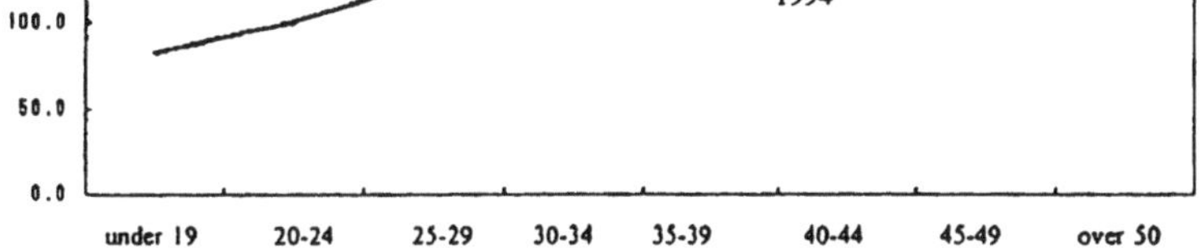

Source: The Economic White Paper, 1996, p. 346

Figure 20: Shapes of Wage Profile (Age 20–24 = 100)

(1) Incentive Mechanism: Checking changes in the wage profile, we compare the wage profile in 1984 with that in 1994 in Figure 20. We recognise that the curve has become slightly flat recently, but that there is no change in the fact that service years in a company are appreciated very highly in calculating the amount of retirement pay (especially for male/university-graduate workers). Service

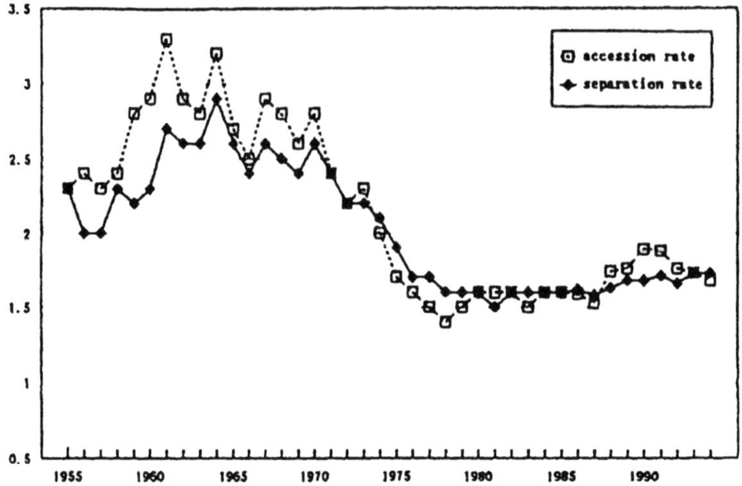

Source: Ministry of Labour, Monthly Labour Statistics

Figure 21a: Accession Rate and Separation Rate, 1955–1994

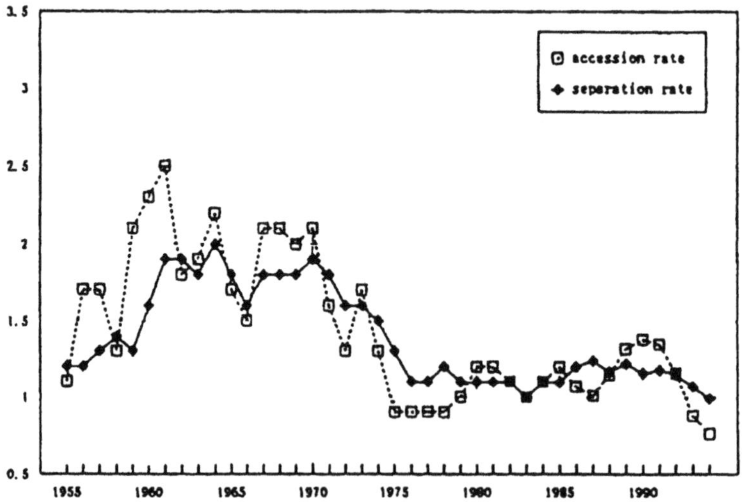

Source: Ministry of Labour, Monthly Labour Statistics

Figure 21b: Accession Rate and Separation Rate, 1955–1994
Over 500 Employees, Manufacturing

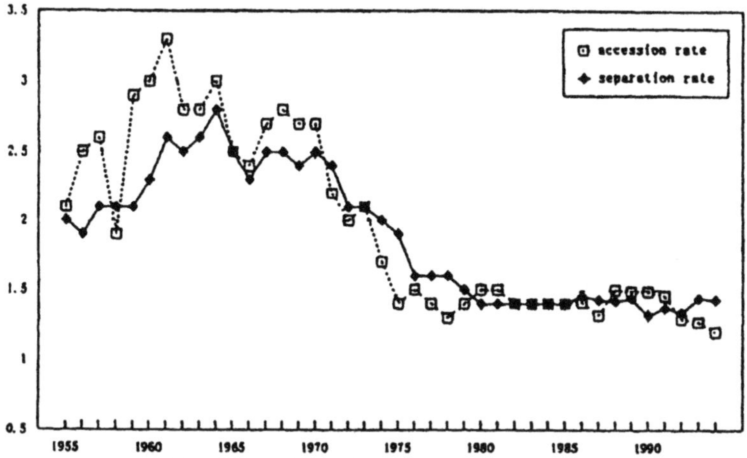

Source: Ministry of Labour, Monthly Labour Statistics

Figure 21c: Accession Rate and Separation Rate, 1955–1994
100–499 Employees, Manufacturing

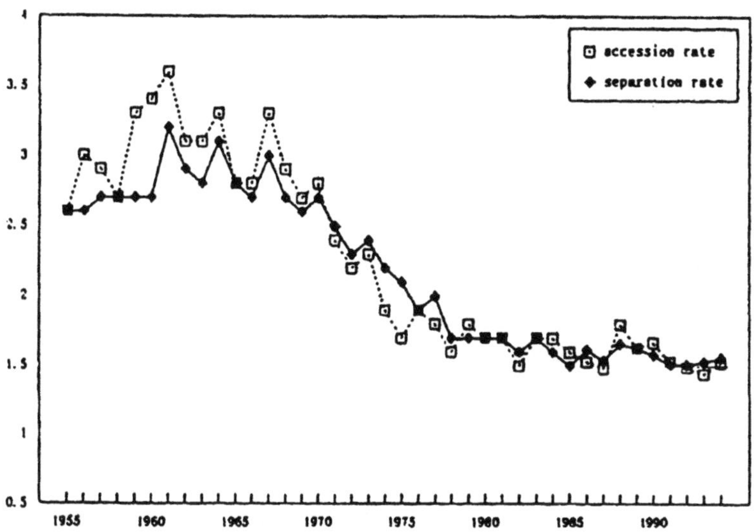

Source: Ministry of Labour, Monthly Labour Statistics

Figure 21d: Accession Rate and Separation Rate, 1955–1994
30–99 Employees, Manufacturing

years have been even more highly appreciated recently. The ratio of retirement pay after a separation for private reasons to that after a separation for company reasons is 51.4 % for workers with 5 years of service, and the ratio increases to 97.1 % with 35 years of service (White Paper of Labour 1996). In short, there is no change regarding the fact that incentives are structurally embedded in the employment system and they prevent mid-career job change. Looking at labour mobility, we can see that the ratio of workers who move from one company to another in the form of separation or transfer has been rather declining, so that mid-career separation has not increased. On the contrary, job-rotation is still pursued very actively within a firm organisation. As a result, we cannot see any remarkable change in the separation rate in the different sizes of firm (Figure 21). Therefore, we can conclude that the incentive mechanism based on "institutionalised job loss-costs" is still maintained and it prevents core workers from quitting their company in the Hierarchical Market-Firm Nexus, even if the long-lasting recession may influence the Japanese people's way of thinking in a wider socio-economic context in the long run.

(2) Structural Compatibility: The following complicated situation can be observed concerning "structural compatibility". As we mentioned above, there is no great change in the shape of wage profile, the appreciation of service years in the assessment of wages and retirement pay and the movement of the separation rate. In other words, the incentive mechanism is maintained, supported by the complementarity of intra-firm-organisational factors and inter-firm-organisational ones. What we must especially pay attention to is the fact that there is a decrease in the accession rate in large firms in the manufacturing sector. This restraint of accession is partly due to the effect of the rapid increase in employment at the period of the "Bubble Boom" and the insufficient adjustment of employment. As a result, companies keep a lot of "labour hoardings" in the manufacturing sector. Therefore, we can conclude that companies are making an effort to maintain employment and so-called "life-time employment", especially concerning core workers, has not collapsed in this recession. The employment structure in the Hierarchical Market-Firm Nexus which is shown in Figure 5 is not likely to be changed drastically (see Table 1). Of course, the percentage of non-regular workers has increased in these seven years. Therefore, the flexibility of employment, which is a "structural effect" produced by the Hierarchical Market-Firm Nexus, has not changed greatly. However, without proper institutional arrangements, the increasing number of non-regular workers may cause instability in the labour market. This may bring about very serious problem especially for the employment of female and elderly workers, so the tendency toward an ageing society and the increasing instability in the labour market may be factors undermining the structural compatibility of the Japanese socio-economic system.

Next, we will investigate inter-firm relations which are the indispensable basis of "structural compatibility". The subcontractor system is experiencing a "structural" change, influenced by this long-lasting recession and the appreciation of the Yen. This is called the "increasing fluidity" of subcontractor structures in The White Paper of Small and Medium-size Firm (1996). The number of subcontractors and the percentage of parent companies' transactions with subcontractors do not show remarkable change as a whole, while subcontractors' transactions with parent companies and the amount of acceptance of order has decreased. This decrease in the amount of acceptance is caused by the selection of subcontractors by parent companies which reduces the number of parts and use their common standard, while the decrease in the subcontractors' transactions with parent companies shows that there is "de-subcontracting" which is initiated by subcontractors. This kind of selection of subcontractors has been pursued before, but it is unusual that parent companies have strong requirements for their subcontractors, facing the increase in imported goods competing with subcontractors in the rapid appreciation of the Yen. Parent companies require subconductors to realise not only high quality and low costs but also to adapt to small-lot production, the shortening of the time for delivery and to new products and technology. Naturally, there are, on the one hand, subcontractors which cannot keep up with the high level of those requirements, and, on the other hand, there are subcontractors which can keep strong ties with their parent companies, responding to their requirements, on the other. In this way, we can see the "increasing fluidity" of the subcontractor system as well as the "polarisation" of subcontractors in this recession. We depict this structural change in the subcontractor system in Figure 22.

Summarising the above discussions, we can conclude the following. Until now, we cannot observe any drastic structural change in the incentive mechanism and the "structural compatibility" of the Hierarchical Market-Firm Nexus. The only remarkable change is the "increasing fluidity" and "polarisation" in the subcontractor system. These changes are brought about by the restructuring of a parent company, the increase in its foreign direct investment, and such long-term environmental changes as the ageing of both managers and employees in subcontractors. In these circumstances, the most important thing is the influence of the extension of overseas businesses on both large firms and small and medium-size ones. What we want to emphasise here is the fact that there is "irreversibility" in the extension of overseas businesses, because Japanese firms will not be able to return their plants to the home country, even when faced with the reverse movement of the exchange rate. This "irreversibility" might destroy the co-ordinating mechanisms promoting the flexibility and dynamism of the economy which the subcontractor system has been realising in its hierarchical structures to cope with industrial transformation. It is decidely premature to draw a conclusion regarding the question, how the "irreversibility" of the shift in capital accumulation combined with the fluctuation in the exchange rate might change the structural com-

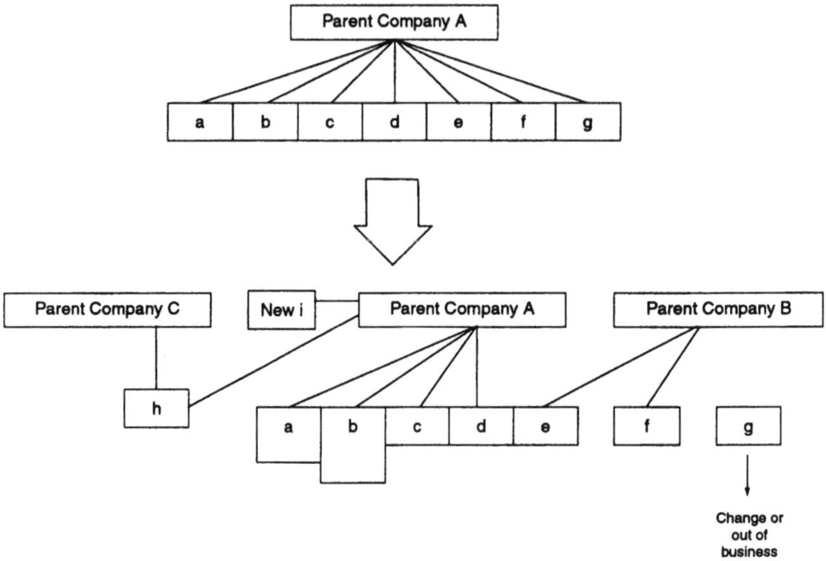

Note: While there is an increase in orders from the parent company at a and b firms, there is a decrease in orders from the parent company at c, d and e firms
Source: White Paper of Small and Medium-size Firm (1996), p. 108

Figure 22: Transformation of Subcontractor Systems in the 1990s

patibility of the Hierarchical Market-Firm Nexus in this path-dependent process, but this must remain a quite important research topic for further researches.

D. Concluding Remarks

Finally, we will refer to two important problems concerning structural changes in the Hierarchical Market-Firm Nexus which we have to consider in further researches.

First, our hypothesis of "institutionalised job-loss costs" should be refined to explain its historical evolution, so time-series quantitative data to reflect it should be organised well on the basis of various kinds of statistics. It must be an indispensable task to analyse how such structural changes as the globalization of production and the ageing society will influence the incentive mechanism based on "institutionalised job-loss costs". We have concluded that there are no drastic changes in the incentive mechanism based on "institutionalised job-loss costs" and articulated structures to ensure flexibility at the macro-economic level, but there is one important problem which has not been solved here. There still remains the question, "Why doesn't productivity recover, although the incentive mechanism based on 'the institutionalised job-loss costs' is maintained generally?" In other words, this is the problem, whether the "structural compatibility" established in the Hierarchical Market-Firm Nexus may lose its productivity-enhancing mechanism, when faced with structural shifts in the Japanese economy.

Second, we should investigate more carefully whether there are changes in the "structural compatibility" in the Hierarchical Market-Firm Nexus. The important question here is what kind of influence the rapid increase in foreign direct investment to Asian countries has on the Hierarchical Market-Firm Nexus. This shift in capital accumulation is going to cause on "increasing fluidity" of the subcontractor system in inter-firm relations, but we have not seen any major changes in the structures of the Hierarchical Market-Firm Nexus except minor ones. This is because there exists institutional complementarity between firm organisation, the labour market and inter-firm relations, and there is also the compatibility of different incentive mechanisms which directs the behaviours of workers in line with the existing social order. Therefore, we cannot help admitting that the institutional complementarity has shown great strength in maintaining itself against environmental changes. However, we have not analysed capital-labour relations and incentive mechanisms in small and medium-size firms thoroughly, so we cannot give a clear answer to the question, how the changes in subcontractor networks due to the extension of overseas business will have an effect on the incentive mechanism in small and medium-size firms, at the same time, influencing the compatibility of incentive mechanisms in the Hierarchical Market-Firm Nexus in a much wider socio-economic context.

If there is no change in the "structural compatibility" of the Hierarchical Market-Firm Nexus, the growth pattern of the Japanese economy may remain the export- investment-led one. In this growth pattern, however, there exists a serious possibility of "vicious circle" (see Uemura 1996). Namely, the mutually enforcing mechanism between the export-led demand formation and productivity growth in the export goods sector may bring about great productivity-growth differentials and unproportional rise in prices between the export goods sector and the non-export goods one, and this may cause the more appreciation of the exchange rate, putting much pressure on manufacturing firms to make a desperate effort to promote productivity growth. In fact, this has been reflected by the problem of so-called "inside-outside price differentials". The general increase in prices in the non-export goods sector in this kind of uneven development is a mechanism to equalise domestic incomes, so we should not necessarily get rid of it only from the viewpoint of international competitiveness. However, this will surely make the conflict of interest more antagonistic between the export goods sector and the non-export goods one, and it might have a negative influence on the incentive mechanisms in the Hierarchical Market-Firm Nexus and social consensus on welfare in the Japanese socio-economic system. If this happens, it can be regarded as "the limit after its very maturity" of the Hierarchical Market-Firm Nexus. However, it is much more premature to make a decisive conclusion, and this is also another important topic for further researches.

References

Aglietta, M. (1976): Régulation et crise du capitalisme, Calmann-Lévy, Paris.

Aglietta, M., and A. *Brender* (1984): Les métamorphoses de la société salariale, Calmann-Lévy, Paris.

Aoki, M. (1988): Information, Incentives, and Bargaining in the Japanese Economy, Cambridge University Press.

— (1992): The Japanese Firm as a System, The Economic Study Quarterly, Vol. 43, No. 5.

— (1996): Towards a Comparative Institutional Analysis: Motivations and Some Tentative Theorizing, The Japanese Economic Review, Vol. 47, No. 1.

Aoki, M., and R. *Dore* (eds.) (1994): The Japanese Firm: The Sources of Competitive Strength, Oxford University Press.

Ariizumi, T. (1995): The Japanese Economy after the 'Heisei Recession', Ibaraki University, Jinbungakubu-kiyo, No. 28, (in Japanese).

Asamuma, B. (1989): Manufacturer-Supplier Relationships in Japan and the Concept of Relationship-Specific Skill, Journal of the Japanese and International Economics, Vol. 3.

Asamuma, B., and T. *Kikutani* (1989): Risk Absorption in Japanese Subcontracting: A Micro Econometric Study of the Automobile Industry, Journal of the Japanese and International Economics, Vol. 6. No. 1.

Atokinson, J. (1987): Flexibility or Fragmentation? The United Kingdom Labour Market in the Eighties, Labour and Society, Vol. 12, No. 1.

Bowles, S. (1985): The Production Process in a Competitive Economy: Walrasian, Neo-Hobbesian, and Marxian Models, American Economic Review, Vol. 75, No. 1.

Bowles, S., and R. *Boyer* (1990): A Wage-Led Employment Regime: Income Distribution, Labour Discipline and Aggregate Demand in Welfare Capitalism, in: Marglin, S., and Schor, J. (eds.), The Golden Age of Capitalism, Oxford University Press.

Boyer, R. (1981): Les transformations du rapport salarial dans la crise: une interprétation de ses aspects sociaux et économiques, Critiques de l'économie politique, no. 15/16, avril–juin.

— (1986): La flexibilité du travail en Europe: Une étude comparative des transformations du rapport salarial dans sept pays de 1973 a 1985, La Deconverte, Paris.

— (1988): Formalizing Growth Regime, in: Dosi, G., et al. (eds.), Technical Change and Economic Theory, Pinter Publishers.

— (1990a): The Capital Labour Relations in OECD Countries: From the Golden Age to the Uncertain Nineties, CEPREMAP, No. 9020.

— (1990b): The Economics of Job Protection and Emerging Capital Labour Relations: From the Perspective of 'Regulation Theory', CEPREMAP, No. 9015.

— (1992a): Rapport salarial et régime d'accumulation au Japon, Mondes en Developpement, Tome 20.

— (1992b): Labour Institutions and Economic Growth: A Survey and a 'Regulationist' Approach, CEPREMAP, No. 9218.

— (1995): Is the Japanese Wage-Labour Nexus Decaying or Evolving? Part One: Theoretical and Historical Background, Paper presented to the International Seminar Regulation Approach to Japanese Typed Capitalism at Hitotsubashi University.

Boyer, R., and B. *Coriat* (1986): Technical Flexibility and Macro Stabilization, Ricerche Economiche, Vol. 40, No. 4.

Boyer, R., and M. *Juillard* (1991): New Endogenous Growth Theory versus a Productivity Regime Approach: One Century of American Economic History Revisited, CEPREMAP, No. 9210.

Calmfors, L., and J. *Driffil* (1988): Bargaining Structure, Corporatism and Macroeconomic Performance, Economic Policy, No. 6.

Coriat, B. (1991): Penser à L'envers: travail et organisation dans l'Entreprise japonaise, Christain Bourgois Editeur.

Ebizuka, A., and A. *Isogai* (1991): Analytical Perspectives on the Current Economic Crisis: SSA versus Regulation Approach, Keizaigaku-zasshi, Vol. 91, No. 5/6, Vol. 92, No. 1 (in Japanese).

Ebizuka, A., *Isogai*, A., and H. *Uemura* (1995): Reconsidering 'Hierarchical Market-Firm Nexus': A Preliminary Discussion, Paper presented to the International Seminar Regulation Approach to Japanese Typed Capitalism at Hitotsubashi University.

— (1996): A Regulation Approach to the Postwar Japanese Economy: The Theory of 'Hierarchical Market-Firm Nexus', Keizaigaku-zasshi, Vol. 96, No. 5/6, Vol. 97, No. 2/3 (in Japanese).

Hanada, M. (1996): Capital-Labour Compromise and Wage Determination: The Regulation of Capital and Labour in Japan, in: Boyer, R., and Yamada, T. (eds.), Rapport Salarial, Fujiwara-shoten (in Japanese).

Higuchi, Y. (1991): The Japanese Economy and Employment-Seeking Behaviors, Toyokeizaishinposha (in Japanese).

Hirano, Y. (1993): Growth and the Wage-labour Nexus in the Post-war Japanese Economy, in: Boyer, R., and Yamada, T. (eds.), Capitalism in Crisis, Fujiwara-shoten (in Japanese).

— (1996): Japanese Institutions and Economic Growth, Fujiwara-shoten (in Japanese).

Hollingsworth, J. R., and R. *Boyer* (1997): Contemporary Capitalism: The Embeddedness of Institutions, Cambridge University Press.

Ishida, M. (1990): Social Science of the Wage, Chuo-keizaisha (in Japanese).

Ishikawa, T. (1981): Dual Labour Market Hypothesis and Long-Run Income Distribution, Journal of Development Economics, Vol. 9, No. 1.

— (1991): Income and Wealth, Iwanamishoten (in Japanese).

— (1993): Labour Market Structures in Japan, in: Itami, H., et al. (eds.), The Firm System in Japan, Yuhikaku (in Japanese).

Ishikawa, T., and T. *Deshima* (1994): Dual Structure in the Japanese Labour Market, in: Ishikawa, T. (ed.), The Distribution of Income and Wealth in Japan, Tokyo University Press (in Japanese).

Isogai, A. (1993): An 'Institutional' Analysis of the Japanese Type of Economic System, Keizaigaku-kenkyu, Vol. 59, Nos. 3–4 (in Japanese).

— (1995): The Japanese Type of Corporate System and the Regulation Theory: In Search for an Analytical Framework of Regulation of 'Company-ism', Keizaigaku-kenkyu, Vol. 60, No. 5–6 (in Japanese).

— (1996): Towards an Institutional Analysis of the Socio-economic System: A New Approach to 'the Economics of Institutions', Annals of the Society for the History of Economic Thought, No. 34 (in Japanese).

Isogai, A., and H. *Uemura* (1996): 'The Economics of Institutions' and the Dynamics of Money–Labour, Keizaigaku-kenkyu, Vol. 63, No. 2 (in Japanese).

Itami, H. (1994): The Japanese Automobile Industries: Why were they braked suddenly?, NTT Publisher (in Japanese).

Itami, H., et al. (eds.) (1993): The Firm System in Japan, Yuhikaku (in Japanese).

Ito, H. (1991): Japanese Human Resource Management from the Viewpoint of Incentive Theory, Richerche Economiche, Vol. 45.

Koike, K. (1988): Understanding Industrial Relations in Modern Japan, Macmillan.

— (1991): The Economics of Work, Toyokeizai-shinposha (in Japanese).

Kumazawa, M. (1992): Two Kinds of Flexibility: An Approach to the Japanese Way of Management, Mado, No. 12 (in Japanese).

— (1993): An Image of Workers in Japan (New Edition), Chikuma-shobo (in Japanese).

Minami, R. (1970): The 'Turning Point' in the Japanese Economy, Sobunsha (in Japanese).

Miyamoto, M. (1991): A Theory of Enterprise and Organization, Shinseisha (in Japanese).

Miyazaki, Y. (1985): Structures and Behaviors in the Japanese Economy, Chikuma-shobo (in Japanese).

Muramatsu, K. (1995): The Employment Adjustment in Japan, in: Inoki, T., and Higuchi, Y. (eds.), The Japanese Employment System and the Labour Market, Nihonkeizai-shinbunsha (in Japanese).

Nakamura, K. (1991): Subcontracting System and Strata of Labour Market (1)(2), Musashi Gakuen Ronshu, Vol. 38, Nos. 5–6, Vol. 39, No. 1 (in Japanese).

Odaka, T. (1984): The Analysis of the Labour Market: The Evolution of Dual Structures in Japan, Iwanami-shoten (in Japanese).

Okina, K., *Takeuchi*, E., and H. *Yoshikawa* (1989): On the Determination of Real Wage in Japan, Keizaigaku-Ronshu, Vol. 55, No. 2 (in Japanese).

Ono, A. (1973): Wage Determination in the Post-war Japan, Toyokeizai-shinposha (in Japanese).

— (1983): The Japanese Way of Employment Practice and the Labour Market, Toyokeizai-shinposha (in Japanese).

Osawa, M. (1993): Beyond Company-centered Society, Jijitsushin-sha (in Japanese).

Otaki, M. (1994): Theory of Business Cycles: A Structural Analysis of the Contemporary Japanese Economy, Tokyo University Press (in Japanese).

Ozawa, M. (1985): The Era of New 'Hierarchical Consumption', Nihonkeizai-shinbunsha (in Japanese).

Petit, P.(1988): La croissance tertiaire, Economica, Paris.

Ramaswamy, R., and R. E. *Rowthorn* (1991): Efficiency Wages and Wage Dispersion, Economica, Vol. 58.

Rebick, M. E. (1993): The Persistence of Firm-Size Earnings Differentials and Labour Market Segmentation in Japan, Journal of the Japanese and International Economics, Vol. 7, No. 2.

Rowthorn, R. E. (1992): Centralisation, Employment and Wage Dispersion, The Economic Journal, No. 102.

Rowthorn, R. E., and J. *Wells* (1987): De-industrialization and Foreign Trade, Cambridge University Press.

Saguchi, K. (1990): Internal Labour Market in Japan, in: Yoshikawa, H., and Okazaki, T. (eds.), Historical Perspectives on Economic Theory, Tokyo University Press (in Japanese).

— (1992): The Transformation of Employment Problems, in: Kurita, K. (ed.), Industrial Relations in Contemporary Japan, Rodokagaku-kenkyujo (in Japanese).

Sako, M. (1992): Prices, Quality and Trust: Inter-firm Relations in Britain and Japan, Cambridge University Press.

Suzuki, Y. (1994): Japanese way of Production System and Corporate Society, Hokkaido University Press (in Japanese).

Tachibanaki, T. (1975): Wage Determination in Japanese Manufacturing Industries-Structural Change and Wage Differentials, International Economic Review, Vol. 16, No. 3.

— (1982): Further Results on Japanese Wage Differentials: Nenko Wages, Hierarchical Position, Bonuses, and Working Hours, International Economic Review, Vol. 16, No. 3.

— (1989): The Determination of the Promotion Process in Organization and of Earnings Differentials, Journal of Economic Behavior and Organization, Vol. 8.

— (ed.): (1994): Labour Market and Economic Performance: Europe, Japan and the USA, St. Martin's Press.

Takasuga, Y. (1965): A Prelude to the Theory of the Contemporary Price System, Iwanami-shoten (in Japanese).

Tsuda, M. (1987): Has the Era of New Dual Structure been Emerging? Nihon-Roudokyokai-zasshi, No. 331 (in Japanese).

Tsuru, T. (1991): Unit Labour Costs, the Reserve Army Effect, and the Collective Bargaining System: A US-Japan Comparison, in: Mizoguchi, T. (ed.), Making Economies More Efficient and More Equitable: Factors Determining Income Distribution, Kinokuniya Company and Oxford University Press.

— (1992): Wage Spillover under the Spring Offensive System, Mondes en Developpement, Tome 20.

— (1995): Contemporary Japanese Unions and the Separation of Union Members, in: Inoki, T., and Higuchi, Y. (eds.), The Japanese Employment System and the Labour Market, Nihonkeizai-shinbunsha (in Japanese).

Uemura, H. (1992): Growth and Distribution in the Post-war Regime of Accumulation: A Theory and Realities in the Japanese Economy, Mondes en Developpement, Tome 20.

— (1996): De-industrialization and Structural Changes in Capital Accumulation, in: M. Ito, M. Noguchi and N. Yokokawa (eds.), Marx's Counterattack: The Rehabilitation of Political Economy, Nihonhyoronsha (in Japanese).

Uemura, H., and A. *Ebizuka* (1994): Incentives & flexibility in the hierarchical market-firm nexus: a prelude to the analysis of productivity regimes in Japan, Japon in Extenso, no. 31, mars–avril.

Uemura, H., *Isogai*, A., and A. *Ebizuka* (1996): A Regulation Approach to the Post-war Japanese Economy: the Hypothesis of the Hierarchical Market-Firm Nexus, International Economic Conflict Discussion Paper (Nagoya University), No. 91.

Uni, H. (1992a): Labor Flexibility in Japanese Manufacturing Industry, The Research and Study, No. 2 (in Japanese).

— (1992b): The Regime of Accumulation on Post-war Japan, Keizaigaku-zasshi, Vol. 92, Nos. 5–6 (in Japanese).

— (1994): On Export-led Growth of Japan, The Bulletin of Japan Society of Political Economy, No. 32 (in Japanese).

Yamada, T. (1991): Regulation Approach, Fujiwara-shoten (in Japanese).

— (1994): Twentieth Century Capitalism, Yuhikaku (in Japanese).

Yoshikawa, H. (1992): The Japanese Economy and Macroeconomics, Toyoukeizaishinposha (in Japanese).

— (1990): On Equilibrium Yen-Dollar Rate, American Economic Review, June.

Williamson, O. E. (1975): Markets and Hierarchies: Analysis and Antitrust Implications, The Free Press.

The Roles of the Public Sector Toward the 21st Century

Tadashi Yagi

A. Introduction

In order to predict the long-run development of the Japanese economy, it is necessary to examine the development of in the fundamental structure of the Japanese society, such as demographic structure, social security system, income distribution and public infrastructure. The purpose of this paper is to consider the factors which change the social structure, and discuss how public policy should be adjusted to the development of fundamental factors toward the 21th century.

B. Public Policies for the Aging Society

I. The Optimal Long-term Care System

Faced with the prospect of a growing elderly population and rising health care expenses, Japan recently introduced a public insurance policy to provide monetary and service benefits to qualified individuals above 65 and in some cases above 40. The cost of such a policy is to be borne by the central, prefecture, and local governments and paid by individual and corporate contributions. Japan has also been trying to expand its program of building up in-house and residential facilities for the elderly (McCarthy 1997).

Japan is not the only country to introduce a public long-term care insurance policy. Under Medicare and Medicaid, the US federal and state governments also provide long-term care benefits such as nursing home care to qualified individuals, especially to those of low income. Denmark focuses its policy on economies of scale by constructing nursing communities that reduce the cost of long-term care per individual recipient. And Canada has a similar program run by the ten provincial governments (Greb et al. 1994, McCarthy 1997). France, Germany, Luxembourg and every OECD country either has separate long-term care programs or is in the process of introducing them.

But is government intervention in this area necessary? If so, which form should it take? Should it focus on the demand side, lowering the financial burden of long-term care to households, or should it be on the supply side, lowering the cost of long-term care? How should it be financed?

The need for government intervention in the provision of long-term care can be rationalized in different ways. On the supply side, long-term care services are subject to economies of scale, i. e., their provision is more efficient when provided collectively in a hospital or in a nursing community. On the demand side, the provision of public long-term insurance is necessary to reduce the burden on the family, especially in countries with rising female labor force participation, or to fill in the gap of the absence of private insurance. Indeed, even in the US, where health insurance markets are well developed, only a very small fraction of the elderly have long-term care insurance (Scanlon 1992). Some economists attribute the failure of individuals to buy long term insurance to the lack of awareness of the public about the potential benefits of long-term care policies (Bacon et al. 1989). Others attribute the lack of demand for long-term care insurance to the strengthening of relations between parents and children and the provision of bequest as a substitute for long-term insurance (Zweifel and Wolfram 1996). A third group attributes the low demand for long-term insurance to the lack of interest on the part of private insurance providers to underwrite long-term care policies due to high risks and the provision of certain government programs for long-term care. Cutler (1993), for instance, argues that private insurers are reluctant to underwrite long-term care policies due to the large intertemporal variability of the cost of long-term care that makes it difficult for underwriters to diversify risk within a cohort. But Pauly (1990) argues that individuals will not purchase long-term care insurance even if it is available at actuarially fair premiums because the main purpose of the coverage is to enhance the expected value of one's estate. Pauly further argues that Medicaid lowers the expected utility of private insurance and therefore reduces the demand for it.

Another important controversy surrounding the public provision of long-term care is financing. Some countries like Finland, New Zealand and Great Britain rely mainly on tax-funding of long-term care. Other countries such as Germany, France, and Japan rely on social insurance contributions levied on employers and employees. Joining the controversy surrounding the provision and financing of long-term care, Yagi, Miyazawa and Moudoukoutas (1997) rationalize the need for public insurance within an overlapping generations model, explore the implications of different forms of financing, and investigate the impact of public insurance on the demand for private insurance.

Specifically, the paper finds that, (i) under the funded insurance program, there is no justification for a public insurance program on efficiency grounds, (ii) the role of the public sector should be confined to the lowering of the cost of the provision of health services rather than into monetary transfers to long-term care recipients, and (iii) the demand for both higher infrastructure spending and private insurance is directly related to the probability of long-term illness.

The model used in Yagi, Miyazawa and Moudoukoutas (1997) is as follows:

The two production sectors are specified as follows:

(1) $$y_1 = rK + wL_1,$$

(2) $$y_2 = L_2G,$$

where y, K, L stand for output, capital and labor, and subscript 1 and 2 stand for the private commodity and the long-term care service producing sectors. G is a public infrastructure for care service production.

The production of a public long-term care sector is assumed to display a number of characteristics: (i) it is more labor-intensive than the private goods sector, (ii) it does not employ any private capital, (iii) it increases labor productivity. Given these assumptions, and setting the price of consumption goods as numeraire and the price of care service as q, the value of the marginal products of labor in the care service sector is given by qG. Assuming perfect labor mobility between sectors, the values of the marginal products of labor in both sectors equate.

The paper considers the two-period overlapping generation model. The budget constraint for the household during the working period is:

(3) $$(1-\tau)w = c_1 + s + a,$$

where w is wage income, τ is income tax rate, c_1 is consumption during the working period, s is savings, and a is long-term insurance payments.

The budget constraint for the retirement period is divided into two cases according to the state of health during the retirement period. The case where the state of health is good is:

(4) $$c_2^G = (1+r)s,$$

where c_2^G is consumption a good state of health, and r is the market interest rate. The case where the state of health is bad and long-term care is necessary is:

(5) $$c_2^B + q = (1+r)s + (1+r^e)a$$

where c_2^B is consumption in a bad state of health, r^e is an actuarially fair rate of return from insurance.

The expected utility function is:

(6) $$EU = v(c_1) + (1-p)u_G(c_2^G) + pu_B(c_2^B),$$

where p is the probability of being ill.

Equilibrium conditions for care service market, labor market, capital market, goods market, and government budget constraint are given by the following equations:

(7) $$y_2 = p$$

(8) $$L_1 + L_2 = 1$$

(9) $$s + a = K$$

(10) $$y_1 = c_1 + (1-p)c_2^G + pc_2^B + G$$

(11) $$\tau w = G$$

The optimal level of public infrastructure for long-term care and the optimal tax rate is given by the following equation:

(12) $$G^* = \sqrt{\frac{pw}{1+r}}$$

and

(13) $$\tau^* = \sqrt{\frac{p}{(1+r)w}}$$

The equilibrium price of care service is.

(14) $$q^* = \sqrt{\frac{(1+r)w}{p}}$$

Disposable income is:

(15) $$I^* = w - \sqrt{\frac{pw}{1+r}}$$

Labor supply is:

(16) $$L_1^* = 1 - \sqrt{\frac{p(1+r)}{w}} \qquad L_2^* = \sqrt{\frac{p(1+r)}{w}}$$

An increase in the probability of individuals being ill,p, will result in two effects. On the one hand, a higher productivity in the long-term care sector will result in a higher G^* and a lower price for long-term care service, q^*. On the other hand, a higher probability of illness will lead to a higher optimal tax rate τ^* and a lower disposable income.

By specifying the utility function in a log-form, the demand for private long-term care insurance is derived as:

(17) $$a^* = \frac{pq^*}{1+r} = \sqrt{\frac{pw}{1+r}}$$

It should be noted that the optimal level of a long-term care service tax is equal to the demand for private insurance which supports the co-existence of both public and private long-term care policies. In this sense, we distinguish the roles of private and public sectors in providing long-term care service.

II. Advancement of Women in the Society

In this section, we discuss the saving behavior, focusing especially on the relation with the aging society. Needless to say, saving is one of the most important factors which determine the growth of the economy. In Japan, the saving rate has a declining trend. According to the Annual Report on National Account, the saving rate was 0.31% in 1970, but it decreased to 0.2 % in 1982, and 0.24 % in 1991. Two of the important structural changes which affect the saving behavior are the aging society and the advancement of women. Here, we discuss how savings are affected by the advancement of women in the society. The key factor which links the aging society and the advancement of women is a "care problem". It is reported that the number of privately managed homes for the aged has been increasing rapidly in Japan. According to "The Survey on the Privately Managed Home for the Aged" compiled by the Ministry of Welfare, one of the most important motivations for entering a home is an anxiety in a case of sickness and long-term bedriddeness. The care system within the family is eroding because of the advancement of women. For a career woman, the opportunity cost of taking taking care of parents is high, because she might have to give up a promotion or even quit her job in many cases.

Recalling that entering the home is a kind of purchasing of an annuity, the rapid increase in privately managed homes for the aged accompanies the conversion of wealth from the bequeathable type to the unbequeathable type, i. e., the annuity. When the bequest is made not from altruistic motives but from gift-exchange motives, the impact of the advancement of women on bequeathing behavior would be not small.

The above argument raises the question of how the saving behavior is affected by the advancement of women. Yagi and Maki (1994) have dealt with this issue in a dynamic setting.

In a society, like Japan, where the working place of women is expanding and the earnings income of women is increasing, the opportunity cost of taking care of parents increases. When the value of bequeathable wealth is smaller than the value of an annuity, the individual sells his or her bequeathable wealth such as real estate and buys an annuity. This implies that bequests decrease as the advancement of women progresses. The decrease in bequests affects the capital accumulation of the economy and affects in the long run seriously economic growth.

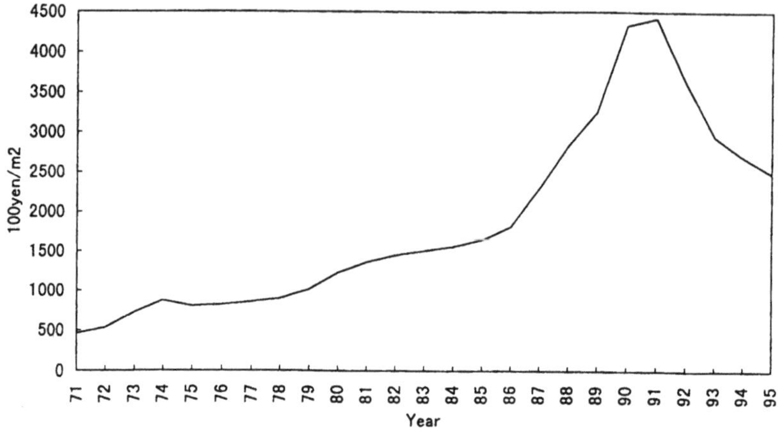

Source: The Japan Real Estate Institute, "Land Price Index in City Area"

Figure 1: Time Trend of Land Price in Tokyo Area

C. The Land Problem in Japan and the Tax System

Japan experienced a drastic increase in land prices in the late 1980s. From 1986, land prices soared rapidly, and attained their peak in 1991 (See Figure 1). After that, land prices decreased considerably and the price level in 1995 was about the same as that of 1987. The surge of land prices from 1986 to 1991 is called the *bubble*, and this period is called the *years of the bubble economy*. Since the consumer price index increased only 7.5 % during 1985–1990, we can understand how land prices increased rapidly in the years of the bubble economy. It is worth noting that the timing of the decrease in land prices corresponds to the timing of the introduction of public policy measures such as a limit on land-related lendings from banks and a land-holding tax.

During the period of the bubble economy, the general sense of inequality increased, especially due to the increased disparity in possession of financial assets and land. The land owners enjoyed an inflated value of their assets, while the renters suffered because of the hike in rental prices. Tachibanaki and Yagi (1994) estimate the contribution of various income sources, including imputed rent, to inequality in total income by decomposition analysis. They also investigate the effect of the Japanese tax system, namely, the separated tax system on income redistribution. The results obtained in their decomposition analysis indicate the relatively weak effect of the separated tax system on the redistribution of income from imputed rent.

Yagi and Tachibanaki (1997) consider a tax reform from the current separated tax system to the comprehensive tax system in order to amend this differential treatment of income sources. Under the current separated tax system, each income source is taxed at a different rate. The purpose of this tax reform is to equalize the taxation for various income sources. It would therefore bring about an increase in tax on imputed rent.

I. The Japanese Tax System for Land Holding

This subsection summarizes a number of aspects of the Japanese land related tax system that are necessary to our discussion (see Ito (1994) for more detailed explanations). First, we explain the different prices for the same piece of land:

1. market price;
2. monitoring price by the Land Agency (koji kakaku);
3. assessment for bequest tax purposes by the National Tax Agency (rosen ka);
4. assessment for the property tax, administered by the municipal government;
5. monitoring for representative places by the prefectural government.

In Japan, the property tax (prefectural tax) rate is 1.4 % (50 % of the property tax is deductible for residential use). However, assessment of real estate varies with prefectures. Homma and Atoda (1990) show that in 1988 the gap between koji kakaku and rosen ka ranges from 33.5 % to 94.1 % with an average of 56.5 % of koji kakaku. Wealthy prefectures tend to assess less. Around 50 % assessment of land value implies that the property tax is subsidized, and encourages hoarding when prices are expected to rise.

The property tax and city planning tax (0.3 %) are levied on landholding, but no tax is levied on imputed income from landholding (a special landholding tax may be assessed by a municipality at the rate of 1.4 %). Four types of taxes for land acquisition exist.

1. The property, including land and structures, is assessed at real estate tax assessment and taxed by a prefecture. The tax rate is 4 %.
2. A special land acquisition tax is imposed by a municipality. The land assessment is the actual purchase price and the tax rate is 3 %.
3. Registration tax is collected at the rate of 0.5 % by the national government.

4. Inheritance tax is imposed on acquisition by bequest. There are three types of capital gains tax, but the application of this tax is very limited.

II. Inequality between Income with and without Imputed Rent

In Tachibanaki and Yagi (1995), the Gini coefficient is calculated for both the income including imputed rent and the income excluding it. The data used by Tachibanaki and Yagi is the Nikkei Needs Raider survey. Total income consists of earned income and income through financial assets. For simplicity, total income is called "pre-rent income", while total income which includes income through imputed rent is called "post-rent income".

The results shown in Table 1 suggest a large difference between the Gini coefficient measured for "pre-rent income" and that for "post-rent income". It indicates that the Gini coefficient increases from 0.32 for "pre-rent income" to 0.371 for "post-rent income". This is a large increase in the inequality of income distribution. The greatest inequality in income distribution is observed for the oldest age class (60 years old and older), and its Gini coefficient for "after-rent income" reaches 0.437.

In Table 2, income inequality in Japan is decomposed by income sources, such as earned income, capital income and imputed rent income (see Fei, Ranis and Kuo (1978) for the decomposition analysis). As is shown in the table, the amount of capital income is around one seventh of imputed rent income. This is one reason why we mainly pay attention to the imputed rent income in the following analysis.

III. The Effect of Taxation on Income Redistribution

Under the current tax system in Japan, imputed rent is not integrated formally as part of the tax base, but is taxed separately as a form of wealth income. Thus, much research on the effect of taxation on income redistribution has been based on income that does not include imputed rent (see, for example, Itaba and Tachibanaki 1987).

Table 3 presents a measurement of the effect of taxes on income redistribution. The effect is measured by comparing the Gini coefficient for pre-tax income (A) with that for post-tax income (B). The coefficient of income redistribution is defined by:

$$\textit{The coefficient of income redistribution} = (A - B) / A \times 100.$$

The estimated coefficient of earned income for all samples is 10.53. For the 40–59 year old age-group, it is 12.01. This will eventually undergo the greatest redistribution.

We examine income which includes both income from imputed rent and income from financial holding (i. e., capital income). The estimated Gini coefficient for pre-tax income for all samples is 0.371, which is significantly higher than 0.304 for pre-tax earned incomes. This implies that when both incomes through imputed rent and capital incomes are added to earned incomes, the degree of income inequality in pre-tax incomes is significantly increased.

The estimated Gini coefficient for post-tax income, including financial wealth income and imputed rent, is 0.353 under the present tax system. This inequality is fairly high, and the coefficient of income redistribution is only 4.85, which is quite small.

These results suggest the following conclusions. When all income sources (including both income through imputed rent and capital income, i. e., property income) are taken into consideration, income distribution is significantly unequal for pre-tax income. Furthermore, although the present tax system works as an instrument for a fairly strong redistribution of earned income, its role is very minor for all income sources, including the above two sources.

IV. Tax Reform to the Comprehensive Income Tax System

The results obtained by Tachibanaki and Yagi (1995) revealed that taxes on financial wealth income and imputed rent play a relatively small role in redistributing income when compared with taxes on earned income. To amend the deficiency of the current tax system in redistributing income, Yagi and Tachibanaki (1997) propose a tax reform from the separate tax system to the comprehensive tax system so that all the income sources would be taxed in an equal manner. Under the proposed comprehensive income tax system, all income sources would be combined and taxed at a single tax rate.

Table 3 summarizes the Gini coefficient for total post-tax income, and compares the tax systems' redistribution effects through the coefficient of income redistribution. In this section, we define total income as the sum of earned income, financial wealth income and imputed rent. The Gini coefficient for the total post-tax income of the whole sample decreases from 0.353 for the separated tax system to 0.344 for the comprehensive income tax system. The coefficient of income redistribution improves from 4.85 to 7.28. The improvement of the coefficient of income redistribution through the tax reform is remarkable for the middle and old age groups. The coefficient of income redistribution improves from 5.46 to 8.62 for the middle age group, and improves from 3.43 to 7.55 for the old age group. The drastic improvement in income redistribution for the middle and old age groups arises from the differential inequality of financial wealth and land holding. The remarkable improvements for the middle and old age groups basically stem from the relatively large inequality of financial wealth and land holding. The simulation results suggest that the comprehensive income tax system redistributes wealth income and imputed rent more effectively than the separated tax system, and decreases the degree of inequality observed in the middle and old aged groups.

Yagi and Tachibanaki (1997) reveal which households are better-off, and which are worse-off. Table 4 describes the incidence of the tax reform by age class, type of tenure and loan size. In the tenure column, renters are represented by 0, and loan holders by 1.

The tax burden decreases the most drastically for young renters, an average of 41 % for this class. These households rent their homes, and their earned income is relatively low. Thus, their living conditions are often difficult and the tax reform should improve their welfare.

The tax burden increases the most drastically for young loan-free home owners, an average of 75 % for this class. This group is not taxed heavily under the separated system since the tax on imputed rent is relatively low. This change in tax burden might be justified because while the heads of these households are often young, they have no loan on their land, which was obtained through inheritance or as a gift. This statement would still be valid even after considering the stiff inheritance tax system in Japan because the value of real estate for inheritance tax is not assessed at the market value (around half) and a large part of the house value for a house of average size is deductible.

Some policy makers might emphasize the changes in the tax burden of the elderly. Taxation of imputed rent is expected to undergo strong opposition from aged land owners with low earned income. While the tax burden for aged renters decreases by 35 % in size, the tax burden for aged land owners increases by 18 %. The importance of this 18 % increase is debatable. Some researchers claim that the aged in Japan are wealthier than any other age group (see Takayama and Arita 1994). In that case, the 18 % tax increase might not be intolerable. On the other hand, the 35 % decrease in the tax burden of the aged renter appeals to our sense of fairness, because they not only have low earned income but also little financial wealth.

Yagi and Tachibanaki (1997) estimate the welfare change caused by the tax reform. The theoretical model of estimating the second round effect is presented by

King (1983). The first round effect is called *cash gain* (CG). Cash gain is defined by

(18) $$CG = y^p - y^0 - (p_H^p - p_H^0)x_H^0,$$

where y^0 is the original income, p_H^0 is the original tax inclusive price of housing services, p_H^p is the post-reform tax inclusive price of housing services, x_H^0 is the original quantity of housing services consumed and y^p is an estimate of the postreform income consistent with a revenue-neutral reform given unchanged behavior. For a revenue-neutral reform, the mean value of cash gain is zero. Since the cash gain is measured by ignoring behavioral responses, the cash gain only provides information about the distributional consequences of the tax reform, and gives no information about efficiency aspects of the reform. In order to incorporate the behavioral responses, we introduce the concept of *equivalent gain* (EG) which is defined by,

(19) $$v(y^0 + EG, p_H^0, p_c) = v(y^p, p_H^p, p_c),$$

where p_c is the tax-inclusive price of the composite commodity. This measures the welfare gain of the tax reform.

Table 5 summarizes the welfare change of the tax reform. Post-reform post-tax income which includes post-tax imputed rent is calculated by multiplying the post-reform income tax rate which is 70 % of the original tax rate with pre-tax income. The weighted average of the equivalent gain for the whole classes is –95,054 yen, and the relative size of the equivalent gain to post-reform income is –2.38 %. This tax reform increases the tax rate on housing service, which induces the welfare loss of the house owner. Our analysis suggests that the welfare loss of house owners exceeds the welfare gain of renters, although the average relative size of welfare loss is not large enough to invalidate the equity improvement caused by the tax reform discussed in the above subsection.

D. Building of Information Infrastructure

In his literature, Aschauer (1990) called the declining of public investment in the U.S. "the third deficit". He argues that not only trade deficits and budget deficits but also insufficient public capital is a cause of decline in the U.S. economy. From his analysis, we can see a close association between changes in productivity and public capital in the U.S., and conclude that the rate of return to private capital is positively affected by changes in the stock of public capital per worker.

In Japan, public capital has been gaining much attention during these years for reasons different from those in the U.S. The shortage of public capital for amenity has been a major point criticized not only by the Japanese but also by the U.S. The excess concentration of industry and population in the Tokyo Metropolitan area has been a serious problem coupled with the land price problem. In addition, the drastic development of computer networking throughout the world requires of us a larger capacity of information infrastructure.

Theoretically, these issues have been analyzed in the context of the optimal allocation of public investment. Nishimura, Yagi and Yano (1995) give some insight into the optimal pattern of public investment over time. The conventional analysis such as Arrow and Kurz (1970) predicts that the optimal pattern of accumulating public capital is monotonic. Some experiences such as the building of the highway network in the U.S. show, however, that accumulating public capital is not monotone but exhibits non-linear features. That is, huge resources were devoted to the building of the interstate highway network in the 1950s, and the building of the highway network was completed in a short period. The intuition for the non-linearity is as follows. When the role of public capital in economic activities is considered, it is optimal to concentrate resources into building public capital in the early period, and enjoy the fruit of the investment in the later period. Some argue that the role of the interstate highway network in the U.S. contributed much to the development of the U.S. economy after World War II. Faced with the development of the computer network society, we need to recall the lessons of the U.S. in building infrastructure in a non-linear way.

The model developed in Nishimura, Yagi and Yano (1995) provides us with the theoretical foundation for the non-linear pattern of building infrastructure. In the following, the model is summarized.

I. Model

In this economy, per capita income y is produced by labor input L. We assume that the labor endowment of the economy is constant and time-independent. We consider a government which accumulates public capital by controlling the income tax rate τ_t for the period t. Thus, $(1-\tau_t)y_t$ is the disposable income used for producing consumption service, and $\tau_t y_t$ is the per capita tax revenue used for the production of public capital. For convenience, we define the per capita income used for consumption as

$$y_{Ct} \equiv (1-\tau_t)y_t \tag{20}$$

and the per capita tax revenue used for the production of public capital as

$$y_{Gt} \equiv \tau_t y_t \tag{21}$$

Since it is assumed that income is produced only by labor, and the labor supply is constant over time, the per capita income y_t is constant over time and equal to y, i. e.,

(22) $$y_{C_r} + y_{G_r} = y$$

In this context, control of the tax rate directly means the control of y_{C_r} and y_{G_r} with the constraint (22).

Consumption C is produced by public capital G and disposable income y_{C_r}. For example, even if one owns a car, one cannot drive without a road. Consumption activity in this example is the movement from one place to another, and the road is public capital. Another example is TV viewing. In this case, watching TV is consumption activity, the satellites are public capital.

Denote by C_t the output of consumption C in period t. In this model, the consumption generating function is specified to the Cobb-Douglas form,

(23) $$c_t = F^C(G_{t-1}, (1-\tau_t)y) = (G_{t-1})^{\alpha_1}((1-\tau_t)y)^{\alpha_2},$$

where $\alpha_1 \geq 0$, $\alpha_2 \geq 0$, and they satisfy

(24) $$\alpha_1 + \alpha_2 = 1$$

The public capital is produced from the existing public capital and tax revenue. Denote by G_t the public capital G in period t. A public capital production function is also specified to be of the Cobb-Douglas form,

(25) $$g_t = F^G(G_{t-1}, \tau_t y) = (G_{t-1})^{\beta_1}(\tau_t y)^{\beta_2}$$

where $\beta_1 \geq 0$, $\beta_2 \geq 0$, and they satisfy

(26) $$\beta_1 + \beta_2 = 1$$

Public capital at the end of period t, G_t, is given by

(27) $$G_t = g_t + (1-\delta)G_{t-1}$$

where δ, $0 < \delta \leq 1$, is an exogeneously determined rate of deterioration in the public capital.

II. Optimal Public Investment Path

We consider the linear utility function $u(c) = c \geq 0$. The government's objective function is a discounted sum of social welfare which is given by the utility of a representative individual. With these preparations, the optimal accumulation of public capital is described by the following maximization problem,

(28)
$$\max \quad \sum_{t=1}^{\infty} \rho^{t-1} c_t$$
$$\text{s. t.} \quad g_0 \le \bar{g} \qquad \text{and constraints (22) through (27)}$$

where ρ (0 < ρ < 1) is a time discount rate. The government maximizes the discounted sum of social welfare by controlling the tax rate in each period subject to the consumption generating function, the production function, the resource constraints and the initial conditions.

In order to analyze the dynamics of the above model, it is convenient to introduce a reduced form of the utility function

(29)
$$v(G_{t-1}, G_t) = max(G_{t-1})^{\alpha_1}((1-\tau_t)y)^{\alpha_2}$$
$$\text{s. t.} \quad G_{t-1} \ge 0, y_{C_t} \quad \text{and} \quad y_{G_t} \ge 0$$
$$G_t = g_t + (1-\delta)G_{t-1}$$

The reduced form utility function provides an attainable utility given by the existing public capital at the beginning of the period. The above formulation indicates that an increasing tax rate implies a decrease in consumption at period t but an increase in public capital. Since consumption depends on the public capital for a fixed period of time, an increase in the tax rate increases future consumption. Thus, the optimal tax rate is determined at the point where the marginal benefit of an increase in the tax rate balances the marginal cost of the increase in the tax rate. In this model, a stream of the public capital stock, G_t represents a public investment policy, and a consumption path is considered to be a growth pattern of the economy.

The domain of the reduced form of the social welfare function is

(30)
$$D = \left\{(g, m) \in R_+^2 \middle| m \le g^{\beta_1}\right\}$$

Given an amount of public capital, G, $v = G(g_{t-1}, G_t)$ captures the consumption possibility frontier. With this expression, the optimal public investment policy described by (28) can be transformed into the following form.

(31)
$$V(G) = max \sum_{t=1}^{\infty} \rho^{t-1} v(G_{t-1}, G_t)$$
$$\text{s. t.} \quad G_0 = G$$

Functions $v(G_{t-1}, G_t)$ and V(G) are often called, respectively, reduced from utility and value functions. These functions allow one to express the infinite-time horizon optimization problem as a period-by-period optimization problem

(32) $$V(G_t) = max_{G_t}[v(G_{t-1}, G_t) + \rho V(G_t)]$$

(Bellman's principle of optimality). Denote by $G_t = \theta(G_{t-1})$ the solution to the optimization problem in (32). In other words, if the public investment policy is optimal, then it satisfies

(33) $$G_t = \theta(G_{t-1})$$

In this sense, θ can be called an optimal public investment function.

Denote by D^0 the interior of the domain of v. The following results are useful for characterizing the global behavior of the optimal public investment function (see Benhabib and Nishimura 1985).

Lemma 1-A: Let $(G_{t-1}, \theta(G_{t-1})) \in D^0$. If $v_{21}(G_{t-1}, \theta(G_{t-1})) > 0$, the optimal public investment function $\theta(G_{t-1})$ is monotone decreasing in a neighborhood of G_{t-1}.

Lemma 1-B: Let $(G_{t-1}, \theta(G_{t-1})) \in D^0$ If $v_{21}(G_{t-1}, \theta(G_{t-1})) > 0$, the optimal public investment function $\theta(G_{t-1})$ is monotone increasing in a neighborhood of G_{t-1}.

The economic interpretation of these two lemmas is as follows. From Bellman's principle of optimality, the optimal condition derived from (32) is

(34) $$-v_2(G_{t-1}, G_t) = V'(G_t).$$

The left-hand side of this optimality condition represents the marginal cost of public investment in period t via the decreases in consumption in period t. The right-hand side of the optimality condition represents the marginal benefits of public investment in period t which will be gained in the future through an increase in public capital. Thus, v_{21} is negative (positive) when the marginal cost of public investment in period t increases (decreases) as the initial public capital in period t (i. e. G_{t-1}) increases, respectively.

Lemma 1-A implies that the graph of the optimal public investment function must be multi-modal if $v_{21} < 0$. If $v_{21} < 0$ globally, then the graph of the optimal public investment function is mountain-shaped with one peak as shown in Figure 2. In this figure, the upward sloping part of the optimal public investment function, G, is the maximum public capital which is attained by increasing the tax rate as much as possible. If the initial level of public capital is sufficiently low, then the government accumulates as much public capital as possible in the early period of planning. Moreover, even after the consumer starts to enjoy the fruits of public capital, it is possible for the government to return to accumulating as much public capital as possible during the planning period.

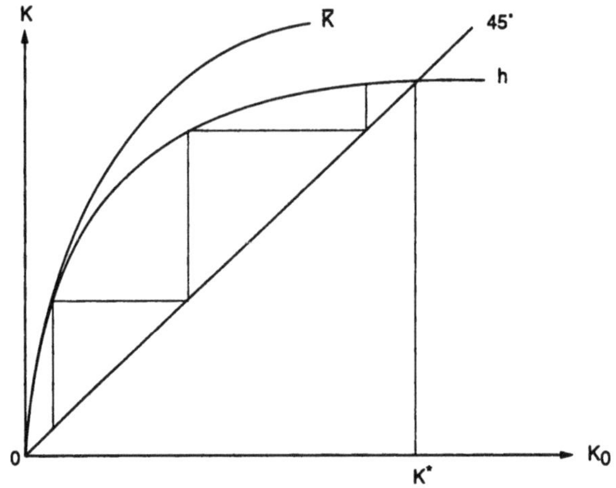

Figure 2: The Optimal Public Investment Pattern

From Lemma 1-B, the public investment function is monotonically increasing if $v_{21} > 0$ globally. If the stationary state is unique and locally stable, and if the initial level of public capital is lower than the stationary level, G^*, then the public capital gradually increases to G^*, as is illustrated in Figure 3. In general, the worker's consumption increases simultaneously throughout this process.

The non-linear dynamics in our model describe various pattern of public investment policy. The optimal public investment pattern described by Figure 2 suggests an alternation between periods of high and low tax rates. Governments which keep the tax rate constant may follow public investment function curves like the one in Figure 3.

III. Public Investment in the Optical Information Highway

Our society is rapidly orienting itself towards computer networking, and the necessity of implementing an infrastructure to support this computer networking is increasing. For example, the building of an optical information highway may make it possible to improve TV viewing, shopping, recreational planning, political discussions, care for the aged, and so on.

A computer network is a form of public capital in the sense that rivalry in consumption is relatively low and the density of networking is crucial to the quality of service. In this respect, it is similar to telephone lines or highways. If the computer network drastically improves the quality and efficiency of consumption activities from one unit of income, if the computer network can be produced only

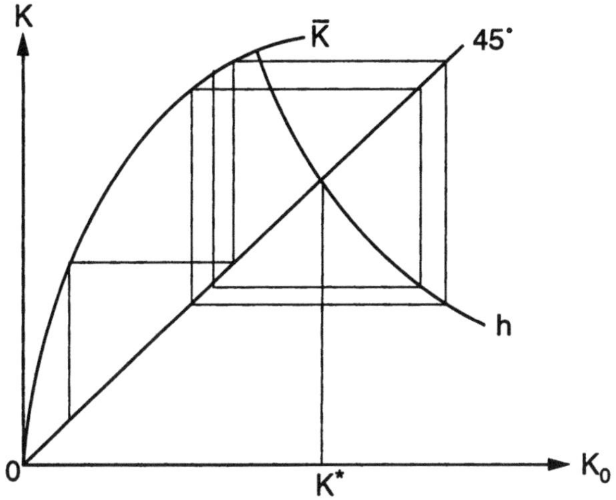

Figure 3: The Public Investment Function Curves

by income and if the depreciation of the network facility is large, then the analysis indicates that it may be optimal to alternate a period of intensive public investment in the network system and a period of enjoying the fruits of the network system. That is, the current intensive public investment in the computer network system is necessary for future activities in a computer society from the efficiency point of view.

Appendix

Table 1

Comparison of Degree of Income Inequality before and after Adding Imputed Rent

	Whole Sample	20–39	40–59	60–
Rent income before adding imputed	7,641	5,903	9,155	7,349
Rent Gini coefficient before adding imputed	0.320	0.270	0.300	0.391
Rent income after adding imputed	9,574	6,907	11,540	10,780
Rent Gini coefficient after adding imputed	0.371	0.308	0.348	0.437

Source: Yagi and Tachibanaki (1997).
Note: Unit of income is one thousand yen.

Table 2

Decomposition of Income Inequality by Income Source

Age Class	Income Source	Mean Income	Gini coefficient	Quasi Gini Coefficient	Degree of contribution to total inequality
Whole sample	earned income	765.73	0.289	0.277	0.9067
	Imputed rent	76.90	0.397	0.188	0.0618
	capital income	11.18	3.77	0.668	0.0319
	Total income	853.81	0.277	0.274	1
20–39	earned income	589.43	0.212	0.206	0.9020
	Imputed rent	48.89	0.604	0.279	0.1012
	capital income	-6.35	-4.502	0.0694	-0.0033
	Total income	631.97	0.214	0.213	1
40–59	earned income	868.11	0.254	0.247	0.9124
	Imputed rent	84.64	0.328	0.141	0.0508
	capital income	6.47	6.539	1.303	0.0359
	Total income	959.22	0.246	0.245	1
60–	earned income	725.98	0.401	0.386	0.9136
	Imputed rent	97.03	0.282	0.123	0.0389
	capital income	53.39	0.981	0.279	0.0486
	Total income	876.40	0.352	0.350	1

Source: Yagi and Tachibanaki (1997).

Table 3

Comparison of the Redistributive Effects of the Separated Tax System and the Comprehensive Income Tax System

	Whole Sample	20–39	40–59	60–
Gini coefficient for pre-tax earned income	0.304	0.259	0.283	0.380
Gini coefficient of post-tax earned income	0.272	0.240	0.249	0.339
The coefficient of income redistribution	10.530	7.340	12.010	10.790
Gini coefficient for pre-tax income	0.371	0.308	0.348	0.437
Gini coefficient for post-tax income under the separated tax system	0.353	0.295	0.329	0.422
The coefficient of income redistribution	4.850	4.220	5.460	3.430
Gini coefficient of post-tax income under the comprehensive income tax system	0.344	0.291	0.318	0.404
The coefficient of income redistribution	7.280	5.510	8.62 0	7.550

Source: Yagi and Tachibanaki (1997).

Note: The coefficient of income redistribution is defined by the coefficient of income redistribution = (A – B) / B ¥ 100, where A is the Gini coefficient for before-tax income and B is the Gini coefficient for after-tax income.

Table 4

Who Benefits from the Tax Reform

Age class	Tenure	Loan	Frequency	Rate of tax change
20–39	0	0	749	-0.41
	1	0	117	0.75
		1	21	-0.04
		2	64	-0.02
		3	41	-0.11
40–59	0	0	536	-0.35
	1	0	404	0.15
		1	132	0.01
		2	179	-0.09
		3	68	0.12
60–	0	0	96	-0.35
	1	0	190	0.18
		1	10	-0.02
		2	11	0.39
		3	11	0.41

Source: Yagi and Tachibanaki (1997).

Note: 1. The data in the column "Tenure" represent the following:
Renter: 0
Land holder: 1
2.The data in the column "Loan" represent the following:
No loan: 0
The ratio of annual loan payment to annual income is less than 0.1:1
The ratio of annual loan payment to annual income is less than 0.2:2
The ratio of annual loan payment to annual income is more than 0.2:3
3.The rate of tax change is defined by Rate of tax change = (C – S) / S, where C represents tax payment under the comprehensive income tax system, and S represents tax payment under the separated tax system.

Table 5

Welfare Change from the Tax Reform

Age class	Tenure	Portion	y^0	y^p	EG	EG/y^p
20–39	renter	0.285	4,001,985	4,110,057	108,072	0.0075
20–39	owner	0.092	5,422,754	5,418,192	-231,475	-0.0427
40–59	renter	0.204	5,545,616	5,785,074	239,458	0.0084
40–59	owner	0.298	6,966,383	6,905,063	-452,488	-0.0655
60–	renter	0.036	4,688,359	4,885,746	197,386	0.0015
60–	owner	0.084	6,109,126	6,054,012	-304,482	-0.0503

Source: Yagi and Tachibanaki (1997).

References

Arrow, K. J., and M. *Kurz* (1970): Public Investment, the Rate of Return, and Optimal Fiscal Policy, Johns Hopkins Press, Baltimore.

Aschauer, D. A. (1990): Public investment and private sector growth, Economic Policy Institute, Washington.

Bacon, P., et al. (1989): Long-term catastrophic care: A financial planning perspective, Journal of Risk and Insurance, March.

Benhabib, J., and K. *Nishimura* (1985): Competitive equilibrium cycles, Journal of Economic Theory, Vol. 35, pp. 284–306.

Cutler, D. (1993): Why doesn't the market fully insure long term care?, NBER Working Paper, No. 4301, March.

Fei, J. C. H., *Ranis*, G., and S. W. Y. *Kuo* (1978): Growth and the family distribution of income by factor components, Quarterly Journal of Economics, Vol. 92, pp. 17–53.

Greb, J., et al. (1994): Interprovincial comparisons of public and private long-term care facilities for the elderly in Canada, Canadian Public Policy, Vol. 20, No. 3.

Homma, M., and M. *Atoda* (1990): Empirical Research on Tax Reform (in Japanese), Toyo Keizai Shinpo sha, Tokyo.

Itaba, Y., and T. *Tachibanaki* (1987): Measurement of tax progressivity when the forms of both income distribution and tax function are given, The Economic Studies Quarterly, Vol. 38, no. 2, pp. 97–106.

Ito, T. (1994): Public policy and housing in Japan, in: Y. Noguchi and J. M. Poterba (eds.), Housing Markets in the United States and Japan, pp. 215–237, The University of Chicago Press, Chicago and London.

King, M. A. (1983): The distribution of gains and losses from changes in the tax treatment of housing, in: M. S. Feldstein (ed.), Behavioural Simulation Methods in Tax Policy Analysis, pp. 109–132, Chicago: Chicago University Press.

McCarthy, Sh. (1997): Aging of Japan, The Toronto Star, April 13th.

Nishimura, K., *Yagi*, T., and M. *Yano* (1995): Optimal public investment: Consumption technology and non-linear dynamics, mimeo.

Pauly, M. V. (1990): The Rational nonpurchase of long term-care insurance, Journal of Political Economy, Vol. 98, No. 1.

Scanlon, W. (1992): Possible reforms for financing long-term care, Journal of Economic Perspectives, Vol. 6, No. 3, Summer.

Tachibanaki, T., and T. *Yagi* (1994): Recent trend of income inequality in Japan: The effect of imputed rent on income inequality and the measurement of accrued income from stock, in: T. Ishikawa (ed.), Income and Wealth Distribution in Japan (in Japanese), pp. 23–58, Tokyo University Press.

Takayama, N., and F. *Arita* (1994): The distribution of household wealth and its historical changes, in: T. Ishikawa (ed.), Income and Wealth Distribution in Japan (in Japanese), pp. 59–78, Tokyo University Press.

Yagi, T., and H. *Maki* (1994): Costs of care and bequest, in: T. Tachibanaki (ed.), Savings and Bequests, University of Michigan Press.

Yagi, T., *Miyazawa*, T., and P. *Moudoukoutas* (1997): Public versus private insurance for long-term care: Why is public insurance necessary?, mimeo.

Yagi, T., and T. *Tachibanaki* (1997): Income redistribution through the tax system: A simulation analysis of tax reform, Review of Income and Wealth, Vol. 44, no. 3, September 1998, pp. 397–415.

Zweifel, P., and S. *Wolfram*, (1996): Long term insurance and bequests as instruments for shaping intergenerational relationships, Journal of Risk and Uncertainty, January, Vol. 12, No. 1.

Accounting for Stock Options in Japan

Akihiro Noguchi

A. Introduction

1995 was a very important year for the history of stock-based compensation plans in Japan. In September, SONY introduced a special compensation plan by using stock purchase warrants issued with debt. In October, the New Business Promotion Act was amended so that small high-tech companies could adopt stock option plans in regardless of the restriction by the Japanese Commercial Code.[1]

In both cases, in exchange for the service received, call options are granted, which means in future if exercised, the companies will be required to issue shares at the specified price. In that sense, the substance of the compensation plans are same. However, because of the difference in their form, the accounting treatments are different. In case of the compensation plans under the New Business Promotion Act, compensation expense will not be recognized. On the other hand, compensation expense will be reported in the income statement for the compensation plans which use stock purchase warrants issued with debt.

In May 1997, the Japanese Commercial Code was amended so that the Japanese companies could offer American-style stock option plans.[2] Two ways to grant stock options were introduced by that amendment. One is to use treasury stocks, and the other is to use stock purchase rights. The former might result in recognition of gain or loss from the reissue of treasury stocks, but the latter would not. So the situation that the difference in form results in difference in accounting treatment did not change.

As the differences in form made accounting treatments different in Japan, the main issue in this paper is the problem of the inconsistency among the accounting treatments for compensation plans using call options.

---

[1] See The Economist (1996) and Weinberg (1995).

[2] See The Economist (1997).

B. Plans by Issuing Stock Purchase Warrants With Debt

Before the amendment in 1997, the Japanese Commercial Code did not allow companies to grant stock options for compensation purpose. So it was necessary for the companies to issue debt with detachable stock purchase warrants, which were allowed by the Commercial Code, and then repurchase those warrants and granted them to the top executives or to the key employees. Example 1 will be used to explain the accounting treatment for this scheme.

Example 1

Assume that bond (per value 100 million yen) with stock purchase warrants was issued at 104 million yen. The fair market value of those warrants were estimated to be 4 million yen and repurchased and granted to the top executives immediately.

The entries for this compensation plan will be as follows:

Dr.	Cash	100,000,000	
Cr.	Bond payable		100,000,000
Dr.	Cash	4,000,000	
Cr.	Stock warrants		4,000,000

The consideration for bond and warrants are recorded separately.

Dr.	Treasury stock warrants	4,000,000	
Cr.	Cash		4,000,000

As warrants are not canceled by the repurchase, some kind of asset account has to be used to record the acquisition for those repurchased warrants, if the accounting treatment follow the form of the transaction.

Dr.	Executive compensation	4,000,000	
Cr.	Treasury stock warrants		4,000,000

When the options are granted, expense or distribution of retained earnings will be recorded.

Above entries are based on the form of the transactions instead of their substance. When the warrants are repurchased, the substance of that transaction is redemption of the warrants. However from the legal point of view, as long as those warrants are not formally canceled, they continue to exist, and have to be treated as assets, just like treasury stocks.[3] If that transaction is recorded based on the substance, it will be as follows:

Dr.	Stock warrants	4,000,000	
Cr.	Cash		4,000,000

As those warrants were repurchased right after they were issued, there would be little, if any, price difference. So the transaction can be recorded based on the original issue price of those warrants. If there were any material difference, that amount should be treated as gain or loss from redemption of warrants.[4]

When the warrants are granted, the substance of the transaction is a grant of stock options. The amount of executive compensation should be determined independently from the original issue price of the warrants. As the measurement of the compensation cost is highly controversial, that issue will not be address in this paper.[5]

If the fair value of non transferable warrants was 2 million yen, the entry to record the grant of those stock options by the fair value based method would be as follows:

Dr.	Executive compensation	2,000,000	
Cr.	Stock options		2,000,000

Because the warrants granted to the executives were made non transferable by the agreement, the fair value of those warrants must be smaller than the warrants that are transferable. The present practice in Japan to record executive compensation based on the fair value of transferable warrants overstates that amount.

On the other hand, if the intrinsic value based method was used, and if that was zero for the non transferable warrants granted, it would not be necessary to record executive compensation.

[3] Treasury stocks are treated as assets in Japan. See Regulation Concerning Balance Sheet and Income Statement of Joint Stock Companies Article 12. If the company prepares consolidated financial statements, the problem becomes more complicated, because, in Japan, treasury stocks are treated as contra equity account on the consolidated balance sheet (Japanese Consolidated Financial Accounting Standards, note 21). In that case, same treasury stocks will be presented as assets on the balance sheet of the parent company and contra equity on the consolidated balance sheet.

[4] In Japan, considerations for warrants are treated as liabilities. If the consideration for warrants are treated as equities, like in IAS 32 (International Accounting Standards Committee, International Accounting Standard IAS 32, Financial Instrument: Disclosure and Presentation, 1995) par.21, that amount will be treated as paid in capital or reduction of retained earnings.

[5] See Financial Accounting Standards Board (1995) and Samuels and Lymer (1996). Because of the lack of international consensus, recognition and measurement standard for stock options was not included in E54 (International Accounting Standards Committee, Exposure Draft E54, Proposed International Accounting Standard, Employee Benefits, 1996).

C. Plans by the New Business Promotion Act (Before Amendment in 1997)

The Japanese Commercial Code Article 280-2 prevented companies from adopting stock option plans, because it required the companies to issue their shares within 6 months after the approval by the stockholders meeting if the shares are issued at the price below the fair value. In October 1995, the New Business Promotion Act was amended so that the designated private high-tech companies could adopt stock option plans. As for those companies, above mentioned 6 months period were extended to 10 years.[6]

As the legal form of this stock option plan utilizes ordinary issue of shares, instead of granting stock rights or warrants, the entry will be made only at the time when the shares are actually issued.

Example 2

Stock options with total exercise price of 3 million yen were granted, and exercised when the market value of those shares were 10 million yen.

When those stock options are exercised, the following entry will be made.

Dr.	Cash	3,000,000	
Cr.	Capital stock		3,000,000

As the stockholders approved to issue shares at the price less than market value, only the fact that the shares were issued has to be recorded. Under this scheme, no compensation cost will be recorded. This accounting treatment is different from recording compensation cost with intrinsic value of stock options at the grant date, like APB Opinion No. 25.

If non transferable warrants (assume that the fair value of the warrants at the grant date was 2 million yen) were granted by the scheme explained in example 1, the entry when those warrants were exercised would be as follows:

Dr.	Cash	3,000,000	
	Stock warrants	2,000,000	
Cr.	Capital stock		5,000,000

[6] See the New Business Promotion Act Article 8. This article was amended again in May 1997, when the Commercial Code was amended to introduce stock options. Now the scheme of the plans by this Act became same as the plans using stock purchase rights by the Commercial Code.

The difference is the amount of contribution by receiving service from the executives. As for the stock options by the New Business Promotion Act, executive compensation will not be recorded.

Although there is a difference in form, whether the plan uses detachable stock purchase warrants or the plan based on the approval to issue shares at the price less than their fair value, the substance is same – to grant stock options to the executives or key employees in exchange for their service.

D. Plans by Using Rights to Purchase Treasury Stocks

By the amendment of the Japanese Commercial Code in May 1997, two kinds of scheme to grant stock options were introduced. One is to grant rights to purchase treasury stocks and the other is to grant stock purchase rights. The former will be explained in this section, and the latter in the next section.

Example 3

Assume that the company repurchased its shares at 3 million yen to grant stock options to the employees. Stock options (total exercise price 3 million yen) were granted and they were exercised when the market value of the shares was 10 million yen.

Based on the present practice in Japan to treat treasury stocks as assets, the entries will be as follows:

Dr. Treasury stocks	3,000,000	
Cr. Cash		3,000,000

Repurchase of treasury stocks are recorded as acquisition of assets.[7]

Dr. Cash	3,000,000	
Cr. Treasury stocks		3,000,000

Exercise of stock options are recorded as sale of assets. If there was a difference between the repurchase price and the exercise price, that amount would be treated as gain or loss.

As the substance of the transaction to repurchase treasury stocks is reduction of stockholders' equity, accounting treatment should not be the acquisition of assets. Even if it lacks the formal procedure to reduce capital stock, treasury stocks should not be reported as assets on the balance sheet. They should be reported as

---

[7] See Regulation Concerning Balance Sheet and Income Statement of Joint Stock Companies Article 22-2.

reduction of stockholders' equity following the substance of the transaction. And when the options are exercised and treasury stocks are reissued, that should be treated as an independent transaction to issue shares.

If the transaction is recorded based on the substance, it will be necessary to record that fact when the stock options are granted.

E. Plans by Issuing Stock Purchase Rights

The amendment of the Japanese Commercial Code in May 1997, made it possible to introduce stock option plans by granting stock purchase rights for compensation purpose after October 1997.

Example 4

Stock options with total exercise price of 3 million yen were granted, and exercised when the market value of the shares were 10 million yen.

As compensation costs were not recognized for the stock option plans under the New Business Promotion Act, it is likely that same practice would be adopted for this scheme. Following entry will be made when the stock options are exercised.

Dr.	Cash	3,000,000	
Cr.	Capital stock		3,000,000

The above entry ignores the fact that the stock options were granted, and service were rendered. As a result, the contribution by service will not be reported.

Although the measurement problem remains, it is necessary to record the fact that the stock options were granted and service were rendered on the financial statements.

F. Plans Other Than Above

There are two other forms to grant stock options in substance. One was adopted by SOFTBANK, where the principal stockholder of that company granted options by using his own shares.[8] The other was adopted by foreign companies where the stock options of the parent company were granted to the executives and employees of the Japanese subsidiary.[9]

---

[8] See Kageyama (1996) and Kobayashi and Kobayashi (1996).

[9] See NIKKEI Newspaper (1996), December 19.

I. Plans by the Principal Stockholder

As call options are granted directly by the principal stockholder to the executives or the employees, no entry will be made on the books of the company according to the form of the transaction.

However, if the substance of the transaction is that the principal stockholder makes a capital contribution to the company and the company grants stock options, there will be entries to be made.[10]

Example 5

Assume that the principal stockholder granted call options with fair value of 2 million yen to the executives.

According to SFAS No.123, the entry will be as follows:

Dr.	Executive compensation	2,000,000	
Cr.	Paid in capital		2,000,000

This entry is a combination of following two entries.

Dr.	Call options	2,000,000	
Cr.	Paid in capital		2,000,000
Dr.	Executive compensation	2,000,000	
Cr.	Call options		2,000,000

However, call options donated from the principal stockholder are call options of the own shares. So, just like treasury stocks, they should be considered as a reduction of capital. As they are options, they should be considered as a contingent reduction of capital. When they are granted, that is a reduction of the contingent reduction of capital. Paid in capital of the company increases when the service are rendered by the executives or the employees who received those options. The donation by its own shares is quite different from the donation by assets.

II. Plans by the Parent Company

Foreign parent company might be able to grant stock options to executives or employees of the Japanese subsidiary. Although the entry or disclosure might be

[10] Accounting treatment based on this interpretation is adopted in SFAS, No. 123, par. 15. See also AICPA Accounting Interpretation 1, "Stock Plans Established by a Principal Stockholder" of Opinion 25.

made on the books of that parent company, no entry or disclosure will be made on the books of the subsidiary.

When that subsidiary is a listed company, it will be necessary for the stockholders of that subsidiary to know that those executives or employees are paid more than what is reported in the financial statements.

G. Summary

As there were various forms to adopt stock option plans, and the accounting treatments were affected by the difference in forms, accounting for stock options became inconsistent in Japan. If the companies grant stock options by using stock purchase warrants issued with debt, compensation costs will be recognized, but if the companies designated by the New Business Promotion Act grant stock options, they will not report compensation cost for their stock option plans. The companies which chose plans using treasury stocks might report gain or loss depending upon the repurchase price and the exercise price, and overstate the total assets, but the companies which chose plans by stock purchase rights would not report compensation cost.

In order to make accounting treatment for stock options in Japan consistent, it is necessary to report treasury stocks as reduction of stockholders' equity instead of including them among assets.

It is also necessary to record the fact when stock options were granted. Although the fair value based method seems to be theoretically sound, it seems to be politically controversial.

References

The Economist (1996): August 3rd, p. 56.

The Economist (1997): August 2nd, pp. 63–64.

Financial Accounting Standards Board (1995): Statement of Financial Accounting Standards No.123, Accounting for Stock-Based Compensation, pars. 57–62.

Kageyama, T., (1996): The Trend of the Stock Option Plans in Japan, and its Meaning for Management, Accounting, and Taxation. (in Japanese), JICPA Journal, April, pp. 14–27.

Kobayashi, T., and M. *Kobayashi* (1996): Accounting and Taxation of Stock Options (in Japanese), KEIEIZAIMU, May 27, pp. 15–23.

NIKKEI Newspaper (1996): December 19.

Samuels, J., and A. *Lymer* (1996): The Financial Reporting of Executive Share Options in the UK, British Accounting Review, 28, pp. 249–266.

Weinberg, N. (1995): Small is ugly, Forbes, December 18, pp. 266–267.

Budget Deficits in Japan

Hiroshi Tsukada

A. Introduction

Since FY 1992 the Japanese economy has been stagnant. The overall business conditions are getting better continuously, but the pace of recovery is very slow. Tax revenue declined and has not yet reached the level of FY 1991. The government implemented a series of economic packages to stimulate the economy, which included not only public works expenditures but also a temporary income tax cut which amounts to 1.3 % of GDP. All of this has caused a rapid expansion of fiscal deficits and the Japanese budget situation has become increasingly worse. The outstanding of government bond reached about 49 % of GDP.

At the same time social and economic conditions change so rapidly that it will affect public finance. The aging of the population is expected to proceed more rapidly hereafter and the Japanese responsibility in the international arena is growing heavier. We have to build a sound fiscal structure in order to meet the budgetary needs arising from these socio-economic changes.

B. Historical Trends in Public Finance and Current Fiscal Situation

I. Situation until First Oil Crisis in 1973

Since the end of World War II, until the mid 1960s, the Japanese government followed a balanced budget policy. In FY 1965, severe recession caused a shortfall in tax revenue. The government revised the budget and issued the government bond in order to finance the deficit. From FY 1966 on, the government abandoned its balanced budget policy and began to issue government bonds. But until the first oil crisis in 1973, with a high rate of growth, Japanese government still experienced a rapid increase of tax revenue and tried to fulfill two policy objectives: The first was to expand public expenditures, especially in infrastructure, the second was tax reduction.

II. Fiscal Deficits in 1970s

However, in the mid 1970s, the situation changed drastically. The gap between government expenditure and tax revenue had a tendency to widen. Until now, we cannot manage out the fiscal system without a huge amount of deficit. What were the reasons for this phenomenon?

The following three points were important:

1. The first was the refraction of the rates of growth which stagnated tax revenue. With the increased oil price, returns on investment fell. So, plant and equipment investment went down, and we faced a lower rate of growth in the neighborhood of 5 %, in the latter half of the 1970s, and 3 % or less in the first half of the 1980s.

2. The second was the rapid expansion of expenditures following major improvements in the level of social security services in the 1970s.

In the early 1970s, we introduced several important institutional reforms. The government began to pay the full cost of medical care for the aged, and insurance benefit coverage was raised. Pension insurance payment was raised, and in pension insurance we adopted the inflation slide system, that is to say, linked expenditures with a consumer price index.

As a result, FY 1973 is known in Japan as the first year of high level social welfare.

These expansions of the welfare services were put into practice assuming a high rate of growth and rich tax revenue. But these assumptions were not realized. The social welfare expenditure began to increase rapidly with its own momentum. For example, improvements in medical insurance resulted in the rapid growth of total medical expenses.

3. The third point is international pressure on Japan to stimulate its economy. In the Summit meeting in 1978, it was argued that Japan and West Germany should take fiscal stimulus measures to reduce current account surplus and lead the depressed world economy, playing the role of locomotives.

Taking these arguments into consideration, the Japanese government increased public works expenditures which was financed by a large government bond issue.

Due to these factors, the volume of government bond issue showed a rapid increase in the 1970s. And the ratio of government bond issue to total expenditure hit its peak at 34.7 % in FY 1979. It was a crisis.

But with the coming of the 1980s, the budget deficit stopped increasing and showed an opposite tendency to decrease moderately.

III. Efforts to Reduce Fiscal Deficits in the 1980s

Let us summarize the process of reducing fiscal deficits in the 1980s.

The expansion of fiscal deficits in the latter part of the 1970s was thought to be very serious. At first the government proposed to introduce a kind of value-added tax which was called general consumption tax. But this proposal became a major issue in the general election in 1979, in which the LDP party (the Government Party) suffered a serious defeat. And the proposal was frustrated.

The government changed its strategy. Tax increase was brought to an end and expenditure cuts were stressed. Severe guidelines for budget requests by each ministry were set, which intended to restrain the growth of general expenditure (general expenditure means policy-oriented discretionary expenditures except for national debt service and tax grant for local governments which are legal obligations of the government). We called it a ceiling. In FY 1980, the ceiling was set at 10 %, that is to say, each ministry was obliged to limit its estimate budget request to a 10 % increase as compared to the previous fiscal year. In FY 1982, the ceiling was set at 0 %. Finally a minus ceiling was set, every ministry was asked to cut down their estimate budget request uniformly.

In addition to this general measure, several specific measures were carried out. The pension insurance system was rationalized and unified. In former times, there existed several separate pension schemes. Now a two-layered system was introduced with the first layer, called Basic Pension Scheme, covering the entire population. In medical care insurance, insurance benefit coverage for salaried workers was cut down from 100 % to 90 %.

Also the government made an effort to reduce the number of civil servants and Japan National Railway and two other public corporations were privatized.

Owing to measures just mentioned, from FY 1983 to FY 1987 general expenditure was controlled to maintain the same level. As for the tax system, after a long political turmoil, in 1989 a consumption tax was finally introduced at a rate of 3 %. But this was in exchange for an income tax reduction of nearly the same amount. The net effect was neutral.

But from FY 1986 to FY 1991 the addition in tax revenue was actually remarkable and fiscal situation improved greatly. This was because of the so-called bubble economy at that time.

IV. The Bubble Economy

From FY 1987 to FY 1990, the real rate of growth heightened to between 5 and 6%. Japan enjoyed prosperity after a long period of economic difficulties.

The story of Japanese bubble economy has its origin in the Plaza Agreement of September 1985 when representatives of the Group of Five Industrial Countries met and reached an agreement. They affirmed that a smooth and systematically managed rise in the value of other currencies against the U. S. dollar would be a desirable means of alleviating the bilateral payments imbalances. Following this agreement, the foreign exchange rate of the yen appreciated 60 % in less than a year.

In mid September 1985, the yen was trading in the range of 244 yen per dollar, but after the agreement the yen appreciated. By August 1986, it had risen to 153 yen per dollar. To counter a possible slump which might have been caused by the strong yen, monetary condition was substantially eased, the official discount rate was cut down four times in 1986 alone.

But at that time the labor productivity of the export industries was increasing so rapidly that the negative effect of the appreciation of the yen rate could be absorbed by the main export industries. On the import side, the Japanese industry could import their input less expensively and consumers could enjoy import goods cheaper than before. That is to say, the appreciation of the yen rate worked as a kind of tax reduction in softened monetary conditions.

Due to these forces, Japan enjoyed unexpected prosperity for a while, which was mistakenly believed to last forever.

In this process, land prices and stock prices soared sharply. At that time the growth rate of money stock was 10 % on average, but the real rate of growth was about 5 %, and the interest rate stayed at very low level. At the end of 1985, the total market value of all outstanding shares was 196 trillion yen, and four years later, at the end of 1989, it stood at 630 trillion yen. In these four years the market value had grown by 434 trillion yen, almost one year's worth of GDP.

People were enthusiastic in speculation which eventually led into a crazy situation. For example, by the end of 1987, the Japanese stock market accounted for 42 % of the total market value of stocks all over the world. For the first time the United States was displaced from the top position by Japan, a nation with half its population, and 60 % its GDP. By the end of 1990, the total market value of Japanese land counted four times as much as in the U. S.

In this overoptimistic atmosphere, plant and equipment investment increased 10 % annually in real terms. Since the end of high economic growth, we had not experienced a growth of 10 %. Such a high rate of growth of plant and equipment investment had been compatible only with a much faster economic growth. So, investing so much in a period of a 5 % growth rate, they were accumulating unnecessary overcapacity in their industries which would have repercussions eventually.

Anyway, in those happy days tax revenue increased, and the fiscal situation improved greatly.

V. Current Fiscal Situation

The bubble economy came to an end, because the government tightened monetary policy in response to signs that consumer prices were rising too fast. Similarly urban salaried workers expressed their dissatisfaction with skyrocketing land prices, for in that trend they lost the chance to have their own home and land.

The government placed restrictions on loans to the real estate business, land prices entered a long decline which still continues today. As can be easily imagined, the recession after the bubble economy was very severe.

The record of the real rate of growth was 3.1 % in FY 91, but fell to 0.4 % in FY 92, 0.2 % in FY 93, 0.5 % in FY 94, 1.2 % in FY 95, 2.5 % in FY 96, and is estimated to be about 0 % in FY 97. The OECD called it a "surprising exceptional low rate of growth".

Tax revenue reached its highest point in FY 1991, and from then on steadily decreased for five consecutive years. In FY 1997, it is estimated to be 57.8 trillion yen which is still less than in FY 1991.

Tax revenue has been stagnant. In addition to this, it was necessary for the government to stimulate the economy with fiscal measures.

In FY 1993 the government initiated various economic measures such as a series of large scale public works expenditures. In FY 1994, in order to promptly respond to the damage caused by Hanshin-Awaji Great Earthquake, a supplementary budget was formulated. In FY 1995, in September, the largest scale fiscal package was decided and a supplementary budget was formulated.

But such measures were not limited to expenditures only. In FY 1994, a temporary tax reduction which amounted to 1.3 % of GDP was carried out. In FY 1995 and 1996 a temporary tax cut was continued on the same level as in FY 1994.

The outstanding of government bond was about 37 % of GDP in FY 1990, but it has now reached 49 % of GDP. In FY 1997, the ratio of fiscal deficit to total expenditure of the General Account Budget is 21.6 % and debt service accounts for 21 % of total expenditure.

C. Conclusion

The future of our fiscal system depends mainly on three factors.

The first is the rate of growth of our economy. The general business conditions are getting better continuously. But the pace of recovery is very slow, and we cannot judge clearly what the medium term prospect of our economy is.

The second is the national burden ratio. That is the total tax and social security contribution as percentage of the national income. Although the ratio of social security contributions to national income tax has been increasing steadily, the amount of tax revenue and social security contributions combined as a ratio of national income is expected to remain the lowest among G-7 countries, staying at a level similar to that in the U. S.

The third is the aging of the population in Japan. The percentage of the population 65 or older was 13.5 % 1993, whereas it was only 5.7 % in 1960. This percentage, although slightly lower than in some European countries, is projected to increase very rapidly, reaching 17.0 % in the year 2000 and 25.5 % in 2020.

The Japanese population will age faster than that of all other industrialized countries, and Japan will be the most aged country among these in the next century. As the aging of the population proceeds and social security benefits increase, more attention should be paid to the issue of financing the costs of social security.

Judging from these factors, especially from the second and the third, the budget deficit we face is not a cyclical phenomenon. If the Japanese economy gets into another orbit of steady growth, its burden will be moderated, but the issue itself will not disappear.

Creating consensus among the people on the extent to which they bear tax and social security burdens and to which they tolerate expenditure cuts will be one of our central objects in this society for the next decade.

Appendix

Table 1
Rate of Growth and Government Finance Indicators until the First Oil Crisis 1973

Fiscal Year	Real GDP Growth rate	General Account Budget (settlement)			
		Expenditure A	Tax Revenue	Government Bond Issue B	B/A
	%	100 million yen			%
1961	11.5	20,635	20,176		
1962	7.7	25,566	21,959		
1963	10.1	30,443	25,302		
1964	9.8	33,110	29,497		
1965	6.2	37,230	30,496	1,972	5.3
1966	11.2	44,592	34,058	6,656	14.9
1967	11.2	51,130	40,936	7,094	13.9
1968	12.5	59,371	49,239	4,621	7.8
1969	12.1	69,178	60,243	4,126	6.0
1970	9.6	81,877	72,958	3,472	4.2
1971	5.0	95,611	79,272	11,871	12.4
1972	9.1	119,322	97,701	19,500	16.3
1973	5.1	147,783	133,655	17,662	12.0
1974	Δ0.5	190,998	150,359	21,600	11.3

Source: Ministry of Finance.

Table 2

Rate of Growth and Government Finance Indicators in the 1970s

Fiscal Year	Real GDP Growth rate	General Account Budget (settlement)			
		Expenditure A	Tax Revenue	Government Bond Issue B	B/A
	%	100 million yen			%
1971	5.0	95,611	79,272	11,871	12.4
1972	9.1	119,322	97,701	19,500	16.3
1973	5.1	147,783	133,655	17,662	12.0
1974	Δ0.5	190,998	150.359	21,600	11.3
1975	4.0	208,609	137,527	52,805	25.3
1976	3.8	244,676	156,578	71,982	29.4
1977	4.5	290,598	173,329	95,612	32.9
1978	5.4	340,960	219,205	106,740	31.3
1979	5.1	387,898	237,295	134,720	34.7
1980	2.6	434,050	268,687	141,702	32.6

Source: Ministry of Finance.

Table 3

Rate of Growth and Government Finance Indicators in the 1980s

Fiscal Year	Real GDP Growth rate	General Account Budget (settlement)			
		Expenditure A	Tax Revenue	Government Bond Issue B	B/A
	%	100 million yen			%
1981	3.0	469,212	289,521	128,999	27.5
1982	3.1	472,451	305,111	140,447	29.7
1983	2.5	506,353	323,583	134,863	26.6
1984	4.1	514,806	349.084	127,813	24.8
1985	4.1	530,045	381,988	123,080	23.2
1986	3.1	536,404	418,768	112,549	21.0
1987	4.8	577,311	467,979	94,181	16.3
1988	6.0	614,711	508,265	71,525	11.6
1989	4.4	658,589	549,218	66,385	10.1
1990	5.6	692,687	601,059	73,120	10.6
1991	3.1	705,472	598,204	67,300	9.5
1992	0.4	704,974	544,453	95,360	13.5

Source: Ministry of Finance.

Table 4

Rate of Growth and Government Finance Indicators in the 1990s

Fiscal Year	Real GDP Growth rate	General Account Budget (settlement)			
		Expenditure A	Tax Revenue	Government Bond Issue B	B/A
	%	100 million yen			%
1991	3.1	705,472	598,204	67,300	9.5
1992	0.4	704,974	544,453	95,360	13.5
1993	0.5	751,025	541,262	161,740	21.5
1994	0.6	736,136	510.300	164,900	22.4
1995	2.8	759,385	519,308	212,470	28.0
1996	3.2	788,479	520,601	217,483	27.6
1997	0.1	773,900	578,020	167,070	21.6

Source: Ministry of Finance.

Note: FY 1997: Initial budget basis
other years: settlement basis

Table 5

Yen Rate and the Rate of Growth

Fiscal year	Exchange rate (end of year)	GDP growth rate (real)	Plant and equipment investment growth rate (real)
	yen/dollar	%	%
1984	255.50	4.1	11.6
1985	179.60	4.1	12.0
1986	145.80	3.1	3.2
1987	125.40	4.8	7.9
1988	132.05	6.0	16.5
1989	157.20	4.4	12.3
1990	141.00	5.6	11.3
1991	133.20	3.1	2.7
1992	115.35	0.4	Δ7.2

Source: Economic Planning Agency, System of National Accounts.

Table 6

Growth of Expenditures and Tax Revenue in the 1980s (General Account)

Fiscal Year	%				Tax Revenue
	general account total	National debt service	Local allocation tax grants	general expenditure	
1981	9.9	25.3	23.5	4.3	7.8
1982	6.2	17.7	14.2	1.8	5.4
1983	1.4	4.6	Δ20.8	Δ0.0	6.1
1984	0.5	11.7	21.5	Δ0.0	7.9
1985	3.7	11.7	9.0	Δ0.0	9.4
1986	3.0	10.7	5.1	Δ0.0	9.6
1987	0.0	0.1	Δ0.0	Δ0.0	11.8
1988	4.8	1.6	7.1	1.2	8.6
1989	6.6	1.3	22.6	3.3	8.1
1990	9.6	22.5	14.3	3.8	9.4
1991	6.2	12.2	4.6	47	Δ2.0
1992	2.7	2.6	Δ1.3	4.5	Δ9.0

Source: Ministry of Finance.

Note: Expenditures Initial budget basis
Tax Revenue Settlement basis

Table 7

Ratio of the Number of Aged People (65 Years and More) to the Total Population (in %)

	1960	1980	1990	2000	2020
Japan	5.7	9.1	12.1	17.0	25.5
Germany	11.5	15.6	15.0	16.0	20.9
France	11.6	14.0	14.0	15.7	19.7
U. K.	11.7	15.1	15.7	15.3	18.0
U. S. A.	9.2	11.3	12.5	12.4	16.1

Source: Ministry of Finance, The Japanese Budget in Brief 1996.

Table 8

Total Taxes and Social Security Contributions as Percentages of National Income (in %)

	Japan	U. S. A.	U. K.	Germany	France	Sweden
The ratio of tax burden to national income	23.1	25.9	35.8	31.7	34.2	50.8
The ratio of social security contribution to national income	14.1	10.6	10.3	25.6	28.4	19.8
Total	37.2	36.5	46.1	57.3	62.6	70.6

Source: Ministry of Finance, The Japanese Budget in Brief, 1996.

Note: Japan based upon FY 1996 budget
U. S. A. CY 1993 actual
France CY 1990 actual
other countries CY 1994 actual

Information Technology and Organizational Change
How Stable is the Virtual Enterprise?

Franz Schober

A. Introduction

"Rebuilding of the economic structure towards the 21st century" is the central theme of this 17th joint seminar organized by the Faculties of Economics from the Universities of Nagoya and Freiburg. The subject of the seminar is not only important because of the brief distance in time to the next century, but also and mainly, because we experience today major changes in our society and our personal lives, such as the rebuilding of the world after the collapse of the communist system, the establishment of the European Economic and Monetary Union including its intended expansion to Eastern Europe, the challenge to democracy within an open world of different political systems or the change of the value system in society. Another major change that is experienced today concerns the way in which we communicate, coordinate and cooperate privately and in the business environment.

Changes in communication, coordination and cooperation in business affect small, medium-sized and large companies alike, national as well as international companies. The classical mechanisms of hierarchical coordination within firms and of multilateral competition between firms seem to be no longer valid. Today we experience an increased focus on horizontal coordination within companies, such as team work and horizontally coordinated business processes. We also experience increased cooperation between firms, constellations where the same companies are partners and competitors at the same time.

There are several reasons for this development. One of the reasons is certainly the increased size and dynamics of competition in an economically open world. New competitors have emerged, either from outside the home country or from outside the home business sector. The competitive situation has also become more unstable: competitors come and go. The driving force behind this trend has primarily been the reduction of many national and international trade barriers in recent years. Business today is less shielded by local protective regulations and, as a consequence, is exposed to a more turbulent environment.

Technological progress in transportation and communication adds to the trend of increased competition. Improved transportation and communication technologies reduce geographical barriers and function as a "turbocharger" to the engine of reduced trade barriers and other protective measures.

In order to maintain competitiveness, enterprises have to develop more efficient ways of doing business. There are several options, but today's prevailing paradigm seems to be the concentration on one's "core competencies", i. e. on the pronounced strengths of a company. It is only within a core competence or a small set of core competencies where a long-term chance of gaining and defending competitive advantage exists. At first glance, the strategy of core competence seems to be diametral to the preferred competitive strategy of the Seventies, i. e. the conglomeration strategy. Behind this shift in paradigm is a shift in the perception of efficiency and risk. The strategic approach of the conglomerates had been outside-oriented. Its focus was on optimized portfolios of independent businesses that guaranteed efficiency at a sustainable level of risk as a consequence of the portfolio mix. The core competence approach is inside-oriented. Efficiency and risk are an integral part of the resource strategy of a company.

Conglomeration strategies and strategies of core competence, however, can also coexist in some way. This is the case with holding companies that manage different businesses almost independently in a core competence style. This seems to be the preferred approach in today's large Western enterprises, while small and medium-sized companies concentrate on a single or a few core competencies.

Concentration on core competencies means, on the other hand, that complementary products and services beyond the core competence have to be added to the final market offer in different ways. The integration of products and services across firms is one key area, where new organizational options have been developed, and where new communication and coordination techniques come into play. Other areas concern the strengthening of the internal organization itself.

Information and communication technologies, subsequently abbreviated as IT, are necessary instruments for the support of a core competence strategy and the integrative processes behind this strategy. This is not to say, that the core competence strategy is driven by IT. The mastering of IT is not a sufficient, but a necessary condition with unprecise (fuzzy) validity.

It is interesting to note that the application of IT as a facilitator of coordination processes and of organizational change is quite new. In the past, IT has been mainly used as an instrument for automation of well-defined tasks within a given organizational framework. Now the organizational framework itself is the target. With this new role, IT has finally become a key instrument for organizational design, a development that promoters of IT had always promised in the past but that had never materialized until recently.

In the following we will explore some current organizational trends and the role of IT (chapter B). Chapter C, as the main part of the paper, will analyze interorganizational arrangements such as the virtual enterprise from a formal economic point of view and will study the impact of IT on the stability of interorganizational cooperations. Chapter D will summarize and draw conclusions for further scientific work.

B. Current Organizational Trends and the Role of IT

I. Generic Coordination Mechanisms

In institutional economics basically two generic coordination mechanisms are distinguished: markets and hierarchies or firms respectively. Market coordination is spontaneous and unplanned, it makes use of the information imbedded in the prices of products and services. Coordination in markets, however, involves, besides the pricing system, also coordination costs that have to be payed for each market transaction (transaction cost). These costs are associated with the search for market offerings, contract bargaining and contract fulfillment.

Coordination in hierarchies is purposely designed by an organizational designer, so that the design process can be described as the art of dividing a complex task into several subtasks (configuration) and of developing a coordination mechanism to integrate the subtasks back into the original task (coordination). The objective of the design process is to ensure maximum efficiency under a given level of risk. The efficiency criterion of organizational design is the sum of production and coordination cost. These cost categories correspond to prices and transaction cost in markets coordination.

Recently, a third generic coordination mechanism between the extremes of market and hierarchy has been proposed, namely the interfirm or interorganizational network, frequently also called the virtual enterprise. In an interfirm network a specific task is divided between legally independent companies. Each company makes specific investments to perform the assigned subtask and expects certain profits from this arrangement. Unlike market arrangements, contracts are only incompletely specified, if at all, and the duration of the cooperation is limited, sometimes predefined, but mostly open-ended. Virtual enterprises are governed to a large extent by mutual trust between the cooperating partners. But they can also be rationalized in economic terms, which is the objective of chapter C.

Within all three generic coordination mechanisms one can observe various impacts from IT. We will first explore some of these trends in a more informal way.

II. Intra-Organizational Coordination and IT

Intra-organizational coordination applies to coordination mechanisms installed inside a company or hierarchy respectively.

Vertical Coordination

Larger western companies have substantially reduced intermediate hierarchical levels in recent years, causing the so-called "middle management crisis". The role of middle management is largely information-oriented. Middle management serves as a top-down transmitter of company objectives and programs to ensure implementation and, reciprocally, as a bottom-up filter for top management information on business performance. The transmittance and aggregation of information today is largely supported by computer-based planning and reporting systems into which top management can directly connect. In addition, many of the interdepartmental control responsibilities of middle management are substituted by IT in support of horizontal coordination, as will be shown below. As a consequence, less middle management is required in the future.

Another observation is the increased delegation of responsibilities to lower company levels. Firstly, IT supports the transfer of knowledge to where it is needed in the company, via data bases and other knowledge systems (e. g. technical knowledge for floorshop operation or conceptual knowledge for consulting). Secondly, IT may channel performance reports upwards the hierarchy to provide implementation control. In terms of principal/agent theory, IT supports the principal to better communicate his objectives and to better specify the required tasks (i. e. work contracts are more precisely defined), and IT also supports the control of objective and task fulfillment. Opportunistic behavior of agents and agency control cost are reduced by the use of IT. Increased geographical delegation of decision-making along with the installation of world-wide integrated IT is particularly observed within international companies.

Horizontal Coordination

Information that is contained within IT-based information systems can be easily distributed within the whole company. It is no longer private knowledge in the heads of certain employees or managers but common knowledge accessible to all who have a right to access. As a consequence, information systems are able to support horizontal coordination along business processes, particularly if these processes are well-structured and defined by a set of rules and procedures that can also be controlled by IT, e. g. by Workflow Management Systems. The current discussion on business process re-engineering centers to a great extent around the effective and efficient use of IT.

IT may also support distributed work that is less structured, e. g. distributed development work by simultaneous engineering systems or distributed management decisions by video conferencing and related groupware systems. The intensively studied field of "Computer Supported Cooperative Work (CSCW)" is one approach to these new ways of horizontal coordination. This includes also IT-based telework, where employees work at home or at locations different from the company premises (e. g. at the customers' or suppliers' location) and are linked to the company via computer networks.

III. Interorganizational Coordination and IT

Interorganizational coordination describes the coordination mechanisms within a network of legally independent firms. As in the case of intra-organizational patterns we can here also distinguish between horizontal and vertical coordination, although from a somewhat different perspective.

Horizontal Coordination

Horizontal cooperation takes place between companies who operate in different businesses, but contribute to a common product or service for the market place. Examples are the cooperation of a software and a hardware supplier to develop and market a specific computer application, or the cooperation of a computer firm and a financial services provider to develop a new IT-based financial service. The IT tools in support of interorganizational vertical coordination are similar to those for internal coordination. In addition, however, open systems architectures and common IT standards largely facilitate the IT-based cooperation between firms.

Vertical Coordination

This type of coordination applies along the value chain of a specific product or service. It describes the linkages between a company and its suppliers and/or customers. A typical example is Electronic Data Interchange (EDI) between a company and its suppliers, as found in the automobile industry. Here, the EDI link ensures "Just in Time" supply of purchased parts as well as immediate billing. Connections to customers may also be implemented via EDI, e. g. to provide automated order processing. Again, common standards and interconnective systems are of key importance for the success of EDI applications. Vertical coordination between firms, however, may also rely on proprietary systems developed by one of the partners, usually the larger firm. Typical examples are found in the area of production planning and control. Here the partners may face substantial switching costs if they intend to abandon the partnership. Switching costs play an important role in analyzing the stability of partnership arrangements.

IV. Market Coordination and IT

The application of IT for coordination within the market system leads to "electronic markets". Early examples are airline reservation systems such as American Airline's SABRE. Today these systems have been enhanced to integrated travel service systems that offer not only airline seats but also hotel or rental car reservations as well as theatre tickets, etc. Other examples are computer-based stock exchange systems such as New York's NASDAQ or Frankfurt's EUREX system.

Electronic markets may support only some phases of the market transaction process, particularly the search phase. Other systems support all phases including search, contract bargaining and pricing as well as contract administration and control. Again one may distinguish between horizontal and vertical systems, although most electronic markets exhibit both aspects.

Horizontal Coordination

Here, members in the network relate to different businesses but offer a common product or service package. Such an electronic package may include specific products, product applications and financial services for payment. In the extreme case, a system like the Internet may be considered as one huge electronic shopping mall offering all kinds of products and services.

Vertical Coordination

Some electronic markets work with intermediary agents or brokers, e. g. most of the electronic travel service systems or stock exchange systems. Other systems connect original suppliers and final customers directly, e. g. within the Internet. In general, electronic markets seem to reduce the importance of intermediary agents in the conventional form (travel agencies, stock brokers etc.) or replace them by fully automated electronic agents.

To sum up the current trends in organizational design, we recognize a whole pattern of new coordination mechanisms based on the innovative use of IT. One question particularly interesting to the economist is the dramatically increased relevance of interfirm arrangements in today's business practice. In the next chapter we will investigate the specific case of the virtual enterprises in more depth and try to identify the economic reasons for their existence, for their stability in time, and for their collapse.

C. An Economic Analysis of the Virtual Enterprise

I. Formal Analysis

Research in the area of interorganizational systems is either anecdotical in the form of case studies, or empirical in the form of structured field research and statistical evaluation, or based on formal economic reasoning. The following analysis belongs to the third kind. It uses elements of formal bargaining theory for explanation. For related works, see Kleindorfer/Knieps (1982) or Clemens/ Kleindorfer (1992).

We restrict our analysis to the case of two legally independent companies who cooperate or plan to cooperate as a virtual enterprise to offer some common product or service. The extension to multilateral networks is possible but complicates the analysis and hides the essentials, particularly if one allows alternative coalitions between different members of the network.

We split the decision process into two periods. In period t = 1 both companies make certain investments in preparation of their joint activity. In period t = 2 a decision is taken whether to materialize the cooperation or not, depending on the profit situation at t = 2. There may be contracts in t = 1, but these contracts can be terminated in t = 2 by paying penalties and thus reducing profits. We further assume that at t = 1 the state of the world in t = 2 is unknown to each partner, otherwise there would be no reason for terminating the cooperation at t = 2. Our setup also explains consecutive decisions on extending or terminating the cooperation because each decision at a period t depends in similar form on investment decisions up to period t – 1.

We assume that at period t = 1 the two companies make investments x_1 and x_2 into task-related and other internal activities and investements y_1 and y_2 into activities that concern the coordination mechanisms between both companies.

As an illustrative example, consider a hardware and a software company which jointly plan to develop and market a specific application system, i. e. a system for computer-aided design (CAD) in the manufacturing industry. The investments x_1 and x_2 are primarily concerned with the development of the required software and hardware components. But some coordination-related investments may also be considered, e. g. for internal project management systems. Investments y_1 and y_2 concern the interorganizational links between both companies, e. g. EDI, video conferencing or other groupware systems.

At period t = 2 the state of the world becomes known to both partners and they must re-evaluate their cooperative commitment.

Assume that at period t = 2 the two companies make gross profits P_1 and P_2 from their investments. These profits depend not only on the individual investments but also on the investment of the business partner, i. e.

(1) $$P_1 = P_1(x_1, x_2, y_1, y_2) \quad \text{and} \quad P_2 = P_2(x_1, x_2, y_1, y_2).$$

This formulation obviously takes the network externalities of the joint arrangement into account. The net profits R_1 and R_2 including prior investments are given by

(2) $$R_1 = P_1 - x_1 - y_1 \quad \text{and} \quad R_2 = P_2 - x_2 - y_2.$$

At t = 2 both partners may also evaluate alternative arrangements. We denote the gross profits from the best of these alternative arrangements with P_1^* and P_2^* respectively. P_1^* and/or P_2^* may be better than P_1 and/or P_2 or worse, depending on the state of the world in t = 2. These profits depend also on how each of the companies is able to derive future advantage from their investments in t = 1, i. e.

(3) $$P_1^* = P_1^*(x_1, x_2, y_1, y_2) \quad \text{and} \quad P_2^* = P_2^*(x_1, x_2, y_1, y_2).$$

P_1^* and P_2^* depend also on the resource configuration of the alternative partners, but this configuration is not relevant to our analysis.

In the case of terminating the cooperation, each partner has to take switching costs S_1^*, S_2^* into account. These costs may include penalties for disrupting the contract with the original partner. We assume that the switching cost depends on the investments y_1 and y_2 into the interorganizational coordination structure, i. e.

(4) $$S_1^* = S_1^*(y_1, y_2) \quad \text{and} \quad S_2^* = S_2^*(y_1, y_2).$$

Net profits R_1^* and R_2^* from the best alternative arrangement sum up to

(5) $$R_1^* = P_1^* - S_1^* - x_1 - y_1 \quad \text{and} \quad R_2^* = P_2^* - S_2^* - x_2 - y_2.$$

The alternative net profits R_1^* and R_2^* may be used by both partners as threats for re-bargaining their relative economic position vis-a-vis the other partner. E. g., if partner 1 can prove substantially larger net profits from an alternative use of the joint investments compared to partner 2, he may request a compensation in the form of a transfer payment from partner 2 in order to continue the cooperation, and vice versa.

In general, at t = 2 we should therefore expand equation (2) by including a transfer payment T:

(2)' $$R_1' = P_1 - x_1 - y_1 + T \quad \text{and} \quad R_2' = P_2 - x_2 - y_2 - T.$$

Bargaining theory suggests the following equilibrium solution for the fair amount of *T*, see Nash (1950), Myerson (1991, p. 375 f.):

(6) $$\max_T E = (R_1' - R_1^*)(R_2' - R_2^*)$$
for all T within the set $B = \{T{:}R_1' \geq R_1^* \text{and } R_2' \geq R_2^*\}$.

Solving for $dE/dT = 0$ yields the following solution $T°$ to the bargaining problem:

(7) $$T° = [(P_2 - P_1) - (P_2^* - P_1^*) + (S_2^* - S_1^*)]/2,$$ if T° is a member of set *B*.

The solution to the bargaining problem suggests that both partners share the surplus profits from their arrangement equally. In the equilibrium point, if it exists, the net profits of both partners are greater than the net profits from alternative arrangements, even after transfer payments. If no equilibrium point exists, i. e. $T°$ is outside set B, then both partners will terminate their arrangement and the virtual enterprise will collapse.

Note that the transfer payment T° and the set B do not depend on the investments x_1, x_2, y_1 and y_2 which are sunk at time t = 2, but only on the extent to which both partners can draw advantage from these investments in their gross profits, both in the cooperative as well as in the alternative case, and in switching cost. Furthermore, in the equilibrium point, $R_1' - R_1^* = R_2' - R_2^*$, i. e. the differences to the second best option are identical for both companies. This can be easily shown by substituting T° from (7) into R_1' and R_2' according to (2)'.

We now turn in more detail to the alternative options. We assume that for each partner these options can take one of the following three forms: (a) switching to a cooperation with another partner, (b) integrating the partner's business into one's own company, or (c) withdrawing from the market. We can express the situation as a compound game, see figure 1. It consists of a competitive partition (competitive game) which defines the best alternative option, and the interaction between the cooperative and the competitive situation (cooperative game).

For each cell of the competitive game two payoff matrices have to be calculated. First a matrix M* containing the alternative payoffs $P_1^* - S_1^*$ or $P_2^* - S_2^*$ respectively, computed individually for each cell. Note that each cell contains cell-specific and in general different values for P_1^*, P_2^*, S_1^* and S_2^*. The second matrix M contains the payoffs $P_1 + T°$ and $P_2 - T°$ where T° is calculated according to (7) using the cell inputs of M*. The matrix M* contains the profits from alternative arrangements, M the profits from the continued cooperation after transfer payments. The difference D of both payoff matrices

(8) $$D = M - M^*$$

measures the relative advantage of the continued cooperation compared to all alternative arrangements. If all payoffs in D are non-negative, then T° is a member

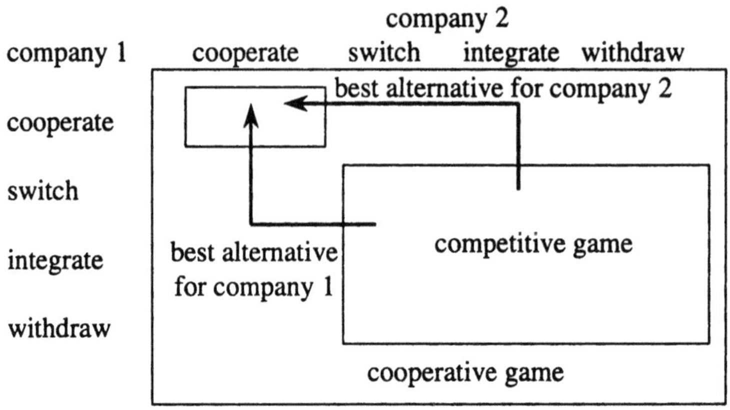

Figure 1: Compound Game Structure

of set B, see (6). Accordingly, the continuation of the cooperation is the economically most advantageous option. If at least one payoff in D is negative, then the cooperation should be terminated. The cell with the smallest negative value defines the best alternative option. More formally, let d° be the minimum payoff for all cells in D, i. e.

(9) $d^\circ = Min\ D$ for all cells in D and $c^\circ = cell$ with value d°,

then the compound bargaining game yields the following solution:

(10) *(a)* the cooperation should be continued, if $d^\circ \geq 0$,
(b) the cooperation should be terminated, if $d^\circ < 0$. The optimal alternative is given by the strategies that correspond to cell c°.

The payoffs in D within a specific cell are always identical for both companies because of the definition of T°.

II. Numerical Examples

Let us consider for the case of cooperation gross profits of $P_1 = 80$ and $P_2 = 100$.

Alternative gross profits P_1* and P_2* are given by the payoff matrix

P_1*/P_2*	company 2		
company 1	switch	integrate	withdraw
switch	70/130	50/140	70/0
integrate	100/50	70/80	120/0
withdraw	0/130	0/140	0/0

and switching costs S_1* and S_2* by

S_1*/S_2*	company 2		
company 1	switch	integrate	withdraw
switch	20/20	20/30	20/0
integrate	30/20	30/30	30/0
withdraw	0/20	0/30	0/0

We assume hereby, that both companies have different gross profits but a similar switching cost structure. Then M* is calculated as $P_1* - S_1* / P_2* - S_2*$:

M*	company 2		
company 1	switch	integrate	withdraw
switch	50/110	30/110	50/0
integrate	70/30	40/50	90/0
withdraw	0/110	0/110	0/0

M is calculated as $P_1 + T° / P_2 - T°$ applying (7):

M	company 2		
company 1	switch	integrate	withdraw
switch	60/120	50/130	115/65
integrate	110/70	85/95	135/45
withdraw	35/145	35/145	90/90

D as the difference M – M* is given by

D	company 2		
company 1	switch	integrate	withdraw
switch	10/10	20/20	65/65
integrate	40/40	45/45	45/45
withdraw	35/35	35/35	90/90

Since all cell entries are non-negative, the continuation of the cooperation is most advantageous, see (10).

As a second example, we keep all inputs unchanged except for the switching costs S_1* and S_2*, for which we assume the "ideal" value zero in all cells, i. e.

S_1*/S_2*	company 2		
company 1	switch	integrate	withdraw
switch	0/0	0/0	0/0
integrate	0/0	0/0	0/0
withdraw	0/0	0/0	0/0

Then we get for M*:

M*	company 2		
company 1	switch	integrate	withdraw
switch	70/130	50/140	70/0
integrate	100/50	70/80	120/0
withdraw	0/130	0/140	0/0

which is identical to P_1* / P_2*.

M is calculated as

M	company 2		
company 1	switch	integrate	withdraw
switch	60/120	45/135	125/55
integrate	115/65	85/95	150/30
withdraw	25/155	20/160	90/90

D finally becomes

D	company 2		
company 1	switch	integrate	withdraw
switch	–10/–10	–5/–5	55/55
integrate	15/15	15/15	30/30
withdraw	25/25	20/20	90/90

As a result, the best solution for both companies is to switch to other partners ($d° = -10$). But the solution where company 1 switches to another partner and company 2 integrates is also better than cooperation. In this case, both companies produce the former product of company 1 and compete on the market (company 1 with a new partner against company 2 alone).

III. Switching Costs

The examples have shown that switching costs are the key to the question how stable a cooperative arrangement will be. Switching costs largely depend on IT-related investments expressed by y_1 and y_2 in equation (4). They also depend on strategic considerations. It may be part of one partner's or both partners' strategy to keep the arrangement stable. In this case electronic links will probably be of a proprietary nature with lock-in effects. An empirical study published by Bensaou (1997) indicates, that e. g. Japanese supplier relations in the manufacturing industry are based on more proprietary interorganizational systems compared to the situation in the U.S.A. Most manufacturers in Japan strive for a long-term nurturing strategy vis-a-vis their suppliers while their American counterparts attempt to create a supplier potential as large and flexible as possible. This leads to investments into open and highly standardized networks.

In the case of non-proprietary, open networks the switching costs of a company depend predominantly on its own investment and only to a negligible part on the partner's investment. Then switching costs for company 1 can be modeled as

$$(11) \qquad S_1^* = \alpha_1 - \beta_1 y_1 + \gamma_1 y_1^2,$$

with $\alpha_1 > 0$ and $\beta_1 >> \gamma_1 > 0$. S_1* is a declining function of investments y_1. The constant α_1 measures the expected switching costs of company 1 in period t = 2, if no investments were made in period t = 1, i. e. $y_1 = 0$. The parameters β_1 and γ_1 may be measured by providing at least two further subjective estimates ($S_{1,1}*$, $y_{1,1}$) and ($S_{1,2}*$, $y_{1,2}$) for the tuple (S_1*, y_1). Depending on the concrete situation, one alternatively may model switching cost using a constant elasticity approach such as $S_1^* = \alpha_1 y_1^\rho$. Here the elasticity ρ has to be estimated along with α_1 for period t = 2.

Similarly, the switching costs of company 2 can be expressed as

$$(12) \qquad S_2^* = \alpha_2 - \beta_2 y_2 + \gamma_2 y_2^2.$$

Let us assume for the example in the previous paragraph, that the switching costs were measured at zero investment level, i. e. are equal to the parameters α_1 and α_2:

α_1/α_2 company 1	company 2 switch	integrate	withdraw
switch	20/20	20/30	20/0
integrate	30/20	30/30	30/0
withdraw	0/20	0/30	0/0

Further, assume $\beta_1 = \beta_2 = 0.07$ and $\gamma_1 = \gamma_2 = 0.001$, i. e. for the reason of simplicity the same decline pattern shall obtain for each cell in the S_1^* / S_2^* matrix. Then we can calculate the optimal strategy in terms of equation (9) for various levels of y_1 and y_2. Figure 2 exhibits the results.

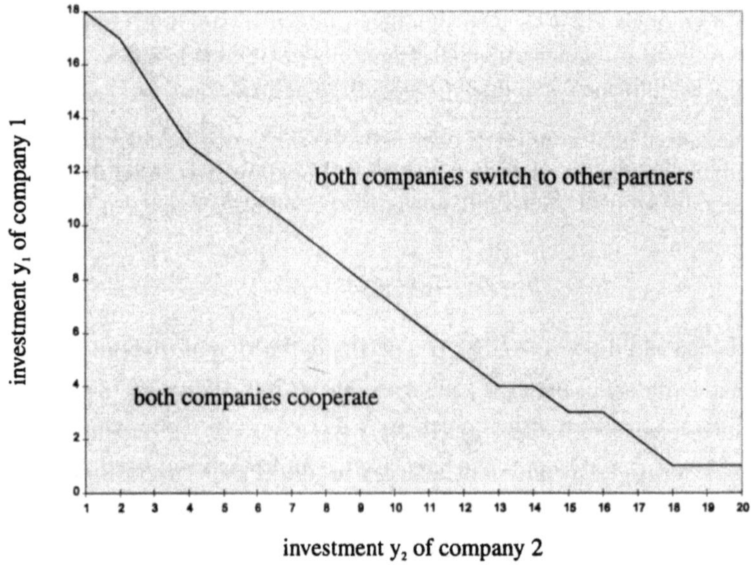

Figure 2: Optimal Strategies and Switching Costs

Figure 2 indicates for the above-mentioned example the levels of investment for each company into open network systems at which the cooperation becomes unstable. Above the separation line the cooperation falls apart.

The investments y_1 and y_2 at period $t = 1$ can be interpreted as investments into larger flexibility at $t = 2$. They definitely reduce net profits in $t = 2$ if this flexibility is unneeded and the cooperation stays alive, see equation (2)'. In the alternative case, see equation (5), the impact on net profits depends on the elasticities of the investments on switching costs which can be only roughly assessed in period t = 1, as mentioned above. Considering the rapid technological progress in IT the investments y_1 and y_2 can also be interpreted as the degree to which each company is willing to keep up with this progress.

D. Summary and Conclusions

In its first part, the paper explored the various potentials of IT for organizational change in general terms. One particular organization that has become more important in recent years is the virtual enterprise as a network of legally independent companies. In the second part of the paper we have analyzed the economics of the virtual enterprise, especially the question of the stability of the cooperation, in more formal ways, using a game theoretic approach. We have concluded that investments into interorganizational networks define the switching costs that impact the stability of virtual enterprises. With more and more open and standardized networks one can expect that virtual enterprises are easier established and also dissolved. On the other hand, proprietary networks can build-up substantial switching costs and lock-in effects, which may be desirable from a strategic point of view for one or all companies involved.

The analysis presented here is quite abstract and stylized. It certainly does reflect the real situation of virtual enterprises only in a very limited way. Therefore, the analysis should be supplemented by work on case studies and structured empirical investigations. Furthermore, the presented approach itself should be extended to the more general case of a virtual network with more than two participants and also with a changing number of companies involved and coalitions within the network. Therefore, the analysis presented here can give only preliminary clues as to the economic performance of virtual enterprises. Nevertheless, it provides a base for a more formal definition of the virtual enterprise, a subject that is very imprecisely and contradictorily treated in the current scientific literature.

References

Bensaou, M. (1997): Interorganizational Cooperation: The Role of Information Technology. An Empirical Comparison of U.S. and Japanese Supplier Relations. In: Information Systems Research 8/2, pp. 107–124.

Clemens, E. K., and P. R. *Kleindorfer* (1992): An Economic Analysis of Interorganizational Information Technology. In: Decision Support Systems 8, pp. 431–446.

Kleindorfer, P. R., and G. *Knieps* (1982): Vertical Integration and Transaction-Specific Sunk Costs. In: European Economic Review 19, pp. 71–87.

Myerson, R. B. (1991): Game Theory. Analysis of Conflict. Cambridge et al.

Nash, J. (1950): The Bargaining Problem. In: Econometrica 18, pp. 155–162.

Restructuring of Co-operation for Small and Medium-Sized Enterprises by Electronic Networks

Günter Müller, Holger Eggs, and Jürgen Englert

A. Introduction

There is a broad consensus that small and medium-sized enterprises (SMEs) are running in a tighter competition, due to globalisation trends. The current discussion demands a restructuring of SMEs. But the realisation of the restructuring will remain purely speculative as long as a large-scale theoretically founded database is lacking. This paper introduces the conception of a large-scale empirical study, projected to investigate the status quo and the economic potential of networking for SMEs, as well as its support by telematic systems.

B. Background of the Study

As early as 1960 McLuhan[1] remarked that the world seems on its way to becoming a global village. In the last decade the so-called Internet has contributed to this development and made this opinion almost realistic.

In the economic environment the changes are especially dramatic. Due to the potential enabled by telematic systems and deregulation we are witnessing a trend of globalisation. Although we are far from a worldwide integrated economy, which would characterise the completion of the globalisation process, we can see that the evolution of important economic variables depends on economic forces that are mainly driven by non-local factors. As a consequence, every enterprise has to deal with new forms of competition and a new economic framework. More and more new and globally acting competitors are entering regional markets and, hence, increasing the intensity of competition for established regional enterprises.

---

[1] McLuhan (1960).

Globalisation has no uniform definition, but rather stands for various observed trends in economic environments. The growing importance of external factors for keeping a firm profitable, supporting local industries and ensuring national competitiveness supersedes what was previously known as internationalisation.[2] Humbert[3] identifies four elements in recent economic evolution that call for the use of the word globalisation:

Formation of regional blocs

The architecture within the blocs of leading countries and their boundaries has changed. This aspect emphasises globalisation as a phenomenon which has emerged from within the blocs of the leading industrialised countries. They have come to form a kind of "triad": three regions, which together are dominating the rest of the world, are trading, producing and consuming the same high value-added and high-tech goods and services.[4]

Some authors analyse the triad landscape as a set of regional trading blocs in a global world.[5] This configuration could be a first necessary step towards multilateralism and a global market place. The development from these regional blocs to real globalisation raises questions about fairness and security. For example, the symmetric access to each region for all countries is a necessary and important condition for overcoming the regional blocs.

The merge of national boundaries

The congruence between a nation-state economic sovereignty domain and its market is coming under pressure. Until recently, national economic interest lay in its set of national firms acting within its market and this market was governed by its national rules. In the past, dominant nations enjoyed national specialisation in manufactured products through their national firms resident in their national territories. They exercised their power via exports. They spread their power across foreign territories perfectly controlling their domestic market and attempting to rule the markets of their national firms abroad. Now the boundaries between national economies are becoming blurred as there is a growing interpenetration of their territorial apparatus of production. This phenomenon questions the idea of national and even regional differences in supply or in national innovation systems and nation-specific regimes of intellectual property rights.[6] The idea that only trade is international seems obsolete and global issues

[2] Humbert (1993).

[3] For a more detailed description see Humbert (1993), pp. 4–9.

[4] Ohmae (1985).

[5] Zysman (1993).

[6] Foray (1993).

go beyond trade issues putting into question the world territorial distribution of production.

The global co-operation phenomenon

In the past the international dimension of production was only taken into consideration by large multinationals which were competing for access to markets and to low labour costs. They continue to do this in a rather traditional manner building oligopolies through concentration in national markets and internationalisation of their production. But recently it is also possible to observe a strong concentration process in many industries which is now taking place at a global level and has resulted in the building of world oligopolies.[7] But even in such world oligopolies, where firms are competing fiercely, they are at the same time searching for co-operation. This search for co-operation results from the limits to continued concentration and from uncertainty both of which have been provoked by a deep industrial transformation.[8] Alliances between big firms are spreading world-wide, especially in high-tech industries, but also in other industries. The result is the formation of world-wide networks.[9] In this time of deep industrial transformation, global involvement is needed to gain access to strategic resources and to learn about generic technologies.

World-wide reachability

Thanks to the development of the communication infrastructure and information networks the world is growing together. The physical distances between people are becoming less important. In addition, the digitalisation of communication, the rise in of capacity and cost reductions are making multimedia communication possible.[10] Based on this technical evolution, more and more aspects of human communication can be technically supported.[11] Hence, innovations in the field of telematic systems will lead to higher reachability and availability of services. With help of the "potential-function of telematics" you can predict the future development of telematic systems (see fig. 1).[12] Reachability means the number of possible locations, or persons, you can reach over a network. The functionality of services describes the degree of information processing a certain network or telematic system offers. For example, the telephone network has a low potential for available services because it allows only the transmission of speech and fax.

---

[7] Chesnais (1993).

[8] Van Tulder (1993).

[9] Nalebuff (1996).

[10] Müller (1996b).

[11] Müller (1996a).

[12] For a more detailed description see Müller et al. (1997), pp. 25–27.

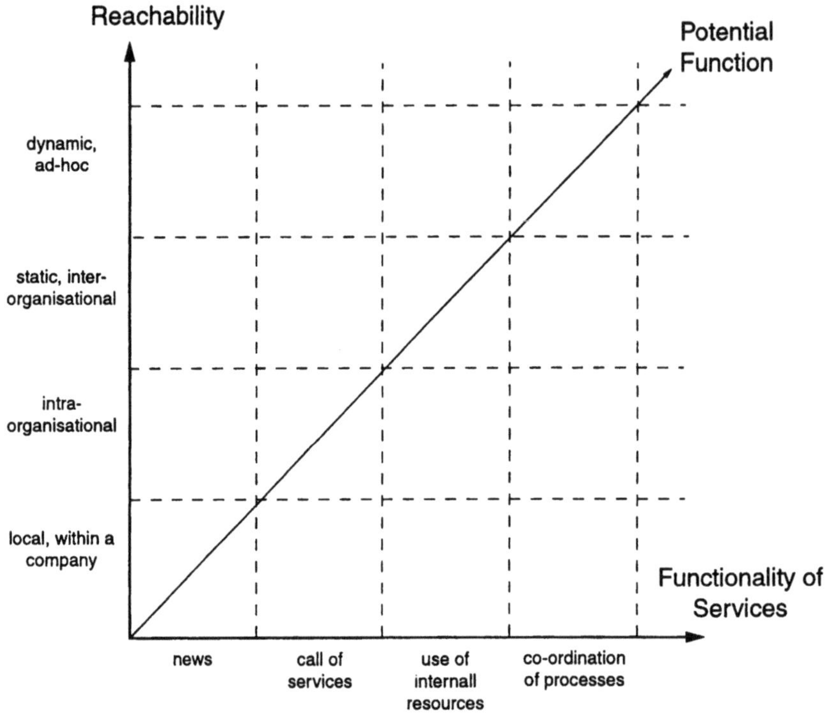

Figure 1: Potential Function of Telematics

But the benefit of the telephone results from the world-wide reachability or connectivity of any person.

C. The Empirical Study

I. Formulation of the Problem

The transformation of the productive system has resulted in a modification of the firms' environmental conditions and vice versa. The changes described above present both an opportunity and a risk for each individual firm. The advantages, or disadvantages, caused by globalisation depend on the specific reactions. It seems that, generally, globalisation is not a major problem for the big and multinational firms. They have acted globally, at least as far as trading is concerned, all along and are prepared for these changes. Multinational firms have their subsidiary companies, or branch offices all over the world. In addition, they have the assets for take-overs or are willing to merge in order to gain global presence. A final reaction of multinational firms is the outsourcing of production in countries with a lower level of production costs, or the building of production plants in such regions.

For many SMEs the situation is different. They are not accustomed to acting globally because usually they are bounded on specific and isolated markets. Consequently, if they want to stay competitive they have to become more globally oriented. But the problem in doing this is their limited size. A single SME is too small for global action and there are a lot of reasons and restrictions which prevent SMEs from reacting in a similar manner to multinational companies:

- They normally cannot afford to open branch offices all over the world.
- They do not have the assets and the experience for take-overs.
- Their restricted capital and know-how exclude them from the possibilities of distributed production.
- In many regions SME have often been founded and are still dominated by one single family. As a result they are very proud of their independence. A merger or being taken over would lead to the loss of that independence.

Our solution for overcoming these restrictions lies in the building of networks between SMEs. The main aspects of networking are, on the one hand, the concentration of core competencies[13] to exploit one's own comparative advantages and, on the other hand, the redefining and optimising of the value chains[14] in an interorganisational context. In our view the term networking consists of different dimensions and we distinguish three aspects of networking: the IT-oriented, the organisational and the institutional/cultural. These three dimensions and their interdependencies will be described in the next chapter.

II. Design of the Study

Research area

The study is initially concerned with SMEs specifically in the REGIO. This will be followed by a global extension and comparison with the help of similar studies in USA and Japan. REGIO is the name of the area located between Freiburg (GER), Strasbourg (F) and Basel (CH). The economic characteristics of

---

[13] For the conception of core competencies see Prahalad/Hamel (1990).

[14] For the conception of the value chain see Porter/Millar (1985).

this region are influenced by a high percentage of SMEs.[15] The main advantages are that it is possible to analyse international aspects within a small regional area:

- First of all there are different political systems. Germany is a federal republic, whereas France is centralized.
- Furthermore, the three countries belong to different economic communities. For example, Germany and France are members of the European Union, whereas Switzerland is not.
- Last but not least, there are a lot of cultural aspects, such as different languages, different ways of tackling problems and a different attitude towards time.

Objectives

The study deals with three main objectives:

- Potential of networking for SMEs.
- Analysis of the existing and intended networked structures and the derivation of a framework for their classification.
- Identification of the requirements for networking in the REGIO.

The first question aims at the economic potential networking can create for SMEs in the REGIO. Here the impact co-operating has on the effectiveness and on the efficiency of SMEs will be examined. In a second step, telematic support for the organizational potential will be analysed. For these two objectives the existing and projected structures of organizational and telematic networking in the REGIO will be surveyed. Afterwards, we will explore the requirements for using the organisational and technical potential. Crucial points are trust, standards, security and legal enforcement.

Topics of questionnaire

At the moment we aim to cover the objectives and aspects of networking by concentrating on six thematic areas condensed from our crucial factors for restructuring SMEs:

- Telematic support
  Telematic systems are enablers for networks. Case studies show that many networks depend on personal relationships rather than on telematic systems. For this reason the first point focuses on the relevance of the telematic support for networking.
- External interlocking of the value chain
  The second point deals with the disintegration of value chains in an interorganisational context. Key words are outsourcing and core competencies.

---

[15] For detailed figures see Wirtschaftsministerium Baden-Württemberg (1995).

- Mass customizing
  Another topic concentrates on mass customizing. The focus is on the embedding of customers in the production process. This refers to networks between SMEs and their customers.
- Organisational flexibility
  The fourth point describes the possibilities for the SMEs in the REGIO to react flexibly to new challenges. The main question is in which way and how fast enterprises are able to transform their organisational structure.
- Globalisation
  The next topic investigates the presence of global competitors in regional markets, as well as the presence of regional SMEs in global markets. In addition, the opportunities for interlocking regional SMEs in global networks are of interest.
- Institutional and cultural aspects
  In addition to the technical and organisational aspects of networking, institutional support is important. Trust generating institutions, risk handling and search institutions are examples for this last topic.

Procedure

For the refinement of this rough framework three case studies are in progress. The insights gained by the case studies will contribute to a questionnaire. After pre-testing this questionnaire, a large-scale empirical study in the REGIO, USA and Japan will be conducted. The results of the empirical study will flow into a consulting concept for SMEs. This will be implemented together with chambers of commerce.

III. Case Studies

The topics mentioned have been investigated in realistic settings by means of three case studies. The case studies aim at developing a concrete design for a large-scale empirical study and a questionnaire which is operational and relevant for both practical and theoretical purposes. The organisational structures and value chains, as well as their support by telematic systems, are investigated. The focus, thereby, will not be on the internal context, but more on the external interlocking of the firms' activities.

The case studies cover main industrial fields, such as the production of physical goods, and information and consulting. The production firm is Endress+Hauser (Reinach, CH) which was founded in the border region of Germany, France and Switzerland in 1953 by Georg H. Endress and Ludwig Hauser. Endress+Hauser is a full range supplier of measurement and automation equipment, with manufacturing, sales and service offices throughout the world. In the information sector the publishing company "Haufe Verlag" (Freiburg) has been investigated. The products of the family-owned company include literature for economists, tax consultants and lawyers. Its headquarters are in Freiburg and it has two branch offices, one in Munich and one in Berlin. Presently the Haufe Group consists of a holding and three subsidiary companies. "International Trade Marketing" (Freiburg) represents the consulting line. Their approach to trade ranges from the search for and the mediation of trade partners to the concrete completion of logistic and financial transactions. ITM acts globally via international co-operation with governments, private companies and international organisations. They have several branch offices in the C.I.S. (e. g. Moscow and Minsk) and in the Asian, as well as in the African area (e. g. Bombay and Tunis).

Each of the three firms is a SME, or has at least strong roots as a SME. They operate internationally and, due to their long-term experience, they constitute a fruitful area of investigation for the study.

D. Crucial Factors for Restructuring SMEs

I. IT Aspects of Networking

The global Information Infrastructure (GII), still in the early stages of its development, is already transforming our world.[16] Over the next decade, advances in the GII will affect almost every aspect of daily life. Disparate populations, once separated by distance and time, will experience these changes as part of a global community. No single force embodies our electronic transformation more than the evolving medium known as the Internet. The Internet is rapidly becoming an appliance of everyday live, accessible from almost every point on the planet.

The Internet is also changing classic business and economic paradigms. New models of commercial interaction are developing as business and consumers participate in the electronic marketplace and reap the resultant benefits. Entrepreneurs are able to start new businesses more easily, with smaller up-front investment requirements, by accessing the Internet world-wide network of consumers. The GII has the potential to revolutionise commerce in all industries by dramatically lowering transaction costs and facilitating new types of commercial transactions. Although the Internet can be seen as a model for the formation of this limitless and global "information world", the availability of sufficient services is still lacking. At the moment we are still far away from a complete realisa-

[16] Clinton/Gore (1997).

tion of the possible potential which telematic systems offer for networking. This state will be reached when any user can

- contact any other person world-wide at any time
- share common data and resources and
- define and work on common tasks.

Ad-hoc-networking between unknown partners is logically the final target.[17]

Besides the technical infrastructures, non-technical aspects will be responsible for the realisation of the potential. Many businesses and consumers are still wary of conducting extensive business over the Internet because of the lack of a predictable legal environment governing transactions. This is particularly true for international commercial activity, where concerns about enforcement of contracts, liability, intellectual property protection, privacy, security and other matters have caused businesses and consumers to be cautious. Consequently, the exploitation of the potential for networking is presently not a technical, but rather an economic and cultural question. Initiatives of the American government and of the EU for the implementation of global and national infrastructures are in progress for tackling these problems.[18] The following chapters describe the non-technical aspects of networking which are relevant for the study.

II. Organisational Aspects of Networking

The concept of networking

The subsequent remarks deal with the organisational aspects of "networking of decentralised organisational units, which take part in a co-ordinated value chain".[19] The concept of the interorganisational network is a broader approach than the term enterprise network in so far as it also contains non-enterprise organisations. The term enterprise network should stand for a coordinating co-operation between legally independent enterprises in which the relationships are complex-reciprocal and cooperative rather than competitive. The enterprise network is directed at the realisation of competitive advantages.[20]

---

[17] Müller et al. (1997), p. 27.

[18] Branscomb (1993).

[19] Picot et al. (1996), p. 395.

[20] Jarillo (1988), p. 32 considers strategic networks as "long term purposeful arrangements among distinct but related for-profit organizations that allow those firms in them to gain or sustain competitive advantage."

Networks can be structurally classified with regard to their scope, functional subdivision, density, diversity, centralisation, multiplicity, connectivity, interdependency, redundancy, stability, openness and rigidity of the organisation.[21]

A crucial issue is the problem of managing power in networks. It is generally accepted that, due to its polycentric structure, management is less hierarchical in networks than in traditional organisational structures[22] and that the managers derive their authority from expertise rather than from rank.[23] The problem solving is decentralised and local which requires specific know-how. In this sense a network can be described as an heterarchical and polycentric system. For appropriate incentives the ownership of and responsibility for the resources should be decentralised as well.

The question of the network boundaries is somewhat difficult. Coase (1937) defines a firm via the co-ordination mechanism "order" as a "system of relationships which comes into existence when the direction of resources is dependent on an entrepreneur."[24] Sydow (1992) describes the network boundaries by means of the exchange contingency. Within a network an exchange will increase the probability of other exchanges. Towards the boundaries of the network this exchange contingency converges against zero. Weber (1994) sees the limits of networks in the self-demarcation of their members given by the shared intention to co-operate and by a common set of targets. Network boundaries are not rigid. Instead they are permanently shifting and permeable. The fading of the boundaries of the firms and networks is accelerated by the increasing use of telematic systems.

Network entities

Profit- as well as non-profit organisations (e.g. economic and political institutions such as chambers of commerce) can be part of organisational networks. Each of the actors contributes his specific abilities to the interorganisationally optimised value chain. The network is, thereby, the result of a continuing process of work differentiation and integration. For optimal synergy effects, there must be a fit between the management and communication culture of the different partners. On the other hand, for vertical integration, the partners have to have a complementary production profile. Each member can belong to different networks, in certain circumstances linking them together.

---

[21] See Sydow (1992), pp. 83–88 and the literature cited there.

[22] Klein (1994), p. 309, Sydow (1992), p. 80.

[23] See for instance Jarvenpaa/Ives (1994).

[24] Coase (1937), p. 393.

Relationships between network entities

Relationships can be classified with regard to their exchange content. The exchanging streams consist of goods, services, financial resources, know-how, human resources, patterns of behaviour and social norms, as well as affects.

The intensity of the relationships extends from strong, long-term and legally codified relationships, to weak, short-term and not legally codified ones. The latter can be interpreted in the sense of Weick's (1976) "loosely coupled systems". This means that one system element influences another one spontaneously rather than continuously and in an negligible rather than an important way. The loose connection, thus refers more to the processes than it does to the structures. To increase the internal market pressure, the relationship to employees is driven by a high degree of performance dependent gratification, as well as by limited working contracts.

Potentials of networking

The potential of networking stems from a better positioning of the value entities in the strategic triangle "costs, quality and time". Quality and time can be included under the term flexibility, which consists of functional and numerical flexibility. Networking enables enterprises to accelerate their processes in order to save time and to shorten the time-to-market. Besides, networking allows more effective alignment with the rapidly changing demands of the customers. Due to their polymorphic structure and their traditional closeness to local markets, the networks of SMEs are especially suitable for exploiting the flexibility potential. The taking up of new enterprises with different or identical skills, is a way to realise functional or numerical flexibility. The adaption is frequently project driven.

Outsourcing as one possible genesis of networks is a way to transform fixed costs into variable costs. Nevertheless, the connected outsourcing of risks may not be total, since the necessary trust within the network would be destroyed.[25] Through repeated transactions with the same partners a digression of fixed transaction costs can be realised.

In addition to from these advantages of networking, Fourcade[26] identifies three reasons for external economies through networks:

- "specialisation economies, which stem from task sharing between firms with complementary activities and production processes;

[25] Jarillo (1988).

[26] Fourcade (1993), p. 213.

- information and communication economies springing from the co-production of non-standardised products, which can be compared to the idea of transaction costs, and
- economies built on labour demand, thanks to the existence of a large pool of specialised workers." A good example for this last point are the positive external effects derived from specialised skilled technicians in Silicon Valley.

By means of concentration on the core competencies several economic advantages can be realised. Economies of scale and progression in productivity can be reached. The co-operation of complementary enterprises can lead to synergy effects and to economies of scope. To illustrate, different business units can use the support of a common sales force. Besides these cost effects, quality can be enhanced through a closer alignment of the value chain with the special needs of local markets.[27]

From an industrial organisation point of view networks are used to gain access to new markets.

Risks of networking

A lot of problems in networks arise from difficulties in managing and controlling them. These stem from a confrontation of different management styles, as well as from the difficulties occurring with the acceptance of common decision finding procedures. These group decision methods are often time intensive and lack mechanisms for sanctioning the decisions. Apart from this, group decision proceedings are often restrained by insufficiently defined competencies. In contrast to markets and hierarchies in which there is no need for debates about the co-ordination mechanisms, additional transaction costs arise in networks which result from the necessity of negotiating the applicable co-ordination mechanism. The embedding of the decision makers in different incentive schemes may cause deviations from a pareto-optimal allocation of the resources.

Different communication and enterprise cultures frequently cause losses due to friction. To match the technological and administrative communication between the partners it is, therefore, necessary to install a suitable conversion and interface management. Telematic systems can support this.

The genesis of organizational networks may be handicapped by unwelcome transfers of strategically critical and valuable knowledge.[28] The preference for independence within a patriarchally managed SME might also contradict the joining of networks. An additional difficulty lies in the profit sharing procedures

[27] Porter (1985), p. 151.

[28] Moermann et al. (1996), p. 462.

in cases where the contribution of the individual partners to the total benefit is not transparent.

The existence of networks is laced with hold-up problems caused by opportunistic behaviour. The danger that a partner will leave the co-operation before its termination may be caused, for example by a strategic redefinition during the co-operation. An early breaking apart of a co-operation would cause sunk costs derived from specific investment in the relationship. Besides, it would lead to an unsatisfactory digression of the fixed costs spent in the co-operation.

III. Cultural and Institutional Aspects of Networking

What are the necessary cultural and institutional conditions for the exploitation of the economic potential presented by organisational networking and broadened by the adequate use of telematic systems? In an uncertain, complex world with bounded rationality[29] and opportunistic behaviour, phenomena like trust must be taken into consideration. A necessary, but insufficient condition for co-operation are win-win-situations. To illustrate, in the so-called prisoner dilemma, the pareto-optimal situation will not be reached, due to opportunistic behaviour on both sides. Trust, in the sense that both players anticipate the co-operative behaviour of the other player, can be a way to realise the additional gains through co-operation. Without trust there is no way to realise the additional gains in non-repeated games.[30] One problem with regard to networks is that some of the relationships are not intended to last for a long period of time, which makes it more difficult to build an atmosphere of trust.[31] Another "trust dilemma"[32] occurs between the objective of high flexibility and fast genesis of networks on the one hand, and the necessity for trust on the other hand, which requires a long-range period of time. A solution could be a trustpool. In this trustpool network no value is created. It is simply a set of enterprises which behaves according to some rules of behaviour. Each enterprise which would like to join the active network has to be recruited out of this pool of "passive enterprises". After the mission for which it joined the active network has been terminated, it falls back to this pool. From there it can be "activated" in new networks for new missions. When it has defected, in the sense that it has lost the trust of the rest of the community, it will be excluded from the trust pool. Participation in any active network is then impossible. A re-entry of

---

29 For the conception of bounded rationality and its interpretations see Simon (1957).

30 Schauenberg (1991), p. 331.

31 Wurche (1994), p. 151.

32 Sydow (1996), p. 12.

the punished enterprise into the trustpool is much more difficult than a new entry of an unknown enterprise.

The building of trust depends on intensive communication in a personal and direct way. It can be supported by telematic systems in so far as telematic systems enable substitutes for direct communication, or expand the opportunities of direct communication, by rationalising the indirect routine communication. In addition, telematic systems can support trusted third parties whose core competency is their trustworthiness.

E. Extensions of the Study

Although the REGIO offers a rich playground for international and cross-cultural studies, the emphasis of this empirical study is still focused on the regional context. So it would be very interesting to extend the study from a regional, although international, to a global analysis. Possible extensions include in particular:

- The shift from Inter- towards Intra- and Extranet.
- The melting of existing regional networks into global networks.
- The application of the results to multinational players.
- Networking between SMEs and multinational firms.

For the purpose of supporting the generalisation and applicability of our results, a comparison to studies with a similar design conducted in other regions would be fruitful. Meanwhile, the contacts to Prof. Sprague of Hawaii University have led to a co-operation in the empirical study. In order to cover all of the most important economic areas, an Asian cooperation partner, especially a Japanese one, is still lacking.

References

Bleicher, K. (1996): Der Weg zum virtuellen Unternehmen, Office Management 1–2, pp. 10–15.

Branscomb, L. M. (1993): The National Technology Police Debate, in: Empowering Technology, MIT Press, Cambridge.

Chesnais, F. (1993): Globalisation, world oligopoly and some of their implications: in: Humbert, M. (ed.): The Impact of Globalisation on Europe's Firms and Industries, Pinter Publishers Ltd., London, pp. 12–22.

Foray, D. (1993): Feasibility of a single regime of intellectual property rights, in: Humbert, M. (ed.): The Impact of Globalisation on Europe's Firms and Industries, Pinter Publishers Ltd., London, pp. 85–95.

Fourcade, C. (1993): Networking strategies for small firms coping with globalisation, in Humbert, M. (ed.): The Impact of Globalisation on Europe's Firms and Industries, Pinter Publishers Ltd., London, pp. 211–218.

Humbert, M. (1993): Introduction: questions, constraints and challenges in the name of globalisation, in: Humbert, M. (ed.): The Impact of Globalisation on Europe's Firms and Industries, Pinter Publishers Ltd., London, pp. 3–11.

Jarillo, C. J. (1988): On strategic networks, Strategic Management Journal, Vol. 9, pp. 31–41.

Jarvenpaa, S. L., and *Ives*, B. (1994): The Global Network Organization of the Future: Information Management Opportunities and Challanges, Journal of Management Information Systems, 10 (4), pp. 25–57.

Klein, S. (1994): Virtuelle Organisation, WiSt Heft 6, Juni, pp. 309–311.

McLuhan, M. (1960): Explorations in Communication, Beacon Press, Boston.

Moerman, P., *Commandeur*, H. R., and F. *Langerak* (1996): Strategische Zusammenarbeit mit industriellen Zulieferern, in: Bullinger, H.-J., Warnecke, H. J. gen (eds.): Neue Organisationsformen in Unternehmen, Springer, Berlin et al., pp. 453–465.

Müller, G., *Kohl*, U., und D. *Schoder* (1997): Unternehmenskommunikation: Telematiksysteme für vernetzte Unternehmen, Add. Wesley, Bonn.

Müller, G. (1996a): Multimedia – Mittler zwischen Menschen: in: Müller, G., Kohl, U., and Strauß, R.: Zukunftsperspektiven der digitalen Vernetzung, dpunkt, Heidelberg pp. 277–292.

— (1996b): Vom Rechnen zum Erkennen – kommunikative Dimensionen von Multimedia, in: Müller, G., Kohl, U., and Strauß, R.: Zukunftsperspektiven der digitalen Vernetzung, dpunkt, Heidelberg, pp. 129–149.

Nalebuff, B., and A. *Brandenburger* (1996): Co-Opetition, Harper Collins Business, London.

Ohmae, K. (1985): Triad Power, The Free Press, New York.

Picot, A., *Reichwald*, R., and R. T. *Wigand* (1996): Die grenzenlose Unternehmung: Information, Organisation und Management, 2. ed., Wiesbaden.

Porter, M., and V. E. *Millar* (1985): How Information gives you Competitive Advantage, Harvard Business Review, July–August, pp. 149–160.

Prahalad, C. K., and G. *Hamel* (1990): The Core Competence of the Corporation, in: Harvard Business Manager 68, May–June, pp. 79–91.

Schauenberg, B. (1991): Organisationsprobleme bei dauerhafter Kooperation, in: Ordelheide, Dieter; Rudolph, Bernd; Büsselmann, Elke (eds.): Betriebswirtschaftslehre und ökonomische Theorie, C. E. Poeschel Verlag, Stuttgart, pp. 330–356.

Simon, H. A. (1957): Administrative Behavior, 2. ed., Macmillan, New York.

Sydow, J. (1996), Virtuelle Unternehmung: Erfolg als Vertrauensorganisation?, Office Management, 7–8, pp. 10–13.

— (1992): Strategische Netzwerke: Evolution und Organisation, Wiesbaden.

Sydow, J. (1996), Virtuelle Unternehmung: Erfolg als Vertrauensorganisation?, Office Management, 7–8, pp. 10–13.

— (1992): Strategische Netzwerke: Evolution und Organisation, Wiesbaden.

Van Tulder, R., and W. *Ruigrok* (1993): Regionalisation, globalisation, or glocalisation: the case of the world car industry, in: The Impact of Globalisation on Europe's Firms and Industries, Pinter Publisher Ltd., London, pp. 22–33.

Weber, G. F., and I. *Walsh* (1994): Komplexe Organisationen, ein Modell für die Zukunft: Die virtuelle Organisation, Gablers Magazin, H. 6–7, pp. 24–27.

Weick, K. E. (1976): Educational organizations as loosely coupled systems, Administrative Science Quarterly, 21, pp. 1–19.

Wirtschaftsministerium Baden-Württemberg (1995): Mittelstandsbericht.

Wurche, S. (1994): Vertrauen und ökonomische Rationalität in kooperativen Interorganisationsbeziehungen, in: Sydow, J., and Windeler, A. (eds.), Management interorganisationaler Beziehungen, Westdeutscher Verlag, Opladen, pp. 142–159.

Zysman, J. (1993): Regional blocs, corporate strategies and government policies: the end of free trade?, in: The Impact of Globalisation on Europe's Firms and Industries, Pinter Publisher Ltd., London, pp. 105–113.

Multiplication of Measurement and Management of Intellectual Capital in Firms

Takeshi Yoshida

A. Introduction

Monetary perspective did and do focus on capturing the company's values on monetary basis, or through inflow and outflow of financial resources. As a result, all other managerial resources (human, material, and informational) are measured in monetary terms, in other words all resources can be converted into financial ones, and it is believed to be a common measure of wealth and can circulate across firms, industries and even nations.

Judy Lewent, who is chief financial officer of Merck & Co. says, "In a knowledge-based company, the accounting system doesn't capture anything really." (Stewart, 1994) Like the organizational chart and hard-wired structure, corporate financial documents are increasingly too static to keep up with the speed of the recent organizational change. As a result, there is an increasing discrepancy between the book value and the market value of the companies, especially emerging young companies (Edvinsson and Malone 1997).

The traditional model of accounting is, however, now failing to keep up with the change or revolution taking place in business world (Edvinsson and Malone 1997). So we will need to change from the traditional monetary perspective to intellectual one quickly.

Intellectual capital is a kind of invisible stock which breeds intangible and intellectual output, or knowledge. It consists of knowledge infrastructure (structural or organizational capital), human brainpowers (human capital), and relationships and linking structures (customer capital) within the focal organizations, and between them and their stakeholders (Edvinsson and Malone 1997, Ross et al. 1997, Stewart 1997, Sveivy 1997).

On the one hand because learning generates knowledge, or intellectual capital (IC), IC accumulation is generated through learning (IC is an outcome). In other words, customer capital, organizational capital, and process capital are built by a human capital. On the other hand, IC may facilitate or prohibit learning (IC is premise). Structural capital is the premise or cause of individual members' learning. They interact with one another and have circulating effects. "In particular, the two initiative complement each other in addition to having important overlaps" (Wiig 1997, p. 400). In this sense, they have already been integrated in a real world. While academicians treated them separately for simplicity of complicated reality so far, their integration should be promoted in a theoretical world.

Human beings are carriers, producers and holders of IC. Only human beings will perform almost all function in knowledge-generation process, through learning by doing, by planning, by reflection and by observing, carrying and storing knowledge. Naturally, other structural or organizational devices also can play a certain part of the whole role. For example, although procedures and routines store knowledge and carry it to the next generation in firms, they can not create knowledge by themselves.

Therefore, three interactions or multiplications is indispensable to taking consideration in the intellectual capital and activities in the firms. Firstly, multiplication of intellectual capital measurement and knowledge management (M1); secondly, of human capital and structural capital (M2); thirdly, of external perspective and internal perspective (M3).

Although three multiplications are indispensable to grasping intellectual activities and assets, this paper focuses on the relation of measurement and management as a starting point for deliberating all of three multiplications.

B. Multiplication of Measurement and Management of Intellectual Capital

Since knowledge era with the following characteristics has already started, there is an increasing need to change perspectives on what real values of the companies are; from monetary to intellectual perspective, and need to acquire a brand-new device for measuring intellectual resources and capital in the modern economy of fast-moving, knowledge-intensive virtual corporations:

- strong and enduring business relationships within networked partnerships,
- the enduring loyalty of customers,
- the role of key employees, upon whose knowledge and competencies the company's future rests,
- the commitment of the company and its employees to learn and renew over time,

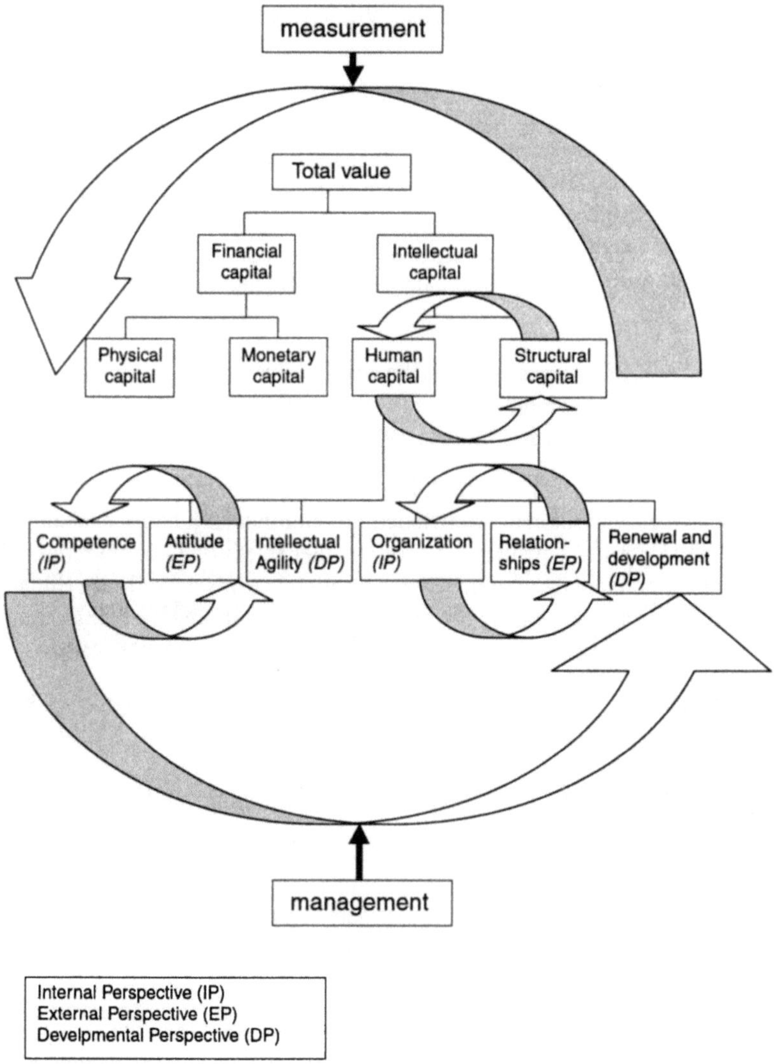

Revised from J. Ross, et al., *Intellectual Capital*, Macmillan Press, 1997, figure 2.13

Figure 1: Interdependencies between Measurement and Management

- and most of all, the character and values of a company, a crucial tool for investors and executives when looking at mergers, acquisitions, alliances, personnel hiring, and partnering. (Edvinsson and Malone 1997, pp. 19–20)

I. Measurement of Knowledge: Visualizing Intellectual Capital

Nowadays throughout the world, managers are gradually noticing that intellectual capital or knowledge is vital for the company's success and moreover aware that it becomes wealth as well as its source instead of financial capital. Customers also realize that they not only acquire hard stuffs such as products, services, materials or money, but also long for the soft ones which would satisfy their own needs, or knowledge. Therefore we should find out another effective viewpoint capable of grasping what the true values, or intellectual resources of companies are.

Thus, analysis of IC turns out to be the study of the roots of a company's value, the measurement of the hidden dynamic factors that underlie the visible building and products (Edvinsson and Malone 1997)

Let's look at what scientist are doing in their communities. Research papers which represent various new knowledge are continuously being exchanged or diffused and rigorously evaluated by peers, other scientists or anonymous referees through the shared paradigms, frames of reference or standards of evaluation. Its effectiveness and real values can be estimated by citation; how many researchers referred to their research papers and how many times they were cited.

Industrial community have already had complete productive engines (i. e. factories, offices and the research lab), circulation mechanism (i. e. Market), measurement devices and evaluation standards for tangible assets. But it does not yet acquire the same devices or yardsticks for intangibles or soft stuffs as the research community had.

For example, most of the tangible resources are decreasing through their exploitation, but intellectual capital do not deteriorate but in some cases increase over time (Ross et al. 1997). In this point, we need different mechanisms for intangible assets.

Most companies, especially those in mega-competition or newly emerging industries are eager to get such devices of evaluating how much intellectual capital they have because they must capitalize and utilize them to possess more competitive edges than their counterparts do. If the capital could be embodied into a company's products or services more quickly and accurately than their competitors, then market would appropriately set higher evaluation on them. Consequently, the demand for their products or services will be much more stronger and finally the price and profit will get higher. In the present accounting system managers and investors were suddenly struck by the outcome of IC (i. e. financial statements) just after a fiscal year passed. But it is too late to make any corrective actions at that point, especially in times of high speed economy.

Intangible assets of a company such as knowledge, good-will, trust and so on, or core competence are playing a more and more important role in gaining and sustaining its competitive advantages than ever. But how do we know to what extent those assets actually influence them? Although knowledge may be intangible, that does not mean it can't be measured. Without common yardstick for measuring such intangible assets, however, we can not know exactly how much they do and will impact on the real value of the companies. Therefore a demand for a new theory and a new measuring method is showing itself.

We should note that IC is not the substitute but the complement to the traditional accounting measures. Whit it people try to measure what could not be measured so far. In other words, for those who had no chance of knowing what kind of knowledge and how much hidden values firms have already possessed, IC make them clear. The quantity and quality of intellectual resources of firms are exposed to their members as well as outsiders such as customers, investors, bankers and other stakeholders.

> "Most, if not all, of a company's intellectual capital could be visualized in some way. In particular, the right empirical indicators could be identified and measured, and the presentational format found, such that intellectual capital could be put on the same strong, objective, and comparative base as financial capital." (Edvinsson and Malone 1997, p. 16)

How can the intangible assets or intellectual capital be measured?

A. Dividing assets into some combination of structural, human, customer capital.

B. Linking those factors both to the future development and to the financial accounting of the firm.

C. Creating some kind of navigational format to move about these factors.

D. Coming up with a body of indicators that measure the same body of intangible assets (Edvinsson and Malone 1997, p. 160–161)

We do not think that intangible assets could be changed into the tangible ones easily. It is difficult, if not impossible. But measuring them with indices and metrics and reporting with numbers make them more visible and understandable, though it is not an easy task.

In a sense, intellectual properties – such as patents, trade marks, and so on – have already been codified and therefore visible, but they occupy small parts of the whole intellectual capital. The metrics and the taxonomy for another intangible assets, or intellectual capital will be necessary.

II. Management of Knowledge

1. Visualizing Knowledge Management (KM) Process

We need not only the balance sheet and profit loss ratio sheet for IC, but also measures for its change on day-to-day basis, that is daily organizational learning. It is true that there is considerable overlap in the scope of theory of IC and KM. But they have different perspective and objectives respectively. KM is concerned with the daily knowledge management process. IC focuses on building, governing and measuring knowledge from the standpoint of the firm as a whole and on the fiscal year basis (Wiig 1997).

> "KM is more detailed and related activities such as creation, capture, transformation, and use. Its function is to plan, implement, operate and monitor all the knowledge-related activities and programs required for effective intellectual capital management." (Wiig 1997, p. 400).

But as IC do not clarify how companies have obtained intellectual resources, we have to obtain another means and theory of knowledge management process in order to understand a detailed story of the process inside the firms.

2. Process Perspectives on KM

Although there are many perspectives on KM, especially two different perspectives are important; Managerial (rational) perspective and process (natural system) perspective. Top-down monitoring and facilitation of knowledge-related activities is central to KM from the managerial (rational) perspective (Wiig 1997). According to Wiig (1997), it includes creation and maintenance of knowledge infrastructure; renewing, organizing, and transforming knowledge assets; and leveraging (using) knowledge assets to realize their value. While Wiig notes that KM is different from IC, intellectual capital management adopts the same as the above activities (Edvinsson and Malone 1997).

If we would make difference between them, as Wiig argued, IC management should be executed from managerial, rational and top-down perspective, but KM from natural, process and bottom-up perspective.

The process (natural) perspective lead to lifecycle model – from creation to scrap – or 7 stage model – of knowledge. The stage model include re-use and re-creation stage which the lifecycle model does not take into consideration. Because both models have the standpoints of frontline members in organizations, in this point they are quite different from the rational model with managerial perspective or top management's standpoint.

Stage 1 (Creation and use): knowledge is created through learning by doing (business process, operation) and through reflecting by using the acquired experience-based skill or know-how on the spot.

Stage 2 (Accumulation): accumulating through master of uncodified skill; or codifying experience-based skill and know-how, transforming them into explicit knowledge, and storing them

Stage 3 (Transfer and absorption): through codification or mastering knowledge can make transfer (traditional and information; Sveivy 1997) much easier.

Stage 4 (Scrap): sorting out knowledge according to usability and scraping unusable knowledge.

Stage 5 (Re-use): reusing the stored knowledge under the similar conditions to one under which it had been used before.

Stage 6 (Re-creation): through learning by adaptation to the different situation or recombination of various existing knowledge, renewing and reviving old knowledge and transforming specific knowledge into general one, or recreating knowledge.

Stage 7 (New combination): Combining a variety of existing knowledge into new one,

3. *New Direction of KM – Frontline or Bottom-up Knowledge Creation*

As with the change from industrial society to knowledge society, some characteristics of KM are altering as follows.

1. From mass-production to mass-customization of knowledge

Codifying a lot of experiences and turning them to general and all purpose knowledge at a time (knowledge mass-production) involves getting rid of nuance which helps understand their true meanings and deteriorating the importance of the specific condition or context where they were acquired and therefore are and will be utilized. It is true the mass-production system did work so far, but will not because many customers or users begin to notice their own needs and search for products, services or knowledge for satisfying them perfectly. As a result, their customization are called for and at the same time firms have to make various kinds of knowledge on a small scale, which amounts to a large volume. Thus we should look for and develop mass-customization system of knowledge.

2. From mere consumer to partial co-producer of knowledge
So far consumers have been those who only consumed goods and services. No doubt they have been passive. Thus consumers or users only have been forced to accept all-purpose functions as well as featureless characteristics of commodities that manufacturer mass-produced. However, they begin to desire customized goods and services. Consumers are gradually transforming themselves into co-producers or co-developers of goods and knowledge with companies.

This indicates the increasing importance of frontline knowledge creation. In general frontline employees have been mere users of knowledge which was created by corporate staffs, who are far away from customers. It was once a strongpoint because they watched the situation of market from a broader point of view, abstracted essence and directed their firms to the seemingly right course, or formed corporate strategy. At present customers realize their different needs and therefore market is ramifying and one small segmented market after another is emerging and disappearing. In this situation the most important knowledge creators or finders are frontline employees as well as customers. Thus bottom-up perspective of KM is of increasing importance.

C. Concluding Remark: Multiplication of Management (KM) and Measurement (IC): Wise Utilization of Knowledge

Because there is no theory underlying IC yet and thereby we can not grasp any reasons why one indices is selected as one of IC measures but others are not, this selection seems arbitrary. We need theoretic basis for selection of metrics. Organizational learning or knowledge management could bring us with them. Because they can explain how learning evolve in organization and how to manage knowledge in everyday operations. IC becomes a strong measure that tells us which company is most intellectual. Numbers or figures have strong power of making implicit things explicit. Most people believe they do not tell a lie. It is objective, macroscopic, non-biased, and easy to handle. Therefore financial data analysts should pay attention to a new measurement technique by which intangible assets are handled, and managerial theorist also should begin to treat knowledge not as invisible and ambiguous concept but as visible and reliable one.

It may be true, but figures do not manifest a real story in firms. Each firms may possess respective unique heroic episodes; how they could create new products, install new equipment, invest in foreign countries, solve hard problems, overcome big crisis and so on. It is a sort of saga, or myth. The reporting with numbers are extremely far from such stories.

Only knowledge management enables us to treat such stories with subtle shade of meanings very well because it focuses on human being, especially frontline employees and customers via case studies or questionnaires research.

We need both objective data and raw (subjective) information, macroscopic standpoint and on-the-spot sense-making, rational planning, goal-setting and natural path-finding process.

Therefore two theories should merge tightly in the near future. IC tells us quantity of knowledge and brings powerful tools by which we will be able to hack our way through unknown territories such as domains where intellectual assets prevails. KM makes clear hidden stories of daily learning inside and outside organizations and bestows rich explanatory powers on us. More importantly, two tools are interacting each other and one continuously improves another and vice versa. There exists multiplication of measurement and management.

References

Edvinsson, L., and M. S. *Malone* (1997): Intellectual Capital: Realizing Your Company's True Value by Finding Its Hidden Brainpower, HarperBusiness.

Ross, J., *Ross*, G., *Edvinsson*, L., and N. C. *Dragonetti* (1997): Intellectual Capital: Navigating in the New Business Landscape, Macmillan.

Stewart, T. A. (1994): Your Company's Most Valuable Asset; Intellectual Capital, Fortune, October 3rd.

— (1997): Intellectual Capital: The New Wealth of Organizations, Doubley/Currency.

Sveivy, K. E. (1997): The New Organizational Wealth: Managing & Measuring Knowledge-Based Assets, Berrett Koehler.

Wiig, K. M. (1997): Integrating Intellectual Capital and Knowledge Management, Long Range Planning, Vol. 30. No. 3, pp. 399–405.

The Holding Company – An Analysis of Its Organizational Form

Tamiki Kishida

A. Introduction

On June 18th 1997, the Anti-Monopoly Act was revised to lift the ban on the holding company in Japan after fifty years. There were almost no arguments against this revision because businesses have been looking for a way out of the long recession, the academicians assumed holding company could not bring such a concentration of the economy as Zaibatsu had done before World War II, and the Fair Trade Commission (FTC) inaugurated "The Workshop for the Chapter Four" to change its attitude in only three months from the prohibition of the holding company to partial permission, and finally to total permission.

Has the holding company altered a democratic national policy for vitalizing modern economy, though Lenin, in his *Imperialism*, attacked holding company as a means of control by monopolistic capital? Why are economists not opposed to the holding company, although they objected to the merger of Yawata and Fuji about thirty years ago?

This article, focusing on the organizational characteristics of the holding company,[1] is organized as follows: Firstly, the merits and demerits of the holding company are evaluated. Secondly, a framework for comprehensively understanding these merits and demerits from the perspective of Organization Design is proposed. Finally, the significance of the lifting of the ban on the holding company to our contemporary corporate society is considered.

---

[1] It seems that some discussions on the holding company refer to their organizational characteristics. However, for example, the separation of strategic decision and operational decision has long been the main characteristic of the multi-divisional organization. In addition, in case of lacking any relatedness as to technology or market, there obtains no synergy effect or economy of scope. Pure holding companies unlike business-related holding companies, try to utilize only the capital relation.

B. Merits and Demerits of the Holding Company

I. Definition

Holding companies have hitherto been defined as companies whose main business is to control the activities of domestic companies through the possession of their stocks. Companies were not allowed to found and become holding companies. In its revision, the holding company is defined as a company whose total value of acquired stocks of its subsidiaries (= companies with more than fifty percent of their stocks owned by their parent company) is more than fifty percent of its total assets. A company should not found any holding company with an excessive control over its business. By excessive control is here meant that (1) the size of the subsidiaries is big across considerable industries, and (2) subsidiaries, through their money transactions and market position, have great influence on the national economy and impede fair and free competition. Thus, the following three cases are not allowed.

The first case is that in which the corporate group is big, and each member company is big in the respective business field. For example, this involves a holding company which has a large corporate group like the biggest six member companies. As a numerical standard, this applies in case that the total assets of the holding company and its subsidiaries amount to 15 trillion yen.

The second case obtains if a holding company owns a big financial company and other business enterprises. This applies for instance in case that a holding company possesses a bank as well as another trading company or a real estate company.

The third case is that in which a holding company has big influence across considerable fields relating each other. For example, by influential is meant a business with more than 10% of the market shares of its field or a business which is among the biggest three. This applies for example in case that a holding company includes Toyota and Shin-Nippon Steel (Mutoh 1997).

The above definition only applies to the pure holding company. The business-related holding company not included at all. Most big companies in Japan today are business-related holding companies. In addition, Japanese companies abroad are in most cases pure holding companies. Those who support the lifting of the ban on the holding company say that holding companies prevail in reality, and that the revision of the Act was merely the confirmation after the fact. In the following, when using the term holding company, we mean the former pure holding company unless specifically stated otherwise.

II. Holding Companies Abroad

Only Japan and Korea have legally prohibited the founding of the holding company. The holding company is not prohibited in the USA, and it is prevalent in Europe.

1. The Holding Company in the USA

The holding company is said to have developed in the beginning of this century in the USA. The US corporations have developed from individual firms, associations, and joint-stock corporations. Then integration led to cartels through "Gentleman's Agreement". The cartel changed into the trust in 1882, when Standard Oil tried to tighten the cartel and avoid illegality, though this trust was judged illegal in 1892. Thus, the holding company as the new form of concentration appeared and diffused.

In the USA, the holding company is most prevalent in finance businesses. This is because no interstate banking businesses are allowed. A bank founds a banking holding company to avoid this regulation in order to conduct its business across several states. In 1994, the banks under the control of banking holding companies were 74 % in number and 93 % in assets. This shows that the big banks, in almost all cases, are operated under holding companies. For example, Citicorp is the holding company of Citibank, Citibank NA, and Citicorp Securities, Bank America Corporation has Bank Of America which is the second largest bank in the US and the largest bank in California, and Shuttle First National Bank, the largest bank in Washington State.

Firstly, however, in most cases American manufacturing companies are business-related holding companies. In 1996, among the top 20 in sales, only four were pure holding companies (Mobil, Philip Morris, Du Pont, and Shevron), though many companies like GE, GM, IBM were business-related holding companies. In the US, the holding company is not prohibited by law, but such a form is not so frequently adopted in case of industrial enterprises.

In addition, the banking holding companies resulted not from their merits in management but from the regulation and the law. Therefore there are few banking holding companies in countries other than the US. In Europe, the universal bank system is prevalent which operates both banking businesses and security businesses.

Secondly, the shareholders' consciousness is usually strong in the USA, and the anti-monopoly climate is ubiquitous.

2. *The Holding Company in Europe*

Holding companies are common in Europe. There are no countries that have any special laws for prohibiting holding companies, and there is no upper limit for the total possession of stocks by large business enterprises, though there are other regulations such as the Law of Fair Trade (England), the *Gesetz gegen Wettbewerbsbeschränkungen* (Law against Restrictions of Competition, Germany), and the Promotion Law of Competition (France). Moreover, there are no special regulations for the holding company in the Maastricht Act.

Well-known big businesses are, in many cases, holding companies. For example, Daimler-Benz AG had been a representative case. The head office, as a holding company, forms the group strategy as a whole, and has managed the firms belonging to the group efficiently, while possessing diversified businesses (AEG, DASA, Debis and Mercedes-Benz). Equally well-known holding companies are Royal Dutch Petroleum in Holland, Shell in England, and Peugeot and ABB in France (Matsushita 1996, Shimotani 1996).

However, in the first place the former Daimler-Benz Group was going to fail in its diversification strategy through the holding company. Daimler-Benz absorbed low performing AEG and divested several divisions with red figures, though its home business, the automobile company, has prospered. In addition, the head office centered around the automobile business. Thus, Daimler has now changed to a business-related holding company with the recognition that decision-making had duplicated under the corporate strategy through the holding company and that management had become inefficient.

Secondly, the research done by FTC[2] in England, France and Germany found that (1) holding companies were not adopted for reasons of efficiency but were the result of the founding of subsidiaries for each country to cope with the respective institutions in the course of European Integration, and (2) holding companies had the effect of shutting off the shareholders' criticism of the performance of subsidiaries, and were utilized as a strategy to protect oneself from shareholders' attacks and hostile take overs. In France, the holding company was usually utilized as strategic maneuvering for shareholder stability, and led to the loss of corporate governance.

---

[2] Research in Holding Company Systems in Europe by FTC.

3. *Merits of the Holding Company*

A report by the Corporate Law System, responding to the request of the Ministry of International Trade and Industry, emphasized the need for the holding company as follows. In the fifty years after World War II, the Japanese economy and the institutional system have become exhausted. Decision-making has been duplicated in the big businesses, which have expanded in accordance with the globalization of the economy. Thus, the need for agile decision-making and business behavior requires a mechanism that, under the corporate head office which forms the corporate strategy, allows flexible management, aims to make full use of resources and treats each business unit as independent. The holding company in this case is the best form for coping with these problems.

Holding companies are said to have the following utility or merits. Firstly, the split between strategic decision-making and operational decision-making or strategic group management and business management releases the top management from day-to-day operation. Therefore, the head office, based on the long-term perspective, makes strategic decisions efficiently. The parent organization receives only its dividend as source of profit from subsidiaries, and can evaluate its subsidiaries by objective indices like ROE (return on equity). Thus, the management efficiency of subsidiaries is indispensable, and this will lead to an increase in efficiency of the group as a whole. In this way, the resource allocation among subsidiaries will be fair and efficient. The independent subsidiaries will minimize the size and function of the corporate head office. Moreover, the chief executive of each subsidiary, as general manager, is motivated by having the responsibility for profit and capital efficiency so that the management accountability is clear. Finally, each subsidiary is managed by the chief executive who is familiar with his own field. Therefore, the holding company can flexibly adapt to its changing environment.

Secondly, the holding company can promote smooth integration without much conflict in organizational and personnel aspects which accompanies, for example, the merger. In the case of the holding company, the responsibility of subsidiaries is made clear and their authority is expanded, and thus the morale becomes high and a smooth personnel management is promoted. This autonomy of the subsidiaries excludes hierarchy consciousness and inferiority complexes, and allows the adoption of the appropriate employment system and working conditions. In addition, unlike with the merger, a leveling of corporate culture and working conditions is not necessary. In this way, the holding company minimizes the resistance to change and costs. That is, the holding company maintains the original unique corporate culture without losing the identity of the respective subsidiary. Moreover, if the company plans a merger in the long run, the transitory use of a holding company can minimize the conflicts in the process of the final merger.

Thirdly, unlike with other organizational forms, the risk is separated, and the failure of one subsidiary does not diffuse to other subsidiaries and the parent company. Therefore, new ventures with high risk can be promoted, and unrelated diversification is easy to implement. This risk aversion allows real restructuring, and the company invests easily into venture businesses. Thus, entries into new fields are activated, and competition is promoted. The increase in corporate activities enlarges the opportunity for employment, and the company can respond to the diverse needs of consumers.

Fourthly, the international harmonization of law is being advanced by lifting the ban on the holding company. The holding company has hitherto been prohibited in Japan. So foreign companies could not form holding companies in Japan, and this has impeded foreign investment. The Japanese firms have been placed in an unfavorable position by the prohibition of the holding company. Therefore, it was necessary to revise article 9, to try to increase efficiency and to accept the foreign investment smoothly (Matsushita 1996, Shimotani 1996).

Fifthly, there is a certain limit to economies of the scale, and one can realize the optimal size for holding companies by splitting into small units and delegating authority.

Lifting the ban on the holding company thus widens the choice of corporate strategy and organizational forms. This will result in a greater freedom of corporate behavior.

4. Demerits of the Holding Company

The holding company has the above merits on the one hand, but on the other hand, the following demerits must also be pointed out. Firstly, it is difficult for a holding company to restructure the whole group as well as each subsidiary. The holding company is a kind of control mechanism only through the capital relationship with its subsidiaries. Each subsidiary is an independent unit, so that in principle the parent company exerts no control over its subsidiaries with some requisite profit.

There is a very famous example in the history of management. In the early 1920s, each subsidiary of General Motors had increased its inventories for the remaining boom of World War II in order to ensure that it got the necessary materials before prices would increase because of inflation and shortage in goods. However, GM, the parent company, cut production because of the tightening of credit sales in installment and the prospects for a decrease in demand. Nonetheless, each subsidiary continued to purchase materials and did not lower the inventories, because it was independent enough to control the use of its operational funds.

At last, on the one hand the demand for the finished cars decreased, and on the other hand, each subsidiary continued to buy materials, which made the excess inventory amount to 70% of the total debt. In this way, Durant, the founder, was finally forced to retire (Chandler 1962).

In the holding company system, each subsidiary has clear responsibility and authority, which gives it motivation, though it sometimes cannot respond quickly to a crisis because of its independence from the parent company. Subsidiaries with high performance have no problems, but subsidiaries with low performance would not change their ways of management once they get worse.

Secondly, especially in Japan, there is a big difference, mainly in terms of wages, working conditions and human resources, between the parent company and its subsidiaries. In case of a merger, the specific conditions have to be taken into consideration, and therefore the organizational and personnel rearrangement becomes difficult, and such considerations might in turn impede a merger. The holding company does not have such problems of integration as in a merger, though the differences in wages and working conditions remain, and the inferiority complex of the subsidiaries with regard to their parent company does not disappear.

Thirdly, in the holding company system through capital control, not all resources are distributed across each subsidiary. Therefore, the holding company does not utilize the synergy effect and the economy of scope. Some argue, in reply to this objection, that the problem may be removed by strategically managing those subsidiaries. For example, the president of Shin-Nippon Steel, Mr. Takashi Imai, has said in a newspaper statement, that the president has to select the business areas, allocate the resources to the selected areas, and the appropriate staffing. He then adds, that the president cannot implement these roles fully without the holding company system.[3] However, at least theoretically, the term holding company refers to a company whose only relationship with its subsidaries concerns capital, and we do not call it holding company if it has some relationship in capital as well as in any other resources with its subsidiaries.

Fourthly, holding companies have difficulties in the utilization of cash flows as in the case of PPM (Product Portfolio Management) used under the system of the multi-divisional organization. Namely, it is difficult for the holding company to

[3] Nihon Keizai Shimbun, April 13th, 1997.

achieve the optimal mix of their whole businesses from a long-range perspective. It entails suboptimization. The multi-divisional organization was at first said to control the discretion of its divisions from a long-range strategic perspective, though, in reality, it was found that the multi-divisional organization impedes investment into the development of new products and new ventures because of the pressure of short-term profit (ROI: return on investment). PPM was thus introduced to check the short-term orientation of the multi-divisional organization. However, the holding company, where each subsidiary is independent from the parent company, has no mechanism for preventing such short-term orientation.

Fifthly, (1) in the holding company system, it is difficult for the stockholders to know the conditions of those subsidiaries that are remote from the parent company, and (2) the holding company is utilized as a means for getting stable stockholders to avoid disclosure. That is, there is no need for the disclosure of the subsidiaries' operational situation in detail in the holding company system, so that it can block the way to pursuing the performance of the subsidiaries, and avoid disclosure by maneuvering the profit and loss of the subsidiaries. In addition, a holding company, through stabilizing its stockholders, economizes on its control by possession. Thus, individual stockholders cannot check the financial conditions of the company, and the company does not have to cope with hostile takeover bids even in case of a decrease in its stock price. These factors will result in a low motivation of the management, who lose the incentive to pursue efficiency (Shimotani 1996, Diamond Harvard Business 1996).

The Workshop on Corporate Systems (1995) replied to these arguments against the holding company as follows: Many objections to lifting the ban on the holding company assert that there is no absolute utility or priority to the holding company, but this is no reason for banning holding companies altogether.

Firstly, it is stated that the division of strategic group management and business management is also possible through the externalized company and the internal company, though the decision which form to select is dependent on the focal company.

Secondly, some criticise the holding company because lifting the ban on the holding company may bring the unnecessary misunderstanding to reinforce the transaction within the corporate group, and there is also some criticism of the insufficient transparency of the Japanese market. However, these criticisms refer to the efficiency of the existing regulation, and not specifically to the problems of the holding company.

Thirdly, some assert that the adoption of the holding company as a substitute for the merger is not only ineffective without any restructuring of organization, but may also lead to the reinforcement of market control. However, restructuring is dependent on the company's judgement, and we can only regulate the merger which is tighter than the holding company, and the holding company cannot be prohibited, because it is looser than the merger.

We have evaluated the merits and demerits. They are the two sides of the same coin. Some argue for it, and others argue against it. For example, unlike the merger, the holding company has the merit of letting differences in wages and working conditions continue, but the distribution of resources across all subsidiaries is not allowed and the differences between the parent company and the subsidiaries tend to remain.

Moreover, the merits themselves may contradict each other in some cases. For instance, the holding company downsizes the administrative unit in order to break the dysfunction of the complicated management in big businesses on the one hand, but on the other hand, the holding company is needed as a substitute for the merger to compete internationally with huge foreign holding companies.

It is indispensable now to see these characteristics from a unified framework. Next, we shall try to formulate a comprehensive explanation from the perspective of organization theory.

C. The Holding Company as an Organizational Form

I. Stagewise Developmental Model of Organization and the Holding Company

There are two essential principles of organizing: differentiation and integration. Differentiation comprises two types: vertical (hierarchical) and horizontal (functional). Integration is also twofold: integration of hierarchy and of functions.

Organizational types or forms can be classified according to these two principles. One is vertical differentiation into autonomous units by hierarchy, and the other is horizontal differentiation by function. The first case needs no other integration mechanisms than hierarchy when authority is delegated to the lower levels, though some integration mechanisms are needed in case of horizontal communication on the same hierarchy level, as in the case of Fayol's gangplank principle. The second case is based on specialization, and needs at least a hierarchy for linking the specialized functions in order to coordinate the whole organization. Moreover, in order to coordinate the serial workflow across functions, there needs to be a new integrating mechanism as well as scheduling.

The representative form based on the first principle is line organization (L), and its developmental form is the multi-divisional organization (MD), which has autonomous divisions. That of the second case is the functional organization (F), and its developmental form is the functionally departmentalized organization (FD), in which specialized functions are departmentalized. Line & staff organization incorporates these two principles to ensure both line authority and specialization in the form of staff services and advisors. Matrix organization tries to integrate these two pronciples in the form of sharing line authority (dotted line). These two forms are integrated by horizontal relations as well as vertical relations (Kishida, 1994).

L and MD are usually said to be decentralized, and F and FD centralized. Explained in detail, line organization and multi-divisional organization are called decentralized in that authority is delegated from the top to the lower levels through hierarchy based on the unity of command principle. Both organizational forms employ vertical differentiation based on the unity of the command principle (structural centralization) which is balanced with the delegation of jobs from the top to the lower levels through hierarchy (managerial decentralization). This type of organizational form, therefore, has the characteristics of structural centralization and managerial decentralization.

In contrast, functional organization and functionally departmentalized organization are organized according to the principle of specialization, so that the jobs and functions are delegated to departments (structural decentralization). The result is a multiplication of command. Thus, what is needed is a central source of authority to coordinate these specialized jobs and functions as a whole (managerial centralization). Hence, this type of organizational form has the characteristics of structural decentralization and managerial centralization.

According to H. A. Simon's metaphor of watchmakers (Simon 1981), line organization and multi-divisional organization share their characteristics with Hora. Here, the organization consists of autonomous, nearly decomposable units differentiated vertically and hierarchically which can respond flexibly to changing environments – accepting orders by call on the way to assemble the parts. This type of organization form has the orientation toward survival and effectiveness. Functional organization and functionally departmentalized organization have parallels to Simon's Tempus. This type of organization is characterized by a horizontal differentiation of functions, and is organized according to the lateral linkage of a group of sequential works. This has the orientation toward the maximum technological rationality – efficiency under stable environmental conditions, different from the negative treatment by Simon. The former is differentiated by vertical hierarchy which integrates autonomous, decomposable units, so that it includes a number of hierarchies. The latter is differentiated horizontally, and only one hierarchy is needed to integrate these differentiated jobs. So this type becomes flatter, less hierarchical.

The above explanation leads us to the conclusion that the holding company belongs to the former type of organization form based on the differentiation by hierarchy. That is, the holding company is a structurally centralized organization under the holding parent company which integrates vertically autonomous, managerially decentralized subsidiaries. Accordingly, the aim of introducing the holding company is to respond flexibly to changing environments to assure survival and effectiveness, but not to economize on cost and to attain maximum efficiency in stable environments.

II. Decentralization versus Centralization and the Holding Company

The holding company is usually said to be decentralized, but this means managerially decentralized, as explained above. Put differently, their characteristics of structural centralization allow the delegation of authority through hierarchy.

As to the antithesis of centralization versus decentralization, the comparison between the holding company and other organizational forms reveals the following points. The functionally departmentalized organization is centralized (managerially centralized), and multi-divisional organization is decentralized (managerially decentralized). Recently, there is a trend toward decentralization through reinforcing the authority of the divisions of multi-divisional organization. The internal company and the externalized company are cases in point. Both serve to introduce the market principle into the relationship between the parent company and the independent units of its companies in order to divide the unwieldy multi-divisional organization into small autonomous and responsible administrative units. The internal company aims at creating small independent units called companies, and the externalized company aims at making these companies more independent from the parent company to give them more autonomy. In this sense, the ideal of the externalized company is closest to that of the holding company. Consequently, the multi-divisional organization, internal company, externalized company, and holding company are the ascent order of the degree of decentralization. The relationships between these four forms are as follows.

Firstly, the multi-divisional organization and internal organization have not yet been externalized, and divisions and companies have to pay the expenditure of the head office. the externalized company and the holding company have externalized their units, which are rather self-regulated and pay the head office in the form of dividend.

Secondly, unlike the pure holding company, the externalized company and the business-related holding company are managed and coordinated by the head office strategy in order to integrate the corporate group as a whole. The business-related holding company has some connections between subsidiaries in terms of technology and market as well as capital. Therefore, it needs the corporate strategy to coordinate inter-business relations to prevent suboptimization. The externalized company serves to heighten the motivation through larger autonomy and responsibility. As the word "setting up in business" shows, some succession of management know-how or technology, and management philosophy is often emphasized (Sakai 1986).

Thirdly, the externalized company always entails downsizing of the size of the constituent units, but this is not always the case for the holding company. Holding companies are formed for two reasons: Either a homogenous business is to be divided, or diverse businesses are to be integrated. The former applies, for instance, in case of a new venture. The latter applies, for example, in case of an international integration of businesses, and is used sometimes as a substitute for the merger. In the first case, the size of the new venture and its constituent units are small. The second case may produce a larger organization.

III. Strategy of Environmental Management and the Holding Company

The holding company, according to the standard of internalization – externalization, is different from other organizational forms in that the holding company consists of separate companies. The holding company may be interpreted as an example of the environmental management strategy as well as a form of organization.

Strategies of environmental management are a kind of interorganizational behavior to assure legitimacy, not by organization design adapting to its environment but by implementing some control over its environment based on the interdependence of resources.

There are three types of strategies of environmental management. The first are the buffer strategies for shutting out environmental effects on the core technology of the focal organization. The representative case is the buffer inventory. The second are independent strategies for decreasing uncertainty and maintaining the autonomy of the focal organization with relying to its own resources and means and without introducing any environmental factors into the decision-making process of the focal organization. Competition, public relations, social responsibility are examples. The third are cooperative strategies for cooperating explicitly and implicitly with the environmental factors in order to resolve the common problems between two or more organizations. According to the degree of dependence, implicit cooperation, contracting and bargaining, co-opting, coalition, and strategic maneuvering are included in this category (Kishida 1985).

The holding company, taken as a substitute for the merger as described earlier, is a kind of strategic maneuvering for absorbing uncertainty by coping with the dependency of resources. Strategic maneuvering is an environmental management strategy for removing dependency and for absorbing important environmental factors, unlike coalition (e. g. cartel and trust) in which two or more organizations coalesce and act jointly for a period of time with each organization maintaining its identity. The holding company is more loosely coupled than the merger.

Firstly, the holding company is not a new form of organization. Historically, the holding company has emerged as a substitute of the trust, when trusts were judged illegal in 1892 (Diamond Harvard Business 1996). Important here is the distinction between coalition (cartel or trust) and strategic maneuvering. The former is a peer group (non-hierarchical group) in which two organizations are tied on the same level. The identity of each organization is maintained, so that this group has no final say to check either organization if it attempts to outwit the other. In contrast, a merger means an hierarchical integration, which has a clear standard for sanctioning and the authority to implement it. So the merger is able to check the free ride. The holding company is the same as the merger in that the holding company hierarchically integrates subsidiaries under the parent company (Kishida 1992). However, in the case of a merger, the interdependence after the merger is close and reciprocal, whereas the holding company shows pooled interdependence only through capital possession.

Therefore the holding company (1) is a kind of strategic maneuvering to absorb part of its task environment, (2) unlike the coalition (cartel, trust) hierarchically integrating its subsidaries, and having some standard for sanctions to check the free ride.

Secondly, the holding company is looser in its coupling than the merger, so that the holding company cannot control the market if we regulate merger activities. However, on the other hand, we can say that the holding company allows to maintain the present market control with looser linkage (lower cost) and that it allows to broaden the range of market control with a lower degree of control. The effect of the merger or the holding company depends on the degree of control of the market needs. In addition, the holding company is based on the principle of vertical differentiation (unity of command). This leads to structural centralization, which assures the unity of command by the parent organization.

Thirdly, when we consider the holding company as an interorganizational relation based on vertical differentiation, consisting of autonomous, independent units, the separation of subsidiaries is to be emphasized. The holding company, so to speak, adapts to its diverse environments by the requisite variety. In that sense, the holding company, as compared with the merger, duplicates its resources, so that it does not assure efficiency and cost minimization.

Fourthly, the holding company usually has a lower performance than any other organizational form. R. P. Rumelt (1974) found that the holding company or conglomerate is lower in all performance indices. This is because this type of organization form cannot enjoy the synergy effect or of economies of scale by sharing of resources between independent units. The multi-divisional organization, on the other hand, shows high performance in most indices relating to profitability and growth. This is so, in turn, because the multi-divisional organization, utilizing the relatedness of technology and market, can avoid the duplication of resources.

O. E. Williamson (1975) reaches the same conclusion. The multi-divisional organization, unlike the holding company, has the information and management necessary for strategic planning and internal control. Although the holding company can also allocate cash flows from low to high yield units, it is viewed as being little different from the capital market (Galbraith and Nathanson 1978).

Generally speaking, vertical differentiation is appropriate for coping with environmental change, but horizontal differentiation is suitable for the pursuit of efficiency through avoiding duplication of resources.

D. Concluding Remarks

The merits and demerits of the holding company have been made clear in terms of its organization form. Both are, in many cases, the two sides of the same coin, so it is necessary for us to see comprehensively both sides in an integrated framework. Consequently, it was pointed out that the holding company is a form based on vertical differentiation, and a structurally centralized and managerially decentralized organization. That is, the holding company emphasizes the differentiation by hierarchy and the autonomy of its units in order to cope with environmental uncertainty. The duplication of resources is characteristic for the holding company and it does not aim to obtain efficiency and integration. Moreover, in terms of interorganizational relation, the holding company as parent organization is an environmental management strategy aimed at giving its subsidiaries autonomy while organizing according to the unity of command. Therefore, in case that the delegation of authority to its subsidiaries is not enough, it is inevitable to centralize power.

There are many facets to the arguments about lifting the ban on the holding company, though few are from an organizational point of view. The fact has been stressed that the holding company is more decentralized and flexible than the internal company and the externalized company. However, the holding company is an organizational form that is tied only in terms of capital. There have been few that have discussed the fact that the organization cannot utilize synergy effects and economies of scale.

Finally, from the perspective elaborated above, we shall now conclude by discussing the relationship between the holding company as an organizational form and corporate power and deregulation.

Firstly, Aoki and Dore (1994), in terms of the relationships between firms and society, view the corporate system as consisting of markets (labor, capital and product markets) and organization (rank hierarchies and horizontal information system). He identifies two types of corporate systems: The American type with a decentralized and competitive labor market and a centralized information system, and the Japanese type with a centralized and cooperative labor market (internal labor market) and a decentralized information system. He then calls this symmetrical relationship "duality principle". However, as described above, there are two principles of organizing, both in Japan and America: vertical differentiation (line organization), and horizontal organization (functional organization). The combination of these two ways of differentiation defines the organizational form. So America also has a horizontal information system and there exists a vertical information system.The holding company is based on the vertical information system, and structurally centralized. If the delegation of authority is not enough, then power is centralized to the parent organization through hierarchy. This point is lacking in Aoki's analysis.

Moreover, not only the influence of the market on the organization, but also the influence of the organization on the market is to be taken into consideration. The holding company is more decentralized (managerially decentralized) than other organization forms on the one hand, but on the other hand, there is another side of the coin, namely the side of the environmental management strategy to handle resource dependency through its constituent units as in the case of Japanese corporate groups. The holding company can be a means to concentrate the power on the parent company, when we consider the holding company as a form of structural centralization and managerial decentralization. Some argue against this point in that a corporate group is a collectivity of organizations, though an industrial group, which is in a sense a successor of Zaibatsu before World War II, is only loosely coupled. However, it may have substantive control over group firms with only a loose tie. In that sense, the holding company may be a means of control without paying the cost of reorganization.[4]

Secondly, some argue for the holding company because of international harmonization and the need for strategic and organizational choice. However, institutions are established by social custom and culture. Different cultures and habits need different institutions. In America, the banker's holding company is prevalent. This is not because of economic and managerial requirements but is the result of laws and regulations. In Europe, banking operations are usually not separated from security operations, so the usual case is the "universal bank" in which the bank manages both banking operations and security operations.

In addition, broadening the strategic choice of organization decreases the dependence on other organizations, which increases the power of the parent organization. Big manufacturing companies in Korea and Japan are stronger than those in other countries. Prohibition of holding companies in these two countries may have been partly responsible for this.

Thirdly, an increase in the range of strategic and organizational choice relates to the trend toward deregulation today. Deregulation will encourage competition, and cut prices. It is sure that a competitive market will emerge in the process of deregulation. However, the result may be a situation favorable to big businesses.

If the price is the same, consumers will prefer brand goods. This may lead to middle and small-sized firms going bankrupt.

President Roosevelt, after World War II, decided to allocate huge munition plants not to the existing big businesses but to small indepallocateendent companies. So Tucker borrowed a large plant in Chicago to produce an advanced model based on the Porsche-type concept car. However, he went bankrupt soon because of malicious news in the big newspapers, rejection of loans, and fraud prosecution (Origuchi 1997). Free competition involves dual facets of continuous dynamic entries of new companies as well as of the power logic to use whatever means for defeating rivals. We also observed the following phenomena after the World War in Japan. Notwithstanding the new entries of 5-yen pencils and Eguchi butter, the existing big companies cut their prices to the same level. Thus big companies cut their prices for the moment, in order to make rivals exit. After that, they raised their prices again soon. The prices being the same, consumers will

---

[4] Firstly, in almost all cases, the holding company is said not to lead to the recovery of the Zaibatsu before World War II. However, no mention is made of the point that the holding company is an organizational form of structural centralization based on vertical differentiation. If coordination between subsidiaries is made in strategy as well as in capital, as a lot of managers say, then there can be a power concentration in the parent company. Secondly, many argue that in the age of globalization, there is no possibility for the Zaibatsu to recover. However, is it an aim of the lifting of the ban on the holding company in Japan to establish organizatioins which are large enough to compete with huge European holding companies? Admittedly the discretion of organizational choice may lead to an increase in corporate power.

buy those goods and services that are offered by big companies. Dempsey and Goetz (1992) found that deregulation brought the sheer competition to decrease prices on the one hand, and on the other hand, the quality of services decreased. As a result, the oligopoly situation came back again. Deregulation, that is sure, will lead to a decrease in prices in the course of competition. However, what is the result of that competition? It is also necessary for us to create fair competition through the appropriate relation.

Broad strategic and organizational choice for big businesses, through a decrease in dependency on others, allows them to implement some control over their market. The holding company is a means to internalize a degree of market risk. It can freely externalize those subsidiaries with low performance, while entering into new, unrelated areas.[5] The market mechanism is not a panacea. Social control is necessary for the market mechanism to function effectively. Therefore, in terms of corporate power, the power of the big businesses over society must be balanced with the power of society over those big businesses. Today the power of the big businesses is prevalent in every sphere of our life, and this balance will be needed more and more from now on.

References

Aoki, M., and R. *Dore* (1994): The Japanese Firm: Sources of Competitive Strength, Clarendon Press.

Chandler, A. D. (1962): Strategy and Structure. The MIT Press.

Diamond Harvard Business (1996): Vol. 21, No. 3.

Dempsey, P. S., and A. R. *Goetz* (1992): Airline Deregulation and Laissez-Faire Mythology, Greenwood.

Galbraith, J. R., and D. A. *Nathanson* (1978): Strategy Implementation: The Role of Structure and Process, West.

Kishida, T. (1985): Management of Organization and Environment (Keiei-soshiki to Kankyou-tekiou), San-rei Shobo.

— (1992): As to the distinction between peer group of coordination among colleagues and coordination by hierarchy, ćonfer Tamiki Kishida, Loosely Coupled System and Organizing, Keizai Kagaku (Economic Science) Vol. 39, No. 4.

[5] When, for example, entering into a new business area, the focal company itself as a subsidiary may belong to the parent company. Thus the focal company is independent from other subsidiaries, so that it can protect them from the influence of the failure in the new business. This is called "fire wall" in America. In American electric power and banking industries, the holding company is not the result of deregulation, but a means to avoid regulation.

— (1994): Organization and Organization Theory: Analytical Framework of Organization Theory, Keizai-Kagaku (Economic Science) Vol. 41, No. 4.

Matsushita, M. (ed.) (1996): Lifting the Ban on the Holding Company (in Japanese), Asahi Shimbunsha.

Mutoh, Y. (1997): Handbook of the Holding Company (in Japanese), Nihon-Keizai Shimbunsha.

Origuchi, T. (1997): The Century for Automobiles (in Japanese), Iwanami Shinsho.

Rumelt, P. P. (1974): Strategy, Structure, and Economic Performance, Harvard University Press.

Sakai, K. (1986): Externalized Company (in Japanese), Asahi Bunko.

Shimotani, M. (1996): Lifting the Ban on the Holding Company (in Japanese), Chuko Shinsho.

Simon, H. A. (1981): The Science of the Artificial, 2nd ed., The Massachusetts Institute of Technology.

Williamson, O. E. (1975): Markets and Hierarchies: Analysis and Antitrust Implications, The Free Press.

Appendix: List of the Publications of Previous Joint Nagoya/Freiburg Seminars

A. Seminar Publications in Germany

(1) Dams, Th.; Jojima, K. (eds.): Ausgewähle Probleme internationaler Wirtschaftsbeziehungen (Selected Problems of International Economic Relations), Berlin 1980.

(2) Dams, Th.; Jojima, K. (eds.): Aktuelle Probleme der Sozialpolitik (Current Problems of Social Policy), Berlin 1982.

(3) Dams, Th.; Jojima, K. (eds.): Wirtschaftliche Anpassungsprobleme bei steigenden Energiepreisen (Economic Problems of Adjustment due to Rising Energy Prices), Berlin 1983.

(4) Dams, Th.; Jojima, K. (eds.): Internationale Wirtschaftsbeziehungen (International Economic Relations), Berlin 1983.

(5) Dams, Th.; Mizuno, M. (eds.): Entscheidungsprozesse auf mikro- und makroökonomischer Ebene (Decision Processes on the Micro-Economic and Macro-Economic Level), Berlin 1985.

(6) Dams, Th.; Mizuno, M. (eds.): Employment Problems under the Conditions of Rapid Technological Chance, Berlin 1988.

(7) Dams, Th.; Matsugi, T. (eds.): Adjustment Problems in Advanced Open Economies: Japan and Germany, Berlin 1989.

(8) Matsugi, T.; Oberhauser, A. (eds.): Economic Cooperation in the 1990s, Berlin 1992.

(9) Matsugi, T.; Oberhauser, A. (eds.): Adjustments of Economics and Enterprises in a Changing World, Berlin 1993.

(10) Matsugi, T.; Oberhauser, A. (eds.): Interactions between Economy and Ecologyy, Berlin 1994.

(11) Matsugi, T.; Oberhauser, A.; Schober, F. (eds.): Integration and Adjustment of Global Economies, Berlin 1996.

(12) Schober, F.; Matsugi, T. (eds.): Labor Market Issues in Japan and Germany, Berlin 1998.

All books were published by Duncker & Humblot, Berlin.

B. Seminar Publications in Japan

(1) Jojima, K.; Dams, Th. (eds.): Chiiki Kaihatsu to Chiiki Seisaku (Regional Development and Regional Policy), Toyokeizai Shinposha 1978.

(2) Jojima, K.; Dams, Th. (eds.): Keizai Kaihatsu to Enjo Seisaku (Economic Development and Policy for Development Aids), Toyokeizai Shinposha 1979.

(3) Jojima, K.; Dams, Th. (eds.): Keiki Teitai to Keizai Seisaku (Economic Policies in Recession), Toyokeizai Shinposha 1980.

(4) Jojima, K.; Dams, Th. (eds.): Shakai Seisaku to Zaisei Mondai (Social Policy and Fiscal Problems), Toyokeizai Shinposha 1982.

(5) Matsugi, T.; Dams, Th. (eds.): Enerugi Mondai to Keizai Seisaku (Energy Problems and Economic Policy), Toyokeizai Shinposha 1983.

(6) Ogawa, E.; Fujise, H.; Matsugi, T.; Dams, Th. (eds.): Kokusai Boueki to Keizai Masatsu (International Trade and Economic Frictions), Nagoya University Press 1984.

(7) Mizuno, M.; Dams, Th. (eds.): Keizai Seisaku to Keiei no Isi Kettei (Decision-Making in Economic Policy and Management), Faculty of Economics, Nagoya University 1985.

(8) Mizuno, M.; Matsugi, T.; Dams, Th. (eds.): ME-ka no Genjou to Koyou Mondai (Microelectronic Development and Employment Problems), Nagoya University Press 1986.

(9) Mizuno, M.; Dams, Th. (eds.): Keizai-Keiei no Kouzou Henka to Taiousaku (Adjustments to the Structural Change in Economy and Management), Nagoya University Press 1987.

(10) Matsugi, T.; Dams, Th. (eds.): Kokusai Keizai ni okeru Nichi-Doku no Yakuwari (The Roles of Japan and Germany in the World Economy), Nagoya University Press 1988.

(11) Matsugi, T.; Dams, Th. (eds.): Hogoshugi ka Jiyuu Boueki ka (Protectionism or Free Trade), Nagoya University Press 1989.

(12) Matsugi, T.; Oberhauser, A. (eds.): EC-Shijou Tougou to Doitsu Touitsu (EC-Integration and German Unification), Faculty of Economics, Nagoya University 1992.

Contributors and Editors

Prof. Dr. *Yuko Arayama,* Nagoya University, School of Economics, Dept. of Business Administration, Furo-cho, Chikusa-ku, Nagoya, 464-8601, Japan.

Prof. Dr. Dres. h.c. *Theodor Dams,* University of Freiburg, Faculty of Economics, Platz der Alten Synagoge, D-79085 Freiburg.

Prof. Dr. *Akira Ebizuka,* Osaka City University, Faculty of Economics, 3-3-138, Sugimoto, Sumiyoshi-ku, Osaka, 558, Japan.

Dipl.-Volkswirt *Holger Eggs,* University of Freiburg, Dept. of Telematics, Friedrichstr. 50, D-79085 Freiburg.

Dipl.-Volkswirt *Jürgen Englert,* University of Freiburg, Dept. of Telematics, Friedrichstr. 50, D-79085 Freiburg.

Prof. Dr. *Akinori Isogai,* Kyushu University, Faculty of Economics, Department of Economics, Hakozaki 6-19-1, Higashi, Fokuoka, 812-8581, Japan.

Privatdozent Dr. *Jürgen Jerger,* University of Freiburg, Dept. of Economic Theory, Platz der Alten Synagoge, D-79085 Freiburg.

Prof. Dr. *Tamiki Kishida,* Nagoya University, School of Economics, Dept. of Business Administration, Furo-cho, Chikusa-ku, Nagoya, 464-8601, Japan.

Prof. Dr. *Günter Müller,* University of Freiburg, Dept. of Telematics, Friedrichstr. 50, D-79085 Freiburg.

Prof. *Akihiro Noguchi,* Nagoya University, School of Economics, Dept. of Business Administration, Furo-cho, Chikusa-ku, Nagoya, 464-8601, Japan.

Prof. Dr. *Franz Schober,* University of Freiburg, Dept. of Information Systems, Platz der Alten Synagoge, D-79085 Freiburg.

Privatdozent Dr. *Alexander Spermann,* University of Freiburg, Dept. of Public Finance II, Platz der Alten Synagoge, D-79085 Freiburg.

Prof. Dr. *Masatsugu Tsuji,* Osaka University, School of International Public Policy, 1-16 Machikaneyama, Toyonaka 560, Osaka, Japan.

Prof. *Hiroshi Tsukada,* Nagoya University, School of Economics, Economic Research Center, Furo-cho, Chikusa-ku, Nagoya, 464-8601, Japan.

Prof. *Hiroyasu Uemura,* Nagoya University, School of Economics, Dept. of Economics, Furo-cho, Chikusa-ku, Nagoya, 464-8601, Japan.

Prof. Dr. *Tadashi Yagi,* Do-shisha University, School of Economics, Dept. of Economics, Karasuma-Maruta- machi, Sakyo-ku, Kyoto, 606, Japan.

Prof. *Takeshi Yoshida,* Nagoya University, School of Economics, Dept. of Economics, Furo-cho, Chikusa-ku, Nagoya, 464-8601, Japan.

MIX
Papier aus verantwortungsvollen Quellen
Paper from responsible sources
FSC® C105338

Printed by Libri Plureos GmbH
in Hamburg, Germany